BLACK SEA POLITICS

BLACK SEA POLITICS

POLITICAL CULTURE AND CIVIL SOCIETY IN AN UNSTABLE REGION

Edited by

AYŞE GÜNEŞ-AYATA

AYÇA ERGUN

IŞIL ÇELİMLİ

Published in 2005 by I.B. Tauris & Co Ltd
6 Salem Road, London W2 4BU
175 Fifth Avenue, New York NY 10010
www.ibtauris.com

In the United States of America and in Canada distributed by
St Martins Press, 175 Fifth Avenue, New York NY 10010

International Library of Political Studies 8

ISBN 1 84511 035 8
EAN 978 1 84511 035 2

A full CIP record for this book is available from the British Library
A full CIP record for this book is available from the Library of
Congress

Library of Congress catalog card: available

Printed and bound in Great Britain
from camera-ready copy edited and supplied by the editors

To all research assistants of KORA

for their enthusiasm, dedication and support

CONTENTS

PART III - CIVIL SOCIETY AND ITS ORGANIZATIONS

PART IV - POWER RELATIONS

LIST OF TABLES

PREFACE

The conference entitled 'Political Culture and Civil Society in the Black Sea Region' which was the catalyst for this book was inspired by the dramatic changes in social distance experienced in the last decade.

The fall of the Soviet Union has been a drastic political change for most of the world. For neighbouring countries, like Turkey, this led to new experiences even on a daily basis. This influx of migrants, some illegal, finding forgotten relatives on door steps, learning that there were other peoples in the world that could speak their own language and with the potential for adventures in new markets, all came with great emotional upheaval. In time, these unprecedented emotions left their place for a more established routine rationality; and later into a systematic search for understanding.

My personal experiences are parallel with this transition. I used to spend my summer vacations in my father's hometown, which is near the Black Sea. As a small child, I remember myself watching the sea, thinking that the other side was never reachable. The Black Sea is rough, does not have isles and gives the impression of endlessness. Even the fact that it was called 'Black' added to its mystery. Countries around the Black Sea did not count among the tourism routes from Turkey. Bulgaria was a country which people would drive through, only to transit to other European countries. Even then, visits would be kept as short as possible, avoiding stopovers, and any unnecessary interaction with other people. Of course, most people knew there were people with similar origins around the Black Sea: the Turkish minority in Bulgaria, Tatars of Crimea, and the Azerbaijanis. But they were relics from a nostalgic past…

A few years ago, I flew from İstanbul to Simpherepol, in less than an hour, and found that the distance was shorter than the time to travel between Ankara and İzmir. During a conversation with a Bulgarian friend, we discovered that my Black Sea hometown was closer to Sofia than it was to Ankara. Talking with a Georgian friend in Tbilisi, I was told that it was easier to get to Batumi from the Turkish border than to travel from Tbilisi. Suddenly the Black Sea turned out to be a large inner lake that led groups of people around it searching for commonalities from language to music.

It was not simply the breakdown of the barriers in social distance that led to this project. Although it was an important source of inspiration, we (editors) think that transnational development of civil society is very much influenced by interaction within the region. The last decade has experienced significant consequences of the interaction amongst these communities. For example, improvements on the freedom of the Turkish community in Bulgaria have made significant contributions to Turkey's developing outlook for its own minorities.

The flow of people within the region has had many effects:

-There have been many families that happily rejoined after decades of minimal interaction.

-There has been significant growth in trade, most of which was carried out informally in street markets.

-There has been a number of mutual enthusiastic visits by NGOs, as well as government officials, promoting cooperation in many areas, from culture to economy.

-There has been the trafficking of women, and illegal migration of labour. In this book, we aim to search for a more systematic study of these issues.

Throughout its history, the Black Sea Region and the surrounding land has not only been a field of battles, but also of social interaction for different cultures that claimed sovereignty, authority and influence on the various parts of the region. The fact that the region had remained under a single authority, the Ottoman Empire, for a significant period reinforced the intensity of interactions and networks. These interactions were significant not only because they gave way to the nascence of new groups, but they also led to a decentralized exercise of power and authority that had diffused into all levels of strata. In this respect, from the very early days of history, when societies were not yet defined by national boundaries and territories, the Black Sea region witnessed a substantive migration and the circulation of population.

The Twentieth century, introduced strict barriers to the region. This created political, social, and economic walls as well as cultural ones. Despite being divided by centralized regimes, which aimed at creating homogeneous populations, all nation-states, having coasts on the Black Sea, contained minorities of the neighbouring states. Interestingly enough, an ethnic group which was the majority in one region, turned out to be the minority of another, such as Turks in Bulgaria and Romania, Muslim population in Georgia, Georgians in Turkey.

Since the history of the region is marked by migrations and resettlements, familial bonds to 'motherland' has always been kept sacred in people's minds. The shifting of boundaries was usually due to occupation and wars, which also led to the continuity of animosity between one group towards another. Many countries gained independence by fighting other countries.

Later they became co-operative neighbours -even allies. Thus, there has been a significant amount of positive and negative interaction; and emotionality. Divided by strict political barriers during most of the Twentieth century, these populations have not had the chance to interact for almost eight decades. In this political context, social science has been negligent in being able to think about the Black Sea region for geo-political analysis.

In this book, we would like to discuss whether the Black Sea, as a region, should be considered as a viable unit of analysis. Besides mentioned regional interaction among the countries, the Black Sea realm carries a political significance as being one of the proposed borders in the development process of the European Union. Countries such as Romania, Bulgaria and Turkey, will be future border states of the EU. This implies a significant role on globalization trends towards the East; Caucasus and Central Asia, for example. The overarching argument of this book is to focus on civil society and political culture that will enable social scientists to reinvigorate this common denominator, which will open the way for further studies about the region.

The literature on the post-communist transition to democracy refers primarily to the role of state actors rather than non-elite and non-state actors. There are studies investigating the role of civil society in democratic transitions in post-Soviet countries. In these writings, the importance of civil-society is recognized in post-communist transformation, only after procedural requirements have been met, and democracy has been consolidated although discovering what kind of 'civil society' is being formed remains vague.

This book presents a variety of experiences of civil society throughout the Black Sea region. The main argument put forward is that the attempt to apply the term 'civil society', which is mainly derived from West European experience to non-Western contexts, is highly problematic as pre-defined categories that oblige readers to understand local realities and experiences through the views of other experiences. In this book, we attempt to bring together both insider and outsider perspectives, we include articles from both regional and international experts. We aim to present comparative perspectives on different experiences of civil society and political culture in the Black Sea region.

Editing a book is always a significant collaborative work needing meticulous attention. We were very lucky to have Middle East Technical University −Alma Mater to all the editors- as a supporting institution. We are indebted to UNESCO for providing a grant to enable the preceding conference. Staff of the Centre for Black Sea and Central Asia (KORA) was very kind in carrying out the tedious work of organizing the conference and compiling this contribution. Throughout the various stages of the endless planning, organizing, and correspondence, KORA research assistants- Bige Yılmaz, Hayriye Kahveci, Işık Kuşçu, Aslıhan Doğanlar, and particularly

Cemre Erciyes, with her word processing skills- gave us very competent and considerate help. We owe them our appreciation. Thanks are also due to Ms. Vasilia Antoniou for her meticulous English editing.

We are grateful to all our colleagues and friends who contributed to this volume and agreed to wait patiently throughout the editorial process and revisions.

Last, but not the least, our families deserve mention for all the encouragement and personal support they have shown us throughout our careers.

I must admit that I take pride in the other editors, both of whom started their academic lives in Centre for Black Sea and Central Asia (KORA) and have become colleagues with great expertise in their areas. There is nothing more gratifying in academic life than this.

Ayşe Güneş-Ayata

Ankara, April 2004

INTRODUCTION

Ayşe GÜNEŞ-AYATA,
Ayça ERGUN & Işıl ÇELİMLİ

The Black Sea area as a region of study has recently become a unit of analysis for comparative research in social science. Recent empirical studies on countries in this region demonstrate that there are comparable experiences in their transition periods. These similarities not only denote a common ground to explore within the social scientific enterprise, but also enable researchers, policymakers and statesmen to think about their own country, reflectively, through an understanding of the experiences of others. The articles in this book are the outcome of an endeavour in which social scientists within and outside of the region attempt to explore various aspects of the transition and consolidation period in the Black Sea area. The contributors provide comparative perspectives on the nature and consequences of regime change, arrays of political transformations, changing political culture and formation of civil society.

The attempt to compare and contrast the countries of the Black Sea region is not, however, an easy task. The first difficulty surfaces when one wants to classify countries in the region, for there is no specific way of doing it. Bulgaria, Romania and Ukraine, for instance, are frequently referred to as Eastern European countries. Armenia, Azerbaijan and Georgia, on the other hand, are three post-Soviet republics of the Southern Caucasus. Turkey, which is often referred to as a Middle-Eastern country, is also considered to be part of Europe. Finally, Russia is either included in the geographical category of the Commonwealth of the Independent States or of a greater Eurasia. To decide which geographical category is appropriate for whom and to what extent such categorization reflects a comparable, homogeneous and coherent regional entity to study are still debatable issues. In this volume, instead of using existing geographical divides we have aimed at examining the specifics of the countries in the region with respect to where they stand in the transition and consolidation phases of political transformation. Despite the fact that each country has their own diverse historical experiences and cultural and socio-political structures, countries of the Black Sea region still share significant commonalities. Most significantly, almost all of them are experiencing transition and consolidation towards democratization at varying degrees since the collapse of the Soviet Union.

It is important to note than the region bears the history of once having been the battlefields of great empires and has been marked by waves of migration and resettlements. In the contemporary settings the ethnic minority of one country can be the majority in the other. This fluidity between countries creates a medium in which reflexivity becomes a significant component of the democratization process. In other words, the experiences societies have within themselves, and with respect to each other, make democratization process a unique one. Eyüp Özveren, in this volume; argues that the Black Sea region 'has always remained a zone of contention between the civilized, settled societies and nomadic challenges stemming from the periphery'. Proximity to Europe, the Eastern Mediterranean, the Caucasus and Central Asia leave the countries of the region open to interaction, exchange and influence. This historical background shapes to some extent the path of democratic political transformation. Predominantly being peripheral-or Eastern-, the countries of the region are particularly keen on being promoted to the centre-or West- and becoming an integral part of the Western world after the anticipated regime changes.

The Black Sea region also carries a political significance, being the last considerations for the enlargement process of the European Union. Countries such as Bulgaria, Romania and Turkey, once they become member states in the EU, will also define the borders of the EU. This implies that the region will play a new role in the international arena. One of our contributors, Tunç Aybak addresses this new role of the region and emphasizes the existing and would-be importance of the Black Sea Economic Cooperation (BSEC). He argues that the region has 'the potential to bridge the gap between the East and the West in Europe as well as facilitating flows between the EU and Russia'. For Aybak, this trend proves to be an example of a new type of regionalism, which will foster the political, cultural and social integration and cooperation in the region. He suggests that the BSEC can be considered as 'a peripheral response to the core regional dynamics of European integration'. Aybak further asserts that the BSEC itself is not an alternative to the EU. On the contrary, it is inspired by the EU since the EU constitutes an example of political, social and economic modernization. In order to have a consolidated democratic statehood, regional countries need the expertise, technological 'know-how', as well as capital investment from the EU. He argues that regional cooperation in the Black Sea region is of vital importance in the promotion of democratic values and in creating a 'common political culture' with the EU countries if the EU successfully completes its enlargement process. Besides achieving regional cooperation for free trade, energy and the environment, the BSEC, with the help of civil societies in the region, is likely to pave the way for the exchange of information and communication.

One of the most important means to achieve internationally recognized democratic standards is to have democratic or at least democratizing political cultures and the formation of a civil society, which would mediate between state and society in order to consolidate the transformation to democracy. Instead of applying Western notions of 'democratic political culture' and 'civil society', the contributors of this volume try to take into account the peculiarities of the Black Sea countries and to highlight their historical experiences while referring to the problems of transition.

The path towards democratization is shaped by the heritage of the prior regime type and newly introduced concepts such as democracy, multi-party system, elections and equal representation of all groups. Free and fair elections are considered as a *sine qua non* for democratization. In all post-socialist countries of the Black Sea region, electoral systems have been established. Countries conduct elections at regular intervals. The formation of multi-party systems does represent a major change in this political sphere. However, non-accountable governments, failures in the implementation of rule of law and ill-functioning political parties appear to be the major challenges that these transitional countries face. The existence of multi-party systems does not necessarily mean that they represent their electorate's interests; political parties are sometimes marked by weak organizational structures and a lack of popular support. In this book, both Sarah Birch and Olga Kesarchuk, for instance, argue that the political party elite in Ukraine benefit from their political power in order to maximize their economic interests by infiltrating the state. For Birch, although political parties are of crucial importance for democratic regimes, in its current form, political parties in Ukraine are far from contributing to democratic transition since the promotion of personal interests are more conducive for the party leaders than serving the public good. As a result, Ukrainian political parties have 'weak links to distinct sectors of the electorate' and fail to represent the electorate's interests. Similarly, Olga Kesarchuk notes that the number of political parties cannot be considered as evidence of democratization since the membership level is low; most parties are either short-lived or those which persist depend on whether the material interests of their leaders are secure or not. This evidently results in disillusionment, distrust and apolitical behaviour on the part of the electorate. Additionally, Kesarchuk argues that political parties in Ukraine do not offer clear programs. Rather, they can be classified either as being pro-government or pro-opposition.

In addition to the characteristics of political parties in Ukraine laid out by Birch and Kesarchuk, Luciana Salagean and Stephan Blackwell, in their article in this volume, introduce another dimension: Romania impinges upon the consolidation of democracy. They argue that the failures in political and economic spheres result in the empowerment of extremist nationalist tendencies as in the case of the election of Vadim Tudor as president of Romania in the elections of 2000. By illustrating the failure of a reformist agenda in Romania, Salagean and Blackwell draw attention to the existence of a dichotomy in the country where the public denies the old political values while the governing elite have internalized little change in their attitudes. These studies demonstrate that the possibility of undemocratic consequences depend on the complex dynamics of the transition periods, demonstrations of which are various. Since transition takes place at three different but overlapping and interrelated spheres - society, polity and economy- transitional governments encounter problems that are outcomes of simultaneous transformations. One also has to note that the transition period is not a linear process and countries in transition might not necessarily end up being fully consolidated democratic regimes.

With the collapse of the Soviet Union, new possibilities of interaction emerged in a wide geographical setting together with long forgotten antagonisms among various ethnic groups. In this context, the relationship between civil society and democratization, and so the resolution of ethnic conflicts, are significant issues to explore. With the transnational character and universal values it entails, civil society surfaces as an important domain on which cultural and social integration can take place. However, it is also important to point out that for the countries of the former Soviet bloc, the emergence of this domain has not been without problems. Civil society, which is considered an essential component of democratic consolidation, is a recently introduced phenomenon in these countries. The establishment of non-governmental organizations is a marker of the patterns of change introduced by the collapse of the Soviet Union. One can witness the growing number of local NGOs dealing with a wide range of issues -human rights, democratization, electoral reforms, women, education, environmental protection, juvenile rights and the protection of refugees. However, heritage of previous rule and the nature of the prior regime-type shape the nature of the organizational sphere and create tensions between civil society organizations and the state. One of the conclusions that the authors have reached is that a Western-type of civil society is yet to be applicable in countries like Armenia, Azerbaijan and Bulgaria since the local NGOs, which play the role of intermediaries between state and society, do not fulfil the same role in these countries. Challenges for the local NGOs originate from a lack of material resources, such as technical equipment, dependency on foreign funding, violations of rule-of-law, arbitrary practices on the part of the governments towards civic activists and the threat of being captured either by pro-governmental or pro-opposition political parties. As a result, civil societal actors cannot develop a sphere of their own.

In this book, articles written by Petya Kabakchieva, Ayça Ergun, Elena Triffonova and Ashot Alexanyan illustrate how the formation of civil society in different settings of the Black Sea region share striking similarities. Local NGOs conduct their activities based on projects funded by international organizations. Their activities are limited to the capital cities. Membership at local NGO levels is considerably low and the resources to recruit new members are scarce. As Ergun and Triffonova note, local NGOs predominantly work like 'research centres' or 'think tanks' rather than being active mediators between state and society. Alexanyan further argues that local NGOs' contribution in decision-making processes remains limited as they fail to operate in various fields of public life and have not established 'objective groups and a base.'

The agenda for democratization in transitional countries includes a strong emphasis on the development of civil society. State-building, institutional arrangements and national law making are designed in order to incorporate civil society with democratic political transformation. Alexanyan, notes that what he calls 'civiliarchic legitimacy' has been achieved through 'the formation of a multi-party cabinet, the establishment of a Political Council and a Human Rights Council under the auspices of the president of Armenia and the legitimate re-emergence of the Armenian Revolutionary Federation Party.' Similarly, in Azerbaijan, the state-building project of the late Heydar Aliyev's government incorporated civil society into political transformation. New units and departments were established within the presidential apparatus and parliament. Yet, the main challenge for the non-profit sector seems to originate from governments' attitudes towards civil societal actors. Ergun, argues that the regime in Azerbaijan encourages the establishment of pro-government organizations in order to create an image of promoting civil society. However, the regime is also cautious toward the activities of NGOs that are connected with opposition political parties. Particularly those NGOs which deal with 'touchy' issues such as promotion of human rights, rights of political prisoners and electoral reforms are labelled as being 'anti-state' or 'anti-government' and are threatened by the arbitrary practices of the government.

In a similar vein, Oktay Tanrısever, in this book, illustrates this dichotomic relationship between state and society with a discussion of the repression of the media in Russia. The main argument he puts forth is that what he calls a 'pathological relationship' between Russian civil society and powerful economic and political groups, which is best seen in the increasing state pressure of the media. Not only are 'disloyal' media institutions and journalists called 'enemies of Russia', but also civil society, which is not under state control, is unacceptable. According to the regime, Russian NGOs funded by international donors or powerful economic groups have their independence under question. This assumption serves as a legitimizing tool for state pressure on both media institutions and civil society organisations.

Another important aspect of the post-Soviet period is the active involvement of international actors, i.e. states, international, governmental and non-governmental organizations and transnational companies in the political transformation of the region. Ergun, Kabakchieva and Triffonova conclude that international organizations are major players in the formation of civil society in the region. Triffonova argues that the Bulgarian NGOs are largely funded through American and European donor organizations and has created a 'political' NGO community. Ergun and Kabakchieva, acknowledging the vitality of the foreign funding for local NGO existence, draw attention to some of its contradictory consequences on the civil society formation in the region. On the one hand, financial contributions provided by the international donor organizations is the main source for the realization of the local NGOs' activities as well as a source of income for the NGO elite. On the other hand, dependency on foreign funding prevents continuity in the activities of local NGOs in cases where they fail to gain subsequent projects. This results in constant competition among NGOs in order to get international funds and prevent collaboration among actors of civil society. Thus, both in Azerbaijan and Bulgaria, a well written project proposal and knowledge of to whom to apply to for funding became more important than the extent of NGO activities, recruitment of new members and actual participation in state-building and the democratization process.

Albeit unconsolidated and premature, civil societies are increasingly becoming active agents of democratization. Ergun notes that civil society in Azerbaijan precedes democratization and is the main place where the issues of how to construct a democratic society are debated. Similarly, Triffonova argues that the NGO sector is the 'reformist niche' and acts as 'the saviour of the democratic agenda' in Bulgaria.

In the region, Turkey is a successful example of democratic political transformation with its consolidated statehood and nationhood and a long history of democratization. Fethi Açıkel's article in this edition focuses on the Turkish case, which is perhaps less comparable, but still shares a number of striking similarities with its post-Soviet and Eastern European neighbours. He situates Turkey's experience at the intersection of the Mediterranean post-military regimes and post-Soviet societies in transition. For Açıkel, bureaucratic elitism of the Turkish state resembles the *nomenklatura*-type of administrations of the post-Soviet period. Yet, the Turkish case is an interesting example of semi-peripheral development with its relatively well-functioning democratic procedures and the formation of a vibrant, self-sustaining and democratic civil society voicing its demands for political rights and civil liberties.

For the development of a democratic political culture and civil society, economic amelioration is of crucial importance for transitional countries. Similar to the failures in establishing democratic statehood and vibrant civil society, economic reforms introduced after regime change have proved to be less successful. Neil Robinson argues in this book that 'partial reform states like Russia and Ukraine suffer the economic cost associated with embarking on the reform without experiencing the benefits of reform that help to lock it in place and create a virtuous reform cycle.' Robinson adds that, especially in countries where presidentialism is the regime type, parliamentary inspection is limited. This in turn results in cases where politicians do care only for the interests of social power holders who would lobby for them. Therefore, neither political consensus behind reform nor the prerequisites for market economy or for economic growth have the chance to develop.

With this book, we tried to bring together the experiences of the countries of the Black Sea region while revealing their similarities and differences in terms of political culture and civil society formations. All case studies demonstrate that neither transition nor consolidation towards democratization has been completed. The challenges facing these countries derive from their attempts to integrate the policies of reform into the not-fully-destroyed political, cultural and social heritage. Common to all countries' shortcomings in achieving successful political transformation to democracy originate from either the governments' reluctance in implementing democratic norms or their anti-democratic practices; immature civil societies lacking necessary tools and resources to mediate between state and society and unsuccessful economic reforms favouring only some segments of the public. These factors result in the emergence of a subsequent dichotomy between state and society; fragmented civil societies dispersed and captured by international donors, governments or powerful economic groups and non-equivocal representation of interests of all groups. However, the region being at the crossroads of Western and Eastern Europe, the Caucasus and Central Asia are extremely open to interchange of experience, knowledge and communication. The extension of regional and international cooperation can be a promoting tool for the development of democratic political culture and civil society in the Black Sea countries.

PART I

BLACK SEA
AS A REGION OF
STUDY

FRONTIER-FUNCTION

&

CIVIL SOCIETY:

THE BLACK SEA WORLD IN THE PAST AND ITS PROSPECTS FOR THE FUTURE

Eyüp ÖZVEREN

The concept of 'civil society' has recently become one of the most fashionable concepts in the social sciences, enjoying something of a renaissance since the collapse of the Berlin Wall (Madison, 1998, pp. ix, 1). Its initial appearance as a 'fashionable' concept occurred during the dawn of modernity, that is, in the late eighteenth and early nineteenth centuries. Interestingly, while the heritage of modernity is coming under attack from all sides, this concept so uniquely dear to the paradigm of modernity remains immune to criticism. The two heydays of 'civil society', approximately two centuries apart, are often conceptualized as similarly chaotic eras symbolized by the making and unmaking of a paradigmatic world order. Whether there is substance behind such a conceptualization remains to be seen. However, there is good reason to suspect that the similarity may be illusory at best.

To my disappointment, much of the literature on 'civil society', including that focusing on the post-Soviet world, the Middle East and Africa, makes limited reference to 'civil society'. Furthermore, they neglect to mention the added explanatory power it yields in deciphering the realities of the parts of the world to which those books refer (Harbeson, Rothchild & Chazan, 1994). In light of this repeated personal experience, I suspect a warning is in order before we begin discussing civil society in the Black Sea world. Ehrenberg, in his work on the fortunes of 'civil society' in the western provinces of the former Soviet Empire, to which the greater part of the Black Sea world was, until recently, attached noted:

As conformity, pretence, and hypocrisy came to mark Soviet-style socialism, it made sense that dissident intellectuals would theorize civil society in the familiar liberal terms of constitutional republics and limited states. But their conflation of economic regulation with political tyranny and their antistatist understanding of civil society blinded them to the dangers of the market. In the end, almost all of their civic forums, citizen groupings, 'flying universities', and social movements were swept away as traditional political structures emerged to apply the iron logic of the market. The once-heady discourse of civil society has long since faded in the region that restored it to the centre of contemporary affairs (Ehrenberg, 1999, p. xv).

Towards the end of this paper, I will return to the so-called 'dangers of the market' in order to make explicit my reservations. At this point, I should clarify what I understand as the 'Black Sea world'. I conceive of the Black Sea world as a social entity that corresponds to the geography surrounding the Black Sea. This social entity has preserved its internal structural unity over the course of history. It is characterized by both a division of labour that cuts across national boundaries and an ecological system that brings a multiplicity of peoples who share a common destiny *vis-à-vis* the natural resources at their disposal into contact (Özveren, 2001). Furthermore, the security arrangements that have prevailed in this geographical area have corresponded to the more general power configurations. It goes without saying that this structure came into increasing contact with the modern world order from the nineteenth century onwards. Even so, while becoming a part of the modern world-system, it has retained its inner characteristics. This geographical and social entity claims to be a region in its own right in close proximity to the European Union, as well as at the nexus of the West, the Eastern Mediterranean and Central Asia. Having thus offered my definition of the 'the Black Sea world', it is time to consider the concept of 'civil society'.

The popular concept of 'civil society' brings together two separate words, namely 'civil' and 'society'. As is apparent at first sight, we are in fact considering 'society'. As such, the limitations and problems that appear when discussing the concept of 'society' (Braudel, 1982, pp. 458-459; Mann, 1986, pp. 1-2) apply equally to the notion of 'civil society'. The modern concept of 'society' emerged in juxtaposition to the concept of the 'individual'. The basic assumption stated that 'society' was essentially something qualitatively different from, and considerably more than, the simple arithmetic summation of individuals. But where would the boundaries of this greater whole be drawn? This question has plagued social sciences since the concept was first employed. The practical solution defined 'society' as a greater whole than ethnic communities and less than humanity at large. The intermediate category was conveniently matched with the boundaries of the modern nation-state. The corollary was that humanity was a conglomerate of multiple societies. This definitional practice could be justified as long as the special historical circumstances continued to operate. Presently, as the global and regional dimensions of social activities gain at the expense of the nation-state and the local, adhering to the long-held definition of 'society' becomes increasingly difficult. In the last quarter of the twentieth century more and more critical sociologists have, understandably, shied away from using the concept of 'society'. We should be courageous enough to ask ourselves: how meaningful is it to refer to Russian, Turkish, Bulgarian or Kazakh societies today and can we reasonably refer to a Black Sea society that embraces all? My feeling of reluctance to do so would take us a long way in the right direction, but also away from the concept of 'society'.

Notwithstanding the aforementioned problems with 'society' as an analytical concept, we should remind ourselves of another commonplace assumption: 'civil society' as a subset of 'society'. In other words, not all societies qualify as civil societies. In fact, very few do, and these are the more privileged ones. Whereas all nation-states by definition entail societies, very few are characterized by the presence of civil societies. This implies that 'civil society' is a superior form of 'society', and therefore, all societies should strive hard to attain this objective. Thus follows the fashionable prescription for globally promoting 'civil society' as the way and means to progress.

But if all societies are not civil societies, then what constitutes a civil society? To this intriguing question no satisfactory answer has yet been given. Numerous works have addressed this question since the dawn of modernity. It should be noted that the exemplary model for discussing this phenomenon was provided by the case of England. In the immediate vicinity of England, the bright minds of the Scottish Enlightenment were the first to discuss at length, among other issues of major concern to political economy, the question of 'civil society' (Hont & Ignatieff, 1983). On the eve of the Industrial Revolution, these scholars noted three ongoing processes occurring in England. Whereas the influence of these processes was spreading quickly into the Scottish Lowlands, the Scottish Highlands continued to display a typical backwardness, which could be compared and contrasted with. Each and every one of these processes held a clue to one factor that could be singled out as the primary cause for the genesis of 'civil society'. On the way from savagery to civil society, communal bonds were loosened and the penetration of the division of labour led to the specialization of some in military tasks. The ongoing overall communal 'demilitarization' was linked with the increasing dissolution of power-based tribal and feudal distinctions. The once martial virtues were subject to a decline. These developments were well noted. The classic work on this was Adam Ferguson's resentful *An Essay on the History of Civil Society* (1767/1966).

Ferguson's work was essentially a prototypical sociological treatment of the subject. However, there was also a positive side to this process when approached from the viewpoint of political economic cost-benefit concerns. There was one geographical factor that made possible this process of communal demilitarization in England. This geographical factor was the insulation of England as an island from the European continent. England was characterized with protection at almost zero cost, illustrating how a locational advantage was converted into an economic advantage. In comparing commonwealth-minded England with Germany that wrote 'state' with a capital 'S', the leading institutionalist Thorstein Veblen (1990, p. 111) emphasized this factor. Despite this, both the sociological and the political economic treatments obscure one salient aspect of the transformation in question. The processes simultaneously taking place were occurring nationally and internationally, namely the radically different reorganization of security concerns within the domestic social space and, in the international space, England's relationship to continental Europe. Once we grasp this truth, we gain an awareness of the hidden international dimension of this security dilemma. Communal demilitarization and the concomitant design of novel security arrangements were two sides of the same coin.

If anything, geography helped deliver a result that was already in the making, in part due to an economic factor simultaneously at work. A contemporary of the Scottish Enlightenment, Adam Smith, was the first to foresee the making of an 'invisible hand', namely the market. The logic of this market would dictate the dynamics of a society in the making. It is no coincidence that another institutionalist scholar of the twentieth century referred to the then nascent social form as a 'market society' (Polanyi, 1944, p. 57). Civil society was a market society. This was so because the market as a 'democratic institution' (Schumpeter, 1942, p. 184) helped sway all distinctions and privileges and treated all as equals as far as buying and selling were concerned. The market was in this sense egalitarian. It promoted the formal equality of individuals as well as eroding ancient privileges and titles. The market undermined power constellations and helped diffuse power among the many participants. Most importantly, individuals in the market process learned to deal with one another without recourse to force. Use of force and violence were unacceptable within a market environment as they would disrupt the very logic of the presumably all-beneficial 'invisible hand' (Hirschman, 1982).

The above assessment leads us to the third definitional aspect of civil society. The word 'civil' is inextricably linked with the concept of 'civilization'. Civil societies are allegedly civilized societies. A civil society enjoys the capacity to learn to do things in a different way in a twofold manner. Firstly, it does things differently from the way it used to when it was not yet civilized. Secondly, it does things differently from other societies in its environment that have not yet developed the same capability. When posed in this light, the power of the market to guide its participants into novel peaceful ways of conduct gains a 'civilizing' attribute (Gordon, 2000).

Each of the above three characterizations of 'civil society' emphasizes a different factor. The list of characteristics can be extended to include factors such as the separation of powers, the existence of autonomous organizations and the now fashionable NGOs. Whereas the separation of powers was an early point of departure for the French philosopher Montesquieu, the emphasis on NGOs refers to a slightly later delineation that sought to re-define 'civil society' as 'organized society outside the state' (Ellis, 2000, p. 105). However, the fact remains that for each of the three basic characterizations one can enlist a number of counter-examples. There are many cases where 'demilitarization' leads to the destruction of the state and the loss of sovereignty. There are cases where the introduction of the market, far from generating a market society, leads to the reign of the Mafia as in the post-Soviet Russia. The same example shows that market transactions and interactions can in fact be forceful rather than peaceful. I contend that the exceptions to the rule point towards a different conclusion, suggesting that none of these factors alone suffices in bringing about a civil society. It is the combined and compounded effect of two or more such factors that characterize the successful cases of 'civil society'. It is the *synergy* that the combination produces that is responsible for the positive performance that we define as 'civil society'. Here lies the problem of perceiving 'civil society' as the key to success, namely the confusion as well as the conflation of cause and effect. It is acceptable to speak of 'civil society' as long as we know that we are actually referring to a *synergy* concomitant upon a combination of factors that can create an innovative capacity. My contention is that insistence on any further specification beyond this point will be counterproductive.

There is one further piece of evidence to support the above position. Throughout its history, the concept of 'civil society' has been defined in various ways. This was partly based on some arbitrariness, but also on the purpose of the scholar in question to bestow upon the definition a strong instrumentality. We have already noted some of these definitions that were specifically developed for the English reality as seen through the lens of the Scottish Enlightenment. In contradistinction, the Continental definitions of 'civil society' emphasize the historical specificities of the various European experiences. The prominent philosopher Rousseau developed a critique of 'civil society' precisely because he was disturbed by the intoxicatingly popular idea of civilizational progress. Rousseau also detested any deviation from direct democracy, the better examples of which could be witnessed in seemingly primitive communities (Coletti, 1972; Grimsley, 1973). The German philosopher Hegel (1942) redefined the concept as the important middle ground between the family and the state. His use of the concept was critical of the British definition insofar as he did not delineate 'civil society' as strictly restricted to the atomizing market. What the market and the division of labour fragmented and atomized was subject to a countervailing tendency towards unifying organization, the roots of which could be observed in civil society and the ultimate expression of which was the state (Hinchman, 1984). Marx's use of the concept lends itself to a multiplicity of interpretations depending on whether one wants to emphasize Kantian, Smithian, Rousseauistic or Hegelian influences. In the early twentieth century, the advent of the concept of 'civil society' reached a new turning point when a renowned Italian Marxist, Antonio Gramsci (1971), entertained the idea of further emphasizing the 'social' at the expense of the 'economic' in defining the concept. 'Civil society' would thus focus on voluntary and organizational undertakings and expressions of society. Only recently, a leading social scientist, Ernest Gellner (1994), warned against getting caught in the intellectual history of the concept and insisted that we subscribe to the commonplace 'operational notion' of civil society as indicative of an 'institutional pluralism of a certain kind' (p. 60). The above trajectory of the concept attests to the fact that if we try to choose any one of the existing definitions at the expense of its alternatives, we also end up choosing a particular problematic that goes with it. The malleability of the concept as such should reinforce our contention that instead of pursuing a mental exercise geared towards conceptual perfectionism we should succumb to benefiting from the inherent volatility of the concept in question.

As social scientists in the twenty-first century, we know only too well that all of the fundamental assumptions and aspects of the so-called 'nineteenth century civilization' (Polanyi, 1944, p. 3) were challenged during the inter-war period. As in all such periods, political and economic experimentation gained a new momentum. It is no coincidence that this period provided the background for two highly original and influential classic works in social science, namely Joseph A. Schumpeter's (1942) *Capitalism, Socialism and Democracy* and Karl Polanyi's (1944) *The Great Transformation*. Neither of these two texts written by institutionalist-minded scholars, worked with the concept of 'civil society'. However, they elaborated a framework within which 'civil society' could be cast in a new light. Schumpeter's text identified a distinction between a private and a political sphere. While the private sphere was primarily, but not exclusively, the realm of the economic, the public sphere was centred around the state as an institution. According to Schumpeter, the state under capitalism was the result of an historical metamorphosis of the pre-capitalist political formation within the context of the great divide between the public and private spheres (Schumpeter, 1942, p. 169). As such, with the eventual future demise of capitalism, the state as we have understood it would also crumble and fall. The implication was clear. The state, and for that matter, the corresponding civil society, could not be expected to last in the post-capitalist future. For the cautious reader a warning is issued here: can we treat the post-Soviet states as if they were of the same substance as the states in Europe during the dawn of modernity? If the answer is 'no', can we then still interpret phenomena taking place in that environment as equivalent to those that constitute 'civil societies'?

In a parallel fashion, Polanyi's work demonstrated how, in the aftermath of the Industrial Revolution, the once all-encompassing social reality was sliced into two separate spheres: the political and the economic. Within the economic sphere, the self-regulating market ruled supreme and dictated the logic of the whole system, whereas within the political sphere, the state appeared as the main institution. The most intriguing part of Polanyi's account was how the institutionalization of the market required the simultaneous expansion of the state. The market was not a natural institutional form but was instead highly artificial. Its creation and operation then necessitated a vast state apparatus that would put in place and provide the legal and operational framework needed for its day-to-day functioning (Polanyi, 1944, pp. 140-141). This insight has an important bearing on liberal dogma. The liberal proponents of 'civil society' often advocate a reduction of the state, assuming that the vacuum created will automatically be filled with 'civil society', which in their view is a market-based society. In light of Polanyi's account, there is nothing further from truth than this naive scenario. In fact, recent history abounds with examples where strong states correlate with strong civil societies, assuming that the strength in question is properly understood:

> The most effective modern economies are those which practice a loose state-economy co-operation, working on the basis of informal networks and pressures, without depriving productive units of their autonomy and liberty of movement, but frankly recognizing the significance of the state as weather-maker, and the inevitably political nature of major economic decisions (Gellner, 1994, p. 92).

Nowhere has the weakening of the state in itself paved the way for the reinforcement of either the market or civil society. It would then be absurd to expect this to happen automatically in the Black Sea region.

As the darkness of the inter-war period gave way to the destruction that the Second World War inflicted upon Europe, among the many eyes that turned to America were Polanyi's and Schumpeter's. Polanyi (1944) in his text singled out the uniqueness of America 'in the age of the open frontier' (p. 249) as a land where '[a] free supply of land, labour, and money continued to be available' (p. 201). The scarcity factor, which did not then apply as it did in Europe, questioned the inevitable conflict between market logic and the instinct of social self-protection. In other words, the exceptional circumstances of the frontier had made possible for a considerable period of time the avoidance of the social hardships of modernity. In a similar vein, Schumpeter (1942, p. 109) discussed more than once the role of 'new land' and 'virgin environments' and agreed with Polanyi that the 'presence of the "frontier" of course greatly reduced the possibilities of friction' (p. 331). He warned: 'That pace of industrial evolution incessantly created new industrial frontiers, and this fact was much more important than was the opportunity of packing one's bags and going west' (Schumpeter, 1942, p. 331). Whereas a geographical frontier

provides a society with a one-time exploitable resource, the metaphorical
use of the frontier as a permanent zone of possibility in all aspects of social
life opens new vistas for us. As in the second half of the eighteenth century
when the first notions of 'civil society' began to circulate, the nascent social
science literature was shaped by the accounts of primitive societies as
observed in the American frontier (Meek, 1976). The primitive cultures of
the New World were contrasted with European civilization in order to
substantiate as well as to criticize the concept of 'civil society'. As such, not
only was the European image formed in the mirror of the ethnographic
description of the Native Americans, but also the concept of 'civil society'
was deeply rooted in this comparative perspective. However, once
European self-confidence was well asserted, this vital link had been lost for
more than a century until the inter-war period when institutionalist scholars
such as Polanyi and Schumpeter resurrected the notion of the American
frontier. This provides us, albeit belatedly, with a window of opportunity.

During the critical period (1500-1800) when attention had been turned to
the discovery and colonization of the Americas, an important phenomenon
was overlooked. Europe had another frontier, residing albeit in obscurity.
The eminent world historian William McNeill rightly brought back to light
this second frontier as 'Europe's steppe frontier' (McNeill, 1964). Motivated
by this historiographical truth, we now look back to the literature only to
find the following somewhat photographic superimposition dating from
1835, to which the author himself referred as 'an imaginary transposition'.
The author who pretended to be a Manchester merchant was in fact Richard
Cobden, a leading member of the Manchester School for free trade:

Constantinople, outrivaling New York, may be painted with a million
of free citizens as the focus of all the trade of Eastern Europe. Let us
conjure up the thousands of piles of railroads carrying to the very
extremities of this empire—not the sanguinary satrap—but the
merchandise and the busy traders of a free State; conveying not the
firman of a ferocious sultan, armed with death to the trembling slave,
but the millions of newspapers and letters which stimulate the
enterprise and excite the patriotism of an enlightened people. Let us
imagine the Bosphorus and the sea of Marmara swarming with
steamboats connecting the European and Asiatic continents by hourly
departures and arrivals; or issuing from the Dardanelles to reanimate
once more with life and fertility the hundred islands of the
Archipelago; or conceive the rich shores of the Black Sea in the power
of the New Englander, and the Danube pouring down its produce
from the plains of Moldavia and Wallachia, now subject to the plough
of the hardy Kentuckian. Let us picture Carolinians, the Virginians,
and the Georgians, transplanted to the coasts of Asia Minor, and
behold its hundreds of cities again busting from the tomb of ages, to
recall religion and civilization to the spot from whence they first

issued forth upon the world. Alas! That this should be only an illusion of the fancy! (cited in Hirst, 1968, pp. 16-17)

Just as the American frontier once served to help elaborate the European concept of 'civil society', the Black Sea frontier, as a result of its loose structural heritage, has been a zone of institutional experimentation and innovation. I go further than either Cobden or McNeill and insist that, in a broader sense, the Black Sea world has been a permanent frontier zone. It was there that the ancient Greeks confronted the Scythians as 'barbarians' and thereby elaborated the first historiographical discourse of civilizational difference (Hartog, 1988). As such, the Black Sea was the first New World long before mankind had the faintest idea of the existence of the Americas. The Black Sea world has always remained a zone of contention between the civilized, settled societies and nomadic challenges stemming from the periphery. These tribal groupings redefined time and again pre-existing urban settlements as a frontier waiting to be ransacked and conquered. However, much more importantly, the Black Sea world has also been a frontier zone in the metaphorical sense. As a response, it was there that the Byzantine, Ottoman, Austro-Hungarian, Russian and, later, Soviet Empires emerged as political entities dealing with multi-ethnic, multi-religious populations in a practical way. It has been the privileged domain of such empires. Even the Soviet Empire, swimming against the tide, was a partial success in holding together for a considerable period of time a number of nationalities when the global trend was towards further fragmentation into conflicting nationalisms. As a political innovation, this mode of governance was invented within the context of this very geography. This conclusion is of utmost relevance with reference to the status of one of the three basic attributes of 'civil society', namely the civilizational dimension and its implications for mutual recognition and peaceful coexistence.

Having thus drawn a conclusion with regards to the Black Sea and one defining characteristic of 'civil society', we should now turn to the next. As we have noted, 'civil society' was linked with 'market society', leading us into the realm of the economic. Before we proceed any further, we should pause for a moment to recall how the actual transition from the realm of civility to that of the economic was reflected in the passage cited at the very beginning of this paper. Economically speaking, the Black Sea world has been host to a number of innovations. When the Italian merchants came into contact with the Mongols in the Black Sea basin, the simple feudal economy was blown into global proportions, thereby necessitating new ways of doing things. The innovative business practices of Italian merchants during the late Byzantine era deserve particular emphasis. The traditionalist economic environment of the Italian city states did not permit such experimentation. In particular, the Genoese merchants turned to the 'frontier', where rigid institutional rules did not apply, in order to benefit from this flexibility and try new entrepreneurial ways that would convert the Black Sea into the central point of international trade (Bratianu, 1969, pp. 224-225, 248-249). We should emphasize that in this example the stimulating environment was native whereas the innovators were foreigners, who were, in fact, the originators of transnational financial capitalism (Arrighi, 1994, p. 84). Even so, the Black Sea world as a whole had benefited from these novelties because the vast area of economic transactions below the capitalist tip of the pyramid was well consolidated. The tragic error of the communist interregnum in the Black Sea history has been a confusion of markets with capitalism. In vengeful despise of capitalism, and unable to distinguish between capitalism and the market, the command-minded authorities attacked the market instead, and subsequently, threw the baby out with the bath water. Despite this, 'black markets' survived, as did the story of enterprising Georgian and Armenian peasants travelling on a regular basis with subsidized Soviet airlines to sell their sacks of farm produce in Moscow (Braudel, 1982, p. 80).

In the immediate aftermath of the removal of obstacles to trade, elementary consumer goods markets have instantaneously flourished to a normal level. However, this has not attracted the attention of myopic yet prestigious economists; they have been concerned with something else. They advocated markets while paving the way for the influx of transnational capitalism, thereby tragically repeating the error of their communist predecessors. The recent thrust for bringing back markets in the place of the command economy has remained largely a figure of rhetoric. What have been brought back are not markets but new forms of transnational capitalism that do not necessarily cultivate the kind of social strata conducive to civility and democracy. Capitalism used in this sense is essentially monopolistic and exclusionist. As such, it is the polar opposite of the market that encourages participation and inclusion as equals. The prominent French historian Fernand Braudel (1985, p. 56) has used this distinction to conclude that capitalism is by definition 'anti-market (*contre-marché*)'. In light of this theoretical characterization, the ongoing economic transformations in the post-Soviet states cannot be taken for granted as automatically conducive of civil formations. On the other hand, the conflation of markets with capitalism leads social scientists to wrongly attribute the 'withering away of civil society' in post-Soviet Eastern Europe to the 'iron logic of the market' (Ehrenberg, 1999, p. xv).

In post-Soviet republics in general but especially in Russia, capitalism and Mafia-type organizations have been making new gains at the expense of markets and transparency. This fact leads us to the third defining feature of 'civil society', namely power and security issues, broadly defined. Throughout its history, the Black Sea world has periodically hosted the confrontation of insurgent peripheral peoples with the settled military powers. As such, Black Sea history oscillated between periods of security and stability identified with the rule of empires that provided 'protection rents' (Lane, 1979) to the economic enterprises they worked with, and periods of chaotic multi-polarity during which 'protection costs' of economic enterprises have sky rocketed. On the whole, the Black Sea world has been a host to an abundance of power and not to a scarcity of power. Consequently, peoples who have inhabited this region have had their share of violence. During the post-World War II period, the bi-polarity of the East-West divide brought to a halt all kinds of exchanges that cut across boundaries of states belonging to rival camps. Many of us have welcomed the dismemberment of the Soviet Empire, in part because it has given momentum to the revitalization of all kinds of exchanges that help contribute to the constitution of the Black Sea world as such. Nevertheless, unless a multinational security arrangement is devised soon, the potential contestation of the interests of Russia, NATO and the European Union, which is on the verge of a new round of enlargement, can seriously jeopardize the chances of peaceful civil cooperation within a Black Sea scope. In my view, lack of security arrangements in the face of intervening external factors poses the greatest imminent threat to the nascent civil formation in the region. Indeed, when it comes to supra-national structures of governance as pertinent to security designs, we are almost always twice removed from democratic participatory processes with a civil resonance.

We have thus seen that the prospects of the Black Sea world as measured against the yardstick of the three fundamental attributes of 'civil society' remain far from certain yet nevertheless open. Notwithstanding the problems noted above, whether a *synergetic* combination of the pluses will work to create the desired effect remains to be seen. In light of this indeterminate state of being, whether there will now emerge another round of innovative social structuring in the Black Sea world also remains to be seen. It should by now be clear that what concerns me more is whether civil formations that can contribute to a synergetic transformation of this region can emerge not so much within the states, as classical theories would envisage it, but across state boundaries (Porta & Scazzieri, 1997), as the exigencies of the current context may require.

The frontier attribute is both a plus and a minus. As a plus, it provides room for flexibility and innovation as we have seen above. As a minus, it helps delay the formation of civil institutions in response to a shared feeling of scarcities and limits. We now observe an example of this. In one respect, the Black Sea world is fast losing its frontier quality. If we recall the inverse relationship between 'frontier-function' and 'civil society' that Polanyi had implied in his discussion of American exceptionalism, this may imply a new opportunity. The level of environmental destruction that is now being inflicted upon the Black Sea as a non-renewable ecological system is bound to impact upon all populations residing in this region. This common threat posed to a people, who has long learned through a process of trial and error how to exploit collectively the scarce natural resources such as fisheries, may initiate a new sense of common belonging. It may lead to the creation of an ecological society (Ascherson, 1995, p. 256) that cuts across the existing national boundaries with which the concept of 'civil society' has until recently operated in. If proven correct, this will demonstrate that the Black

Sea world has the capability to give rise to further originalities and novel institutional forms that will measure up to the standards set by its own past performance. Having thus struck an optimistic note, we should however caution ourselves: the ecological unit in question is not only the innocent world of once self-replenishing fisheries but also the rich nonrenewable energy resources that appeal to the appetite of global powers and their gas and oil companies. With the foray into the power equation of these instruments of transnational capitalism, the chances of regional grassroots civil formations are likely to be reduced. The overall balance of these two countervailing tendencies will in the end determine the likelihood of a better future for the Black Sea world.

References

Ascherson, N. (1995). *Black Sea*. New York: Hill and Wang.

Arrighi, G. (1994). *The long twentieth century*. London: Verso.

Bratianu, G. I. (1969). *La Mer Noire: Des origines à la conquête Ottomane* [Black Sea: From the origins to the Ottoman conquest]. München: Societas Academica Dacoromana.

Braudel, F. (1982). *The wheels of commerce*. New York: Harper & Row.

Braudel, F. (1985). *La dynamique du capitalisme* [The dynamics of capitalism]. Paris: Les Éditions Arthaud.

Coletti, L. (1972). *From Rousseau to Lenin: Studies in ideology and society*. New York: Monthly Review Press.

Ehrenberg, J. (1999). *Civil society: The critical history of an idea*. New York: New York University Press.

Ellis, E. (2000). Immanuel Kant's two theories of civil society. In F. Trentmann (Ed.), *Paradoxes of civil society: New perspectives on modern German and British history* (pp. 105-131). New York: Berghahn Books.

Ferguson, A. (1966). *An essay on the history of civil society*. Edinburgh: Edinburgh University Press. (Original work published in 1767)

Gellner, E. (1994). *Conditions of liberty: Civil society and its rivals*. New York: Allen Lane.

Gordon, R. H. (2000). Kant, Smith, and Hegel: The market and the categorical imperative. In F. Trentmann (Ed.), *Paradoxes of civil society: New perspectives on modern German and British history* (pp. 85-104). New York: Berghahn Books.

Gramsci, A. (1971). *Selections from the prison notebooks*. London: Lawrence and Wishart.

Grimsley, R. (1973). *The philosophy of Rousseau*. Oxford: Oxford University Press.

Harbeson, J. W., Rothchild, D. & Chazan, N. (Eds.). (1994). *Civil society and the state in Africa*. London: Lynne Rienner Publishers.

Hartog, F. (1988). *The mirror of Herodotus*. Berkeley: University of California Press.

Hegel, G. W. F. (1942). *Philosophy of right*. Oxford: Clarendon Press. (Original work published in 1821)

Hirschman, A. O. (December, 1982). Rival interpretations of market society: Civilizing, destructive, or feeble?. *Journal of Economic Literature*, XX, 1463-1484.

Hirst, F. W. (Ed.). (1968). *Free trade and other fundamental doctrines of the Manchester School*. New York: A. M. Kelley. (Original work published in 1903)

Hinchman, L. P. (1984). *Hegel's critique of the Enlightenment*. Tampa and Gainsville: University Presses of Florida.

Hont, I. & Ignatieff, M. (Eds.). (1983). *Wealth and virtue: The shaping of political economy in the Scottish Enlightenment*. Cambridge: Cambridge University Press.

Lane, F. C. (1979). *Profits from power: Readings in protection rent and violence-controlling enterprises*. Albany: State University of New York Press.

Madison, G. B. (1998). *The political economy of civil society and human rights*. Routledge: London.

Mann, M. (1986). *The sources of social power: A history of power from the beginning to A.D. 1760*. Cambridge: Cambridge University Press.

McNeill, W. H. (1964). *Europe's steppe frontier, 1500-1800*. Chicago: The University of Chicago Press.

Meek, R. L. (1976). *Social science and the ignoble savage*. Cambridge: Cambridge University Press.

Özveren, E. (2001). The Black Sea World as a unit of analysis. In T. Aybak (Ed.), *Politics of the Black Sea: Regional dynamics of cooperation and conflict* (pp. 61-84). London: I. B. Tauris.

Polanyi, K. (1944). *The Great Transformation: The political and economic origins of our time*. Boston: Beacon Press.

Porta, P. L. & Scazzieri, R. (1997). Towards an economic theory of international civil society: Trust, trade and open government. *Structural Change and Economic Dynamics*, 8(1), 5-28.

Schumpeter, J. A. (1942). *Capitalism, socialism and democracy*. New York: Harper.

Veblen, T. (1990). *Imperial Germany and the Industrial Revolution*. New Brunswick: Transaction Publishers. (Original work published in 1915)

INTERREGIONAL COOPERATION BETWEEN THE EU AND BSEC

Tunç AYBAK

The aim of this paper is to evaluate the dynamics of the 'new regionalism' in the Black Sea area in comparison to the globalization process taking place in Europe. In doing so, I would like to focus on the evolving forms and functions of inter-regional relations between the EU and the regional cooperation process in the Black Sea area.

Globalization and Europeanization

The stretching of social, political and economic activities across national frontiers and the deepening of the density of patterns of global interdependence on economic, political, social and environmental issues are generally referred to as globalization. It seems that these symptoms of globalization are most acutely felt in the European continent, especially since the end of the Cold War. While the density, extent and evenness of the globalization process are disputed, the increasing patterns of interdependence on economic, political, social and environmental matters impinge on the relationship among societies and states throughout Europe (Axtmann, 1998; Wallace, 2000). As Wallace (2000, p. 370) states: 'Europeanization is not an even process across the continent, although it is not a process confined to those countries that are members of the European Union'. The state still remains as an important unit of analysis in the study of European political economy, but it is no longer the only actor. Non-governmental, supranational and transnational actors also increasingly force states to adjust to new circumstances.

The first characteristic of this development is the coexistence of many trends and levels of activity that appear to create a European space of 'contradictions, paradoxes and great fluidity' (Smith, 2001, p. 808). One can also point to the coexistence of global, regional and local processes of change in rapidly changing political, economic and cultural contexts. As well as nation states, our attention is drawn to the emergence of different realms in the Pan-European arena. In the current literature, these worlds have been described as those of 'boundaries, layers and networks'. This European area is described as an expanding negotiating space. As Smith (2001, p. 809) notes, 'negotiations in a world of bounded activities concern the emergence of new spaces, locations, institutional affiliations and state identities'. These are directly related to the dynamics of the widening and deepening process of the EU.

Apart from the shifting boundaries, another tendency that can also be observed is the emergence of new layers of governance. Layers are spheres of action and interaction among policy making actors that encompass varying scopes and extents of authority and policy making competence in various forms of regional and sub-regional organizations.

Networks on the other hand can be viewed as corporate transactions or alliances; relations between cities; cross-border transactions; information networks and transactions between cities and NGOs. These transnational policy communities also include the knowledge based academic networks and the regional civil society associations. Alongside boundaries, layers and networks, we must also consider flows. These take the form of legitimate flows in the areas of trade, tourism, energy and migration as well as illegitimate flows, such as drug and human trafficking, money laundering, environmental pollution, etc. All these flows are transboundary in nature and cannot be controlled merely by the states. The existence and emergence of networks, policy layers, shifting boundaries and flows indicate that a rapid globalization process has been taking place in Europe since the end of the Cold War. States and their sovereignty are being transformed by these emerging new spaces.

At the core of this globalization process, the EU offers a model of modernization through its Europeanization process, manifested in the supranational deepening and widening process towards a post-Westphalian order. It is pulling the states on the periphery into its integrative modernization orbit. However, the Black Sea states, located on the periphery of Europe, are still 'distant' and 'different' as well as increasingly 'dependent' on the European modernization model. They are distant because most of the Black Sea states are still in the process of state-building and modernization. They are far from the emerging post-Westphalian European order.[1] They are different because they have different structural, cultural, economic and historical trajectories from the states that form the core of Europe. Finally, and most importantly, they are dependent on Europe. They look to Europe for their political, social and economic modernization. They need the technological know-how, capital investment as well as financial and economic incentives to complete their state-building and modernization process. The dilemma here manifests itself between difference and dependence, and on how to complete the modernization process and consolidate state sovereignty while coping with the undermining impact of globalization on the strictly defined Westphalian understanding of sovereignty.

The New European Subregionalism in the Black Sea2

The emergence of the Black Sea Economic Cooperation (BSEC) can be conceived as one of the first signs that the effects of globalization were extending to the Black Sea region. The BSEC can then be seen as a peripheral response to the core regional dynamics of European integration. The demise of the Soviet Union and the disintegration of the Former Yugoslavia, as well as the speeding up of the deepening and widening processes of the European integration following Maastricht, have completely changed the landscape of the Pan-European order. In other words, the states in the Black Sea have been exposed to the initial effects of globalization emanating from the core of Europe. One way that the Black Sea states have tried to adjust to this rapid transition was to participate in the European regional political economic system. Fragile state structures compelled states to adopt new regionalist strategies in order to catch up with developments occurring in the core of Europe. In this sense, regionalization and globalization did not appear to be mutually exclusive strategies, but complementary processes for globalization in Europe.

During the 1990s regions were made and re-made and their form and content were decided by the strategies of state elites as well as social factors (Grugel & Hout, 1999, p. 9). Similarly, region building in the Black Sea area was based on the strategic calculations of states that pushed for integration as a way of positioning themselves in response to the global changes in Europe. Regionalism in the Black Sea was initiated then as a state-led project with the aim of transforming the Black Sea area into a geo-economic region. State elites have thus been crucial in driving region building.[3]

The regionalism in the Black Sea area *vis-à-vis* this European globalization process portrays the characteristic of peripheral regionalism. A rough distinction between core regions and peripheral regions has been noted by scholars (Hettne, Inotai & Sunkel, 1999, p. xvii). Core regions are economically stable, economically and technologically more advanced and dynamic, whereas the peripheral regions are defined as the regions of development. Peripheral regions are peripheral because they are 'economically stagnant, politically turbulent and war-prone'. The only way they can overcome the dilemma of dependence on, distance from and difference with the core region is to become more regionalized, that is to increase their level of regionness. As Hettne et al. suggests, the alternative to this is further political disintegration and economic marginalization. In this sense, peripheral regionalism in the periphery can be seen as a developmental strategy against the effects of globalization. Such a state strategy is conceived to transform peripheral geographies from passive objects to subjects with the capacity to articulate the interests of the emerging region (Hettne, et al., 1999, p. xviii). The states aim to form regions in order to halt the process of marginalization, despite the fact that their regional arrangements are fragile and ineffective. The success of this regionalism exercise is also dependent on regional cohesion and other background factors.

What we are witnessing in the Black Sea area is a new type of regionalism that is distinctly different from that visible during the Cold War. In contrast to closed regionalism, Black Sea regionalism is an open ended and open process. It is about joining Europe and it is not an alternative to European integration. It is a response to globalization in Europe. In this sense, globalization and regionalism in the Black Sea are not mutually exclusive. (Aybak, 2001) Whereas the old regionalism was inward oriented and protectionist in economic terms, the current regionalism in the Black Sea area is characterized as 'open' and thus compatible with an interdependent world economy. This is evident in the Preamble of the Bosporus Declaration of the BSEC, which states that the BSEC hopes 'to create better facilities to integrate the region with the European and World Economy' (BSEC, 1992).

The BSEC also differs from the old regionalism of the Cold War, which had taken shape in the context of a multi-polar world order. The regionalism that the BSEC advocates is not imposed by bipolarity. It aims to overcome the old east-west divisions of Europe. Regionalism in the Black Sea area is the outcome of an 'inside out' approach. It is a spontaneous process from within the Black Sea area where the constituent states now see the need for cooperation to tackle new global challenges. It is especially relevant to note that most states in the region lack the capacity and the means to manage such tasks at a national level (Lake, 2001).

While the old regionalism was concerned with relations among nation states, regionalism in the Black Sea allows for new types of transnational forms where many different non-state actors (regional, private, non-governmental and business networks) are activated and encouraged. Further, the Black Sea regionalism is a European regionalism. Its European character is emphasized on several occasions with reference to European legal instruments and organizations.

The old regionalism was specific with regard to its objectives (some were strictly security focused and others were economically oriented). This new regionalism in the Black Sea however is a more comprehensive and multidimensional process. As a project oriented regional cooperation framework the BSEC deals with diverse issues (such as free trade, energy and environment) and aims to create the foundations for a regional infrastructure in transportation and communications facilities. These projects, if successfully completed, will allow for horizontal engagement between societies and local economies as well as increase the regionalization of transnational interactions during the formation of a regional economy (Aybak, 2001).

As I emphasized earlier, the regionalism in the Black Sea has been conceptualized as an integral part of the emerging European architecture. The process began before the end of the Cold War among Bulgaria, Romania, the Soviet Union and Turkey. As a result of the efforts of Turkish diplomats, the idea survived the initial turbulent years of the Soviet Union's disintegration and led to the formation of the Black Sea Regional Economic Cooperation in 1992. The fact that the newly independent states of the Black Sea sat in the meeting as sovereign equals with other big regional powers for the first time was deemed to be merely symbolic. Despite the initial optimism, for the most part of the 1990s the BSEC remained a loose cooperation process. Greece, for instance, joined the BSEC to counter balance Turkey's weight, and the initial optimism of Russia has given way to suspicions regarding Turkey's motivations, particularly with regards to its southern frontier. For Ukraine, a key Black Sea country, the Black Sea cooperation was secondary to its European aspirations (Aybak, 2001). Another contributing factor to this lack of enthusiasm was the perception that the BSEC was initiated by Turkey to exert its influence on the emerging political vacuum in the region. Indeed, the Black Sea as a loose framework of cooperation was regarded secondary to the overwhelmingly European orientations and ambitions of most Black Sea countries.

By the mid 1990s, the EU developed a set of bilateral cooperation frameworks with the Black Sea countries. European association agreements came into force with Bulgaria and Romania with a vision of full membership. Turkey already had an association relationship with the EU and had signed a customs union agreement. Partnership and cooperation agreements had been signed with Russia, Ukraine, Moldova and the three Caucasian Republics (Lake, 2001; Commission of the EU, 1997). All these countries, with the exception of Russia and the full EU member Greece, expressed their willingness to join Europe. However, given their level of economic development and the political problems of the 1990s, they had to come to terms with their structural distance from the European integration zone. By the end of the 1990s, two different groups of Black Sea countries emerged in relation to European integration. The first group, composed of Bulgaria, Romania and Turkey, were gradually placed within the orbit of the enlargement process, albeit without any fixed time tables and on the condition that they fulfil the political and economic criteria. The second group of countries, consisting of Russia and Ukraine, Moldova and the three Caucasus states, settled for Partnership and Cooperation agreements.

However, what became clear was that the Black Sea area was a new negotiation and policy space for the extension of European governance primarily as a result of the plethora of bilateral ties that were formed with the EU (Friss & Murphy, 1997). These bilateral ties are not static agreements but open ended processes. While an increase in the number of EU members is a challenge, the question of which countries are candidates and which ones are left out is equally relevant. Enlargement is often seen in terms of full membership to the EU, yet it refers to a widening of boundaries in the scope of the EU's competences and in a range of policy areas from the environment to trade and from border controls to energy policies. The competencies and policies have already been extended through the Accession Protocols, as in the case of Turkey, Romania and Bulgaria. The cooperation and partnership agreements can also be seen as an extension of the EU's governance in terms of its negotiation space. In this sense, these Cooperation and Partnership Agreements seem promising given that the EU's eastern enlargement negotiations have just started. As the Luxembourg Presidential Conclusions of the EU stated: 'With the launch of enlargement we see the dawn of a new era finally putting an end to the divisions of the past. Extending the European integration model to encompass the whole of the continent is a pledge of a future stability and prosperity.' At the same time, the prospect for extending EU enlargement to include Romania and Bulgaria (and perhaps Turkey) creates new east-west divisions across the Black Sea, inducing fears of exclusion and existential insecurities.

The Relevance of Black Sea Regionalism to the EU

The increasing relevance of the BSEC for European integration warrants attention. While the Black Sea countries developed divergent bilateral relationships with the EU in the 1990s, the BSEC has also deepened its regional cooperation framework. Three important developments took place in the late 1990s. Firstly, the BSEC completed its formative stage and became a fully fledged regional organization with the ratification of its legal status in the national parliaments of the BSEC countries. Secondly, the BSEC countries expressed their intention to turn the Black Sea area into a free trade area. Last but not least, the BSEC adopted the Platform for Cooperation between the BSEC countries and the EU. In 1999, the Council of Ministers confirmed that 'BSEC attaches particular importance to its cooperation with the EU, with the ultimate aim to progressively shape the EU-BSEC economic area and thereby integrate BSEC into European economic space' (Platform for Co-Operation between EU-BSEC Platform was approved in the 13th Meeting of the Ministers of Foreign Affairs, Tbilisi, 30 April 1999.) One way of interpreting this is that the BSEC countries adopted European integration logic in order to extend the European economic space to the Black Sea (Aybak, 2001).

There has also been a marked change in perceptions. Following the coming to power of the Simitis government, Greece started playing a more active role and ceased to conceive of its membership strictly in terms of counterbalancing Turkish influence. Greece is the only EU country in the BSEC and the compromise to establish the BSTD in Thessaloniki strengthened Greece's position as the facilitator in extending the financial provisions of the EU to the region.

In the late 1990s, as Ukraine gradually felt excluded from the current enlargement process of the EU, foreign policy makers have come to realize that regional cooperation in the Black Sea matters. At a BSEC meeting, held in Yalta in 1998, the Ukrainian Foreign Minister, Boris Tarasyuk, considered 'the formation of a Euro-Black Sea community as BSEC's first task' (Bukvol as cited in Aybak, 2001). Intra-regional economic convergence between the EU and the Black Sea is particularly important for Ukraine. Russia and the CIS as a whole remain Ukraine's largest trade partners. While the EU is the Ukraine's main trading partner outside the new independent states (20 per cent of the Ukraine's trade is with the EU) only 0.3 per cent of EU trade is with Ukraine. In 1998, President Kuchma adopted a decree on the Strategy for Ukraine's Integration into the EU. However, at present this remains a distant objective. Despite the existence of a Partnership and Cooperation Agreement, there is an increasing sense of isolation from the project of European integration in Ukrainian official circles.

As far as Russia is concerned there is no official declaration of intent to join the EU. However, politically Russia and the EU are key partners and immediate neighbours on the European continent. Russia is an important trading partner for the EU. Energy supplies represent 45 per cent of Russia's exports to the EU, which in turn account for 42 per cent of the EU's needs in imported natural gas. Unlike NATO's expansion, influential pragmatists in Russia do not seem to have objections to the enlargement of the EU. A recent study suggests that awareness of the EU among the Russian public is low. Some officials are, however, concerned with the possible negative consequences of the EU enlargement. Russia's trade relations with central and east European countries are expected to be affected adversely. As one Russian analyst has recently stated, the enlargement of the EU will further increase the gap and risks creating a normative divide 'by heightening the feelings of isolation' (as cited in Light, White & Lowenhardt, 2000, p. 82) One of the most important objectives for Russian policy makers is how to incorporate Russia in European economic and social space. BSEC is now seen in some official circles as an integral part of the emerging European political economy. In this sense, regional cooperation in the Black Sea has the potential to bridge the gap between the East and the West in Europe as well as facilitating flows between the EU and Russia.

For the small and vulnerable states of Southern Caucasus, membership to the EU also remains a distant objective. These countries lie at the periphery of the Russian Federation geographically and politically, and are far from the European integration zone. As newly independent states, their claim to national sovereignty is very strong, yet their autonomy is constantly undermined by external and internal factors, such as societal breakdown, ethnic conflict, proxy wars, etc. The transition from a Soviet state to independent statehood has been a painful process. The existence of strong national and ethnic identities in the region, combined with fragile statehood, constitutes a recipe for continuous instability and fragmentation. These relatively small states are now exposed to the dynamics of globalization from above and fragmentation from below. On several occasions the leaders of Armenia, Azerbaijan and Georgia have expressed their aspirations to join the EU. It appears that the only way out of stagnation is to promote regional integration and cooperation in the Black Sea area before the long term objective of joining the European integration process can be achieved. The Southern Caucasus is a highly fragmented and a conflict-ridden area with fragile state structures and strong nationalisms. The notion that historical evidence, rather than international law, is the ultimate factor in determining the strength of the nation's claims to a specific territory continues to dominate, i.e., the 'we-lived-there-first-therefore-it's-ours'. Failure to comprehend that there are various intermediate stages between total subservience and total independence (e.g., degrees of autonomy, federal and confederal arrangements) remains an obstacle for achieving regional peace and stability (Coppieters, 2001). As Ambassador Alex Rondeli of the Georgian Ministry of Foreign Affairs suggested, 'integration in both trade and relations with neighbours within the Black Sea Region is not optional but compulsory, unless the small states in the Caucasus cooperate, they will have little hope against the fragmenting effects of globalization.'[4] Therefore, intra-regional cooperation and stability remains an essential precondition for structural convergence with the EU.

The desire for European integration suggests that regional cooperation in the Black Sea area primarily stems from the rational behaviour of states in the region in order to maximize their national interests. In the process, however, the Black Sea states have focused on whether they should pursue regional cooperation at the expense of their national interest. Instead, they focus on how their national interests are linked to regional development, thus addressing the most pressing issue: marginalization in the European political economy.

Regionalism from Below: Civil Society and Democratization

What distinguishes the new regionalism's approach from the old one is the strong civil society component. Regional dynamics from below are as crucial as the dynamics from above when forming new regional identities.

The strengthening of the national and the local as well as encouraging the involvement of civil society have aided the spreading of democratic values and the Europeanization process in the region. The emergence of a genuine civil society constitutes a crucial stage in the region building process from below. It also increases the legitimacy of regionalism in the eyes of outsiders, in this case of the EU. As Hettne et al. (1999) notes, '*regional community* takes shape when an enduring organizational framework (formal or less formal) facilitates and promotes social communication and the convergence of values and actions throughout the region, creating a civil society' (p. 11).

The organizational framework of the BSEC has been tailored to strengthen the regional civil society dimension. States and, more importantly, non-state organizations can participate in the regional structures and networks. BSEC is a comprehensive and multidimensional regional organization, facilitating frequent vertical, horizontal, bilateral and multilateral contacts and transactions at different levels of society (including governments, parliaments, the private sector, local governments, NGOs, academic and civic institutions). From the new regionalism's point of view, if civil society has arrived in the Black Sea area, it is of importance to discover to what extent this has happened. The networks themselves do not constitute a regional civil society, but they do provide the webs and channels of information and communication for encouraging a regional society within societies.

Cooperation on strengthening democracy and democratic institutions has also been high on the agenda of the Black Sea countries. The creation of the Parliamentary Assembly of the BSEC in 1993 added a democratic dimension to regional cooperation. Regular contacts among parliamentarians with similar ideological and political affiliations have contributed to the formation of a regional political culture. The PABSEC plenary sessions take place at least once a year (generally biannually). It provides the forum for discussions and assesses BSEC's activities. It also adopts reports, specific recommendations, declarations and decisions by an absolute majority.

In line with its objectives, PABSEC provides the legal framework for the realization of human rights, the rule of law and democratic values. It also enacts legislation in order to implement its decisions as well as to strengthen parliamentary democracy in the participating states. The BSEC countries have diverse political traditions and cultures with different experiences of democratization. Despite these structural differences, PABSEC has facilitated an exchange of opinions. The interdependence between democracy and development has been high on PABSEC's agenda. In seminars, organized by PABSEC, on 'Development and Democratic Institutions' and 'Peace and Stability in the Black Sea Region', parliamentary democracy and free elections have been cited as the key principles necessary in creating an environment that is conducive to regional economic development, stability and peace. PABSEC also facilitates regular contacts among national delegates from Black Sea countries. When other bilateral channels are circumscribed by friction and conflict, multilateral forums play an important role in sustaining social and political engagement, thus providing alternative channels of communication. As one observer noted, 'PABSEC's main source of influence derives from the fact that it consists of national parliamentarians who can-when back in their national parliaments-exert influence on their respective governments' (Hartwig, 1997, p. 5). While it is difficult to measure the degree of influence and recognition of the BSEC as an organization in national parliaments, the significance of national delegations discussing and exchanging opinions on regional issues cannot be underestimated.

PABSEC's new regionalist approach to the challenges of globalization is also evident in its deliberations in the words of the national delegations during the general debate on 'Globalization and the Black Sea Region's Challenges':

> Globalization is somehow undermining democracy at the level of the nation state as a result of creating trans-governmental decision making systems, effectively escaping the control of any single nation state. Consequently, in order to avoid the development of international bureaucratic structures lacking democratic legitimacy, a system of global subsidiary must be put in motion and the role of parliamentarians at the international level should increase, thus moving closer to the citizens the decision making process. Here lies the importance of the parliamentary dimension of international organizations as guarantors of democratic values in the activities of such institutions. The Parliamentary Assembly of BSEC plays an important role in providing for this. (BSEC, 2001a)

The rhetoric used in the general debates is surprisingly innovative. Apart from the democratic principle of 'subsidiarity', which allows regions to have a direct role in global governance, the parliamentarians also increasingly make references to 'pluralism, diversity, transparency and accountability'. Although these remain rhetorical, their utterance signifies that the principles of good governance and regional democracy are now being internalized by regional elites as an integral part of the regionalist discourse.

It is also worth mentioning an important report entitled 'The BSEC Economic Agenda for the Future', approved by the BSEC Council of Ministers in Moscow in April 2001. The Report offers crucial recommendations in relation to the potential role that PABSEC can play in regional good governance. While recognizing the need to preserve the independence of national legislation, PABSEC should assist states to develop stage-by-stage legislative acts which facilitate multilateral economic cooperation. Thus, speeding up economic, political and social reforms and whenever possible to approximate and harmonize these reforms with the EU legislation and standards in the areas of (prospective) BSEC-EU cooperation. The Report also invites, alongside other recommendations, PABSEC to focus on the consolidation of democracy, human rights and the rule of law, as well as to encourage and support contacts between NGOs and other civil society organizations (BSEC, 2001b).

In addition to PABSEC, the emergence of NGO networks have created the foundations for a regional civil society. At present, there are at least 16 NGOs recognized as observers by the BSEC participating in the region-wide activities through regular meetings, transactions and communications.[5]

The existing organizational facilities of the BSEC and governmental elites further encourage NGO participation.

Environmental NGOs have played an increasingly crucial role in forming the regional agenda and in participating in local, national and regional activities. As in many other aspects of political life in the post-Soviet Black Sea area, it is difficult to gather empirical information that accurately estimates the nature and extent of civic engagement. However, in the field of environmental activism regional data is relatively easier to obtain. The recently published BSEP NGO directory identifies nearly one hundred environmental organizations in the Black Sea area. At present a Black Sea NGO network exists. But, in general, these networks are externally motivated and sponsored by the EU and other international financial institutions rather than being self-sustained and independent civil society organizations. Unless environmental citizen groups form strong regional and local networks, there is little hope that the ecological identity of the Black Sea will be strengthened from the bottom. It has also been noted that local NGOs do not have the capacity to influence processes on the national - let alone international - level. 'Think globally, act locally' does not apply to Black Sea NGOs (Çevikoğlu & Tugay, 2000). Due to a lack of resources and coherent vision, regional co-operation across borders has proved to be difficult. Nonetheless, despite the social and economic conditions, there are some dedicated NGO groups working successfully in all six countries.

Generally, the concept of civil society is considered an imported notion, but one not fully internalized, by societies in the Black Sea region. As a result of the strong state traditions in the region, civil society has remained largely underdeveloped at the national level. The emergence of a genuine regional civil society and a common political culture in the Black Sea area can only follow from a strengthening of civil society at the national level.

Irrespective of the inherent weaknesses in the national civil society traditions, it is now possible to speak of an emerging regional network society in the Black Sea area. Regional interaction (in terms of movement of ideas, people, goods) at all levels of society is intensifying. The degree to which and ways that people interact in the Black Sea area suggests that it can be considered as a region. Regional civil society groups, alongside governments and states, are crucial agents and instigators of regionalism. It is highly likely that the spreading of regional networks and the multiplying of channels of communication at different levels of society will further facilitate the creation of a genuine Black Sea civil society.

The European Union's Strategic Interests in the Black Sea

The Black Sea region is important for the EU in several respects. An enlarged union will be even more dependent on external supplies of gas and oil from this region. The Black Sea region provides the crucial link with gas supplies from Russia and oil resources from the Caucasian and Central

Asian countries. The majority of Black Sea states are not only consumers, but they also provide energy transportation links with Europe. This will certainly highlight the need to promote political stability in the region.

Furthermore, with a population of 190 million (this figure only includes the number of people living in the immediate hinterland of the Black Sea), the region is an important market for future EU trade. The EU already maintains a trade surplus with many countries in the region. It is almost certain that the enlargement of the EU will increase the significance of Black Sea Regional Cooperation. As Agenda 2000 stated: 'the importance of regional cooperation will increase as the union enlarges as its development will promote the openness of the enlarged Union towards its neighbours'. In this context, the EU has realized that Black Sea Regional Cooperation is fundamental for overcoming the divisions of the Cold War. It also has a potential to overcome the new divisions between north and south in terms of development. In 1997, the European Commission issued a report titled the 'Perspectives for EU Action Encouraging Its Further Development'. In its blueprint common strategy the Commission set some priority objectives: the promotion of political stability and dialogue; the strengthening of human rights, democracy and the rule of law; effective transit through the region and the development of regional infrastructure in terms of transport and telecommunications networks to allow horizontal engagement with European networks; regional commercial cooperation and the creation of favourable conditions to attract foreign investment, including small and medium size enterprises; sustainable development, including the protection of the region's environmental integrity and nuclear safety; and the reduction of drug trafficking, smuggling and illegal immigration throughout the region.

This Commission Report is significant in two respects. First of all, it recognizes the facilitating role of the BSEC in extending of European regional governance to the region. Secondly, there seems to be a departure from strict bilateralism towards a more multilateral approach. As I pointed out earlier, the EU has already been active in the region. Since 1990 the EU has provided financial and technical assistance to the Black Sea countries via the PHARE, TACIS and MEDA programs. This assistance has amounted to nearly a billion euros. Over the same period an estimated 490 million euros in grants were also provided for activities specifically aimed at strengthening regional cooperation, for example; TRACECA (Transport Corridor Europe-Caucasus-Central Asia) project; the INOGATE (Rehabilitation Modernization and Rationalization of Interstate and Oil and Gas Pipelines) and the Black Sea Regional Energy Centre programs in the field of energy; and the Black Sea Environment program, etc. At a recent conference, it was argued that the EU has yet to overcome the problems associated with the allocation procedures for different EU programs in the region. In an interview, it was suggested by the Head of the Centre for Black Sea Studies, Yannis Papanikolau, that the PHARE, TACIS, CIIONTEL, MEDA programs should be designed in a complementary way in order to contribute more effectively to cross-regional cooperation.

In general, inter-regional cooperation between the Black Sea and the EU remains limited and the development of a coherent European strategy is still far from realization. In its reply to the BSEC's invitation to join its activities the EU was cautious. The EU's present position is that cooperation with the BSEC should proceed on an ad hoc basis. The EU still favours bilateralism in its dealings with Black Sea countries and continues to be reluctant to commit itself to multilateralism via a coherent regional strategy. NGOs, the business community and government ministers have expressed their dissatisfaction with the EU's lack of interest in the region at numerous Black Sea conferences and workshops. However, BSEC must similarly undergo a deepening process in order to become more effective as an independent actor with its own voice, particularly given the diverse interests that its members have. Despite the early signs of deep regionalization and increasing interdependence on matters of development, security, energy and environment, there remains a general reluctance to address the interconnection between these issues for future regional development. The compartmentalization of single issues within different regional institutions, with little coordination with each other, limits the possibilities for effective regional governance.

Preliminary Conclusions and Prospects

In the beginning of my paper, I referred to European globalization as a widening negotiation space and a form of governance within which new boundaries, layers of governance, flows and networks interact with each other within and beyond the control of the states. The interregional interdependence between the Black Sea and the EU is uneven and unstable. In this context, Black Sea regional cooperation offers an overall policy framework by which to extend European governance, primarily to manage the increasing yet unstable asymmetrical interdependence between the EU and the Black Sea region. However, the successful management of interdependence between the EU and the Black Sea raises a number of policy-related questions.

The first and most important concerns the issue of boundary maintenance. It is still unclear to what extent the EU will enlarge its post-Westphalian order in the Black Sea area. This suggests an increasing gap between those who are gradually being incorporated into the European integration process and those who are left out. Indeed, in a Europe of shifting boundaries, negotiations are likely to be concerned with inclusions and exclusions. What then are the implications of the growing sense of exclusion in the Black Sea region? Furthermore, what sort of relationship should the EU develop with the three key states in the region, (Russia, Turkey, Ukraine) if the enlargement process does not include them? Once accession takes place with candidates from the Black Sea, the EU's selective enlargement process will fragment and the divisive effects for the regional cooperation process will become more visible.

Secondly, the EU has been developing bilateral relations with Black Sea countries, which operate on the basis of strict conditionality. The nature of the EU's integration policies *vis-à-vis* individual countries in the region creates an uneven integration process and undermines the principle of multilateralism. Multilateralism is an essential ingredient for regional cooperation. In the race to jump on the European bandwagon, the EU's bilateral approach also encourages competition between countries of the region, rather than greater regional cooperation. In a region where full membership of the EU is seen as the ultimate goal, regional cooperation among Black Sea countries appears only secondary to their European aspirations. I argue that this amounts to putting the cart before the horses. If the EU successfully enlarges into the Black Sea region, regional cooperation in the Black Sea region is a crucial prerequisite for the development of democratic values and a common political culture between the EU and the Black Sea region.

References

Aybak, T. (Ed.). (2001). *Politics of the Black Sea: Dynamics of cooperation and conflict.* London: I.B.Tauris.

Axtmann, R. (1998). *Globalization and Europe: Theoretical and empirical investigations.* London: Pinter.

Borisenko, E. N., Kononenko, A. P. & Semonenko, I. V. (1998). *Black Sea Economic Cooperation from regional initiative to international organization.* Istanbul: Uzman Publishing.

BSEC. (June 25, 1992). The Istanbul Declaration and the Bosporus Statement .

BSEC. (2001a) *The Eighteenth PABSEC Plenary Session, Sofia, December 4-6, 2001.*

BSEC. (April, 2001b) Economic Agenda for the Future Towards a More Consolidated, Effective and Viable BSEC Partnership approved by the BSEC Council of Ministers, Moscow.

Çevikoğlu, M. & Tugay, Z. (Ed.). (2000). *Black Sea NGO directory.* (3rd ed.). İstanbul: GEF Black Sea Environmental Programme.

Commission of the EU. (1997). *Regional cooperation in the Black Sea area: State of play, perspectives for EU action encouraging its further development* (No: COM/97/0597).

Commission of the EU. (2000) *Agenda 2000.* Retrieved from http://europa. eu.int//comm/agenda2000/index.htm.

Coppieters, B. (2001). *Federalism and conflict in the Caucasus.* London: RIIA.

East-West Institute. (October 16-17, 2000). *Cooperative efforts in security of the Black Sea Region: Security challenges and cooperative responses.* Bucharest: The Black Sea Strategy Group.

Emerson, M. & Vahl, M. (August 30 - September 10, 2001). *Europe's Black Sea dimension-model for European regionalism.* Paper presented at the Halki International Seminars, Halki Island.

Friss, L. & Murphy, A. (1999). The European Union and Central Eastern Europe: Governance and boundaries. *Journal of Common Market Studies*, 37 (2), 211-232.

Grugel, J. & Hout, W. (1999). *Regionalism across the North-South divide: State strategies and globalization.* London: Routledge.

Hartwig, I. (1997). The Black Sea Economic Cooperation process. *European Institute of Public Administration*, 1, 3-8.

Hettne, B., Inotai, A. & Sunkel, O. (1999). *Globalism and the new regionalism.* London: Macmillan.

Lake, M. (August 30 - September 10, 2001). *BSEC-EU: A Platform for Political, Economic and Social Cooperation.* Paper presented at the Halki International Seminars, Halki Island.

Light, M., White, S. & Lowenhardt, J. (2000). A wider Europe: The view from Moscow and Kyiv. *International Affairs*, 76 (1), 77-88.

Mee, L. D. (August 30 - September 10, 2001). *Protecting the Black Sea environment: A challenge for cooperation and sustainable development in Europe.* Paper presented at the Halki International Seminars, Halki Island.

Neuman, I. B. (1998). European identity, EU expansion and the integration/exclusion nexus. *Alternatives*, 23 (3), 379-416.

Smith, M. (2000). Negotiating new Europes: The roles of the European Union [Special issue]. *Journal of European Public Policy*, 7(5), 806-822.

Valinakis, Y. (1999). The Black Sea Region: Challenges and opportunities for Europe [Chailliott Papers]. *WEU Institute for Security Studies*, 36.

Waever, O. (1995). *Regionalism: Concepts and approaches at the turn of the century.* Bucharest: Romanian Institute of International Affairs.

Wallece, H. (2000). Europeanization and globalisation: complementary or contradictory. *New Political Economy*, 5 (3), 369-382.

PART II

REPRESENTATION, PARTICIPATION AND ELECTIONS

PARTIES AND ELECTORATES IN UKRAINE:

CULTIVATING THE GRASS-ROOTS[1]

Sarah BIRCH

This chapter addresses the development of Ukrainian political parties with reference to the strategies employed by politicians to cultivate grass-roots support bases. One of the key questions in the study of post-communist politics is how parties structure their relations with the citizenry in such a way as to win votes in elections. Popular cynicism and disillusionment with parties in general have hampered efforts in Ukraine to cultivate party identification of the type found in Western societies. At the same time, most parties are too organizationally fragile to be able to establish stable party 'machines'. Finally, perceptions of lack of party accountability for policy limit the credibility of appeals to policy-based voting. This combination of factors presents parties with a difficult task at election time, and the aim of the analysis is to explore how they approach the electorate and which strategies have proved most successful.

Some commentators have discerned a partisan configuration in Ukraine similar to that found in many Western countries (Hesli, Reisigner & Miller, 1998; Evans & Whitefield, 2000; Miller, Erb, Reisenger & Hesli, 2000). Others, however, contend that Ukraine has no genuine parties at all (Bilous, 1997) or no real party system (Kubicek, 2000), with the implication that parties are therefore not important in Ukrainian politics. Questioning both these views, I shall argue that parties are increasingly important in Ukrainian politics but that their nature as organizations and the role they play in politics differs fundamentally from that found in Western democracies.

The Ukrainian party system cannot be fully comprehended if it is situated on a trajectory of party system development that leads from a one-party system to Western-style multipartism (the teleological fallacy of much of the democratization literature). Political parties in Ukraine function in very different ways and serve different functions both from the CPSU under communism and from parties in established democracies; rather than mediating between the state and civil society, many of the most influential parties represent vehicles through which economic elites penetrate the state in order to serve their own economic ends.

Maintaining electoral support is the weak link in the chain of relations through which parties strengthen their positions. To this end they have attempted a variety of means of winning support, which will be assessed here mainly with reference to the 1998 parliamentary elections. The first section will provide an overview of the development of political parties in Ukraine since the communist period. The link between parties and voters will be the topic of the second section. A brief conclusion will summarize the findings of the analysis and draw out their implications for future research.

Political Parties, Democracy, and the Context of Post-Communism

When democracy was first being invented in its modern guise in the eighteenth century, factionalism was seen as an evil to be avoided (Hamilton, Madison & Jay, 1961), but gradually over the intervening years parties representing different groups in society have come to be seen as crucial to democracy. The rise of mass parties with the expansion of the franchise in the late nineteenth and earliest twentieth centuries in the West established them firmly as legitimate players in the democratic process. Their role was to articulate and aggregate interests and thereby provide institutionalized links and two-way channels of communication between the state and civil society. Notwithstanding recent accounts of the professionalization and cartelization of parties in established democracies (Panebianco, 1988; Katz & Mair, 1995), they are seen as necessary to the democratic process. Moreover, when the West exports democracy, parties play a central role in the ideal type promoted.

The role of political parties in the post-communist context is obviously conditioned by their role under communism itself, and this role was characterized by a discrepancy between theory and practice. The leading role of the party was in theory a means of ensuring ideological integrity and policy development that reflected a scientifically-based approach to socio-political development. In practice, however, the party was a hierarchical power structure that served as once as a means of rule and a network of patronage. Patronage relations were especially well developed in Soviet Ukraine, where many of the USSR's most economically important and prestigious components of the military-industrial complex were located (Willerton, 1988; Harasymiv, 1990).

In the post-Soviet context parties have generated considerable antipathy from large sectors of the population while at the same time being relatively attractive to elites. This has led to a proliferation of parties with weak links to distinct sectors of the electorate and fluid identities. Parties tend to be subordinated to individuals and institutions rather than the other way round. Parties do not structure politics; politics structures parties in the sense that politics tends to be fought out in terms of struggles among institutions dominated by individuals. Organized political structures have thus played a weak and marginal mediating role between the state and civil society, and the inherent weakness of independent civil society has further attenuated these links. (See, for example, Miller, White & Heywood, 1998; Birch, 2000; Birch & Wilson, in press).

In schematic terms, there have been three main phases in the development of the Ukrainian party system: (1) the pre-party phase when nascent political groups mobilized around anti-communist causes and began to organize; (2) the period between the legalization of opposition parties in 1990 and the first multiparty parliamentary elections in 1994; and (3) the post-1994 period. Roughly speaking, the first period was characterized by protest, the second period by experimentation and learning, and the third period by the establishment of party-based channels of influence and power-regulation. The Ukrainian parties did not have to face electoral competition until March of 1994, four years after the earliest of them had formed. They therefore developed primarily as parliament-based organizations, without the perceived need to build extensive mass support bases. One of the consequences of this is that party leaders often overestimated their popularity among the electorate. The 1994 elections were a rude surprise to many of the fledgling political structures; prominent new parties such as the Ukrainian Republican Party and the Democratic Party did poorly, while the left demonstrated its continued grip on the popular consciousness (see Table 2.1). Four years later, in the parliamentary elections of 1998, an entirely new crop of parties had formed, and in the run-up to the 2002 elections, the range of parties on offer underwent further transformation.

In ideological terms, the Ukrainian party galaxy bears the birthmarks of its genesis in the late Soviet context. Since alternative political associations were allowed to form in the spring of 1990, the ideological spectrum has been structured around a broad opposition between a left favouring state control of the economy and close ties with the states of the former Soviet Union, and a right more open to the market and intent on shoring up Ukrainian independence. Yet neither the Communists nor the opposition *Rukh* party which spearheaded the independence drive has succeeded in dominating its portion of the political spectrum.

The Communists have had to compete for turf with other leftist parties, most notable among them the Socialist Party of Ukraine, and Rural (*Selyans'ka*) party and more recently the break-away Progressive Socialists, while on the right *Rukh* vies for support with a host of other moderate 'national democratic' and nationalist groups. Between independence in 1991 and the first parliamentary elections in 1994 the left parties maintained relative solidarity, both in elections where they divided the seats amongst themselves, and in parliament where they tended to vote as a bloc. The non-successor parties were considerably more fragmented, suffering frequent splits, short-lived mergers, re-launches, and name changes in an effort to map out viable political spaces and define constituencies. The reason for this is not difficult to fathom: there is only one way back but many ways forward. But more recently, when it has become obvious that the way back is a dead end, leftist cohesion has suffered badly, with many Socialists being pulled toward the centre, the Rural party splitting broadly along regional lines, and even the Communists failing to maintain the discipline they once enjoyed.

When analysing the development of the party system, it is necessary to bear in mind that Ukrainian parties were not starting from scratch. There was a long tradition of coerced political activism in Ukraine, such that the rise of multiparty competition coincided with a decline in party membership from 3.30 million in 1989 to 2.96 million in 1991 (Kuzio & Wilson, 1994, p. 142). At the same time, however, the Ukrainian party system was undergoing a dramatic diversification, and the meaning of party membership was diversifying along with it. After ten years of development, the party system has only one organization that can be described as a mass party in the traditional sense that it represents a distinct sector of the population and has a strong grass-roots support base – the Communist Party of Ukraine (CPU). But the CPU is a residual mass party, and its distinctive social contours – the age and economic deprivation that characterize its adherents – contrast sharply with its profile during the Communist period. The CPSU was banned in 1991 and not allowed to reform until the autumn of 1993. During the interim the Socialist Party of Ukraine, founded in October 1991, took over a large part of the communist party membership, which reverted to the latter in 1993. But this was also a residual membership. The CPSU attracted members largely because of the career ladder it represented. The post-Soviet communist party, by contrast, was formed of members who shared common interests and believed that the restoration of the Soviet system – both in its economic and its geopolitical aspects - would serve those interests. In many sense it has, by default, become much more similar to Western communist parties – anti-system parties of the under-privileged who share common beliefs and values.

Initially, Ukraine appeared to be going down the road of many East European states, where anti-communist umbrella movements gradually broke up into their component parts which began to differentiate themselves ideologically and compete for votes on this basis. But the 1994 parliamentary elections demonstrated the limited reach of the new anti-communist parties. In these elections two thirds of Ukraine's voters opted for candidates with no party affiliation (see Table 2.1), and a further fifth chose one of the parties of the left which had developed in the wake of the demise of the CPSU. The right and the centre together commanded less than 15 per cent of the vote and won approximately as many seats in the new parliament.

Table 2.1 Results of the 1994 parliamentary elections*

Party	Per cent votes (first round)	Number of seats by party member-ship	% Seats by party member-ship**	Number of seats by nomina-tion	% Seats by nomina-tion**
Communist Party	12.72%	86	25.44%	49	14.50%
Socialist Party	3.09%	14	4.14%	4	1.18%
Rural Party	2.74%	19	5.62%	29	8.60%
Total left	**18.55%**	**119**	**35.21%**	**82**	**24.26%**
Party of Democratic Rebirth	0.83%	4	1.18%	0	0%
Labour Party	0.40%	4	1.18%	2	0.59%
Social Democratic Party	0.36%	2	0.59%	0	0%
Civic Congress	0.25%	2	0.59%	0	0%
Total Centre	**1.84%**	**12**	**3.55%**	**2**	**0.59%**
Rukh	5.15%	20	5.92%	12	3.55%
Ukrainian Republican Party	2.52%	8	2.37%	5	1.48%
Congress of Ukrainian Nationalists	1.25%	5	1.48%	3	0.89%
Democratic Party	1.08%	2	0.59%	0	0%
Ukrainian National Assembly	0.51%	1	0.30%	0	0%
Christian Democratic Party	0.35%	1	0.30%	0	0%
Ukrainian Conservative Republican Party	0.34%	2	0.59%	1	0.30%
Total Right	**11.20%**	**39**	**11.54%**	**21**	**6.21%**
Other parties	1.93%	0	0%	0	0%
Independents	66.48%	168	49.70%	217	64.20%
Unknown				16	
Vacant seats		112		112	
Total	**100%**	**450**	**100%**	**450**	**100%**

Source: Calculated from the Vybory-94 database: Petro Mohyla Society of Kiev. (1995). *Khto ye khto v ukraïns'kii pol\u0456tytsi 1995*, Kiev: KIS.

* Results of the March and April 1994 elections.

** These figures are percentages of seats filled.

The Ukrainian parties of the left had maintained their electoral stronghold among the electorate largely due to patronage-based mobilization strategies (Birch, 1997), and it was not long before other parties began to imitate them. The post-1994 period saw the rise of a new kind of party; unlike the parties of the 1990-94 period, which had formed around ex-dissidents and intellectuals, the post-1994 'centrist' parties formed around those who had gradually accrued political and economic power. Parities were means of structuring that power. They also represented mechanisms for transforming economic power into political power that was durable and reliable. Such parties are to networks of political patronage what banks are to mafia-like economic activities: mechanisms of legitimation and regularization. Though the most politically active of Ukrainian citizens have been firmly ensconced in either the left or the right 'camp', approximately half of Ukrainian voters have been shown in surveys to favour more 'centrist' positions or not to have strong ideological leanings. A large number of the deputies elected to parliament in the single-member constituencies in 1994 were also centrist by political proclivity and factional allegiance. In ideological terms these were people who did not have strong views on statehood - which mainly divided the left and the right - and were more concerned with the distribution of state assets.

This rise in organized parties of the centre was accelerated at the time of the 1998 parliamentary elections for three main reasons. Firstly, the adoption of party list voting for half of the seats in parliament provided a strong incentive for centrists to organize along overtly partisan lines. Secondly, as post-communist transformation led to socio-economic differentiation and increasing wealth disparities among the general population, economic cleavages became more prominent; the interests of the 'haves' were more clearly distinguished from those of the 'have-nots'. Finally, the resolution of Ukraine's main statehood problems made this issue less salient. With the adoption of the constitution in 1996, Russian recognition of Ukraine's borders the following year and the resolution of tensions over the status of Crimea and the Black Sea Fleet, politicians and ordinary citizens alike were better positioned to turn their attention to economic issues. The centre of the spectrum benefited as a result, while the balance of strength between the left and the right remained much as it had been in the previous parliament.

A final aspect of the Ukrainian party system that must be noted is its high degree of regionalization, both in terms of party development and party support. 'Partification' of electoral support is much more developed in the west of the country, where the main parties are those of the right and the centre, than in the east and south where competition generally revolves around a centre-left axis. It is also notable that there is no 'red-brown' coalition as in some post-communist countries (Russia, Slovakia, Bulgaria); instead, the structure of the party spectrum more closely resembles that found in many Western countries, with a socially conservative nationalist right espousing economic liberalism and a state interventionist left.

Parties and the Electorate: Strategies of Electoral Competition

As noted above, using party structures to organize and channel networks of clientelist relations is nothing new in Ukraine. This was the norm during the communist period. What is different about the post-communist use of parties is that the decline of the unifying structure of the CPSU led to a fragmentation and diversification of informal networks and the rise of 'clan' politics. These clans are now obliged to compete with each other for power. Much of this competition goes on behind the scenes, but parties also play an important role in structuring that competition. In addition to the basic function of organizing allegiances within parliament, the main function served by political parties is that of identifiability: parties provide a means whereby members of various networks can recognize one another, and they provide a convenient means of identifying different groups to the electorate.

As during the Communist period, the party label is a badge of loyalty that enables the distinction to be made between 'us' and 'them', between those who can be trusted and those who cannot. One of the defining features of clientelist networks is their opacity; they are required to conceal many of their relations to avoid public scrutiny, but in so doing, their structure is often obscure even to members of the same network. Party membership is a legitimate and readily recognizable token in a given network that allows members to distinguish those whom they can trust from outsiders. There are of course many breaches of party trust, resulting in defections, expulsions and splits, but these very processes serve as markers which enable members and non-members alike to track shifting alliances.

Parties are also of great advantage to a network in widening its reach. The usefulness of parties in this regard became apparent at the time of the 1994 elections. Though only 33.52 per cent of parliamentary candidates were party members, 50.30 per cent of those elected held a party card (see Table 2.1). Amid the confusingly long list of names on a ballot, a party label is a convenient way for voters to distinguish one name from another. Even if they have no particular allegiance to a party, the fact that a given party label is familiar through some kind of personal contact of campaign publicity may be enough to incline voters to choose it.

Party membership is thus a convenient means of enhancing identifiability *vis-à-vis* the electorate, but it is also useful in camouflaging the potential negative attributes of a candidate. In this regard the party list system introduced for the 1998 elections was particularly well-suited, for it provided parties with a means of substituting the image of the party - which could be generated by slick advertising – from the image of the individual candidates on the list. The proportion of party-affiliated winners rose from 50.30 per cent in 1994 to 74.22 per cent in 1998 (see Table 2.2).

Yet convenience cannot be equated with a positive attitude toward political parties on the part of the electorate, and the main weakness of Ukrainian political entrepreneurs is their lack of established and reliable mechanisms for maintaining and enhancing their electoral support bases. The proportion of the voting-age population which claimed that there were *no* leaders in Ukraine fit to govern the country rose from 24.7 per cent in 1994 to 35.1 per cent in 1997 (though it declined prior to the 1998 parliamentary elections to 19.8 per cent) (*Demokratychni initsiatyvy*, 1998a, p. 18; 1998b, p. 87). Not surprisingly, disillusionment with politicians in general is also manifest in views of political parties. The same survey organization found that growing proportion of the population also believed there were no political parties in Ukraine who could be trusted with power;

28.0 per cent in 1994 and 34.0 per cent in 1997 (though again the figure declined to 20.9 per cent just prior to the 1998 elections). Parties, like politicians in general, are perceived by many as corrupt and self-serving.

Table 2.2 Results of the 1998 parliamentary elections

Party	List Votes	List Seats	% List seats	SM seats	% SM seats	Total	%
Communist Party	24.65	84	37.33	38	16.89	122	27.11
Socialist/Rural bloc	8.56	29	12.89	5	2.22	34	7.56
Progressive Socialist Party	4.05	14	6.22	2	.89	16	3.56
Working Ukraine	3.06	--	--	1	.44	1	.22
Defenders of the Fatherland	.31	--	--	--	--	--	--
All-Ukrainian Party of Workers	.79	--	--	--	--	--	--
Total left	**40.63**	**127**	**56.44**	**46**	**20.44**	**173**	**38.44**
Party of Greens	5.44	19	8.44	--	--	19	4.22
Popular Democ. P.	5.01	17	7.56	12	5.33	29	6.44
Hromada	4.68	16	7.11	7	3.11	23	5.11
Soc. Democ. P. (United)	4.01	14	6.22	3	1.33	17	3.78
Agrarian Party	3.68	--	--	8	3.56	8	1.78
Together bloc	1.89	--	--	1	.44	1	.22
NEP bloc	1.23	--	--	1	.44	1	.22
P. of Nat. Econ. Development	.94	--	--	--	--	--	--
Soc. Lib. Union bloc (SLOn)	.91	--	--	1	.44	1	.22
P. of Reg. Revival	.91	--	--	2	.89	2	.44
Soyuz	.70	--	--	1	.44	1	.22
Women's' Initiat.	.58	--	--	--	--	--	--
Soc. Democ. P.	.32	--	--	--	--	--	--
Party of Muslims	.20	--	--	--	--	--	--
Spiritual, Econ. and Soc. Progress	.20	--	--	--	--	--	--
European Choice bloc	.14	--	--	--	--	--	--
Total Centre	**30.84**	**66**	**29.33**	**36**	**16.00**	**102**	**22.67**
Rukh	9.40	32	14.22	14	6.22	46	10.22
Reforms and Order	3.13	--	--	3	1.33	3	.67
National Front bloc	2.72	--	--	5	2.22	5	1.11
Forward Ukraine! bloc	1.74	--	--	2	.89	2	.44
Christian Democratic Party	1.30	--	--	2	.89	2	.44
Republican Christian Party	.54	--	--	--	--	--	--
Ukr. National Assembly	.40	--	--	--	--	--	--
Fewer Words bloc	.17	--	--	1	.44	1	.22
Total Right	**19.43**	**32**	**14.22**	**27**	**12.00**	**59**	**13.12**
Against all	**5.26**						
Independents				116	51.56	116	25.78
Invalid	**3.09**						
Total	**100**	**225**	**100**	**225**	**100**	**450**	**100**

Sources: *Uryadovyi kyr"yer,* 1998, April 9, p. 5; 1998, April 21, pp. 4-10; *Holos Ukraïny* 1998, April 18, pp. 3-9; 1998, April 28, p. 3; 1998, August 18, p. 2.

When asked 'In your opinion, does Ukraine need a multiparty system?', 43.3 per cent responded 'no', up from 29.8 per cent in 1994 and 35.5 per cent in 1997. A similar question was asked by the International Foundation for Electoral Systems, which has conducted surveys in Ukraine yearly since 1996. These findings are made only somewhat less gloomy by the fact that those who thought multiparty competition was either 'not very important' or 'not at all important' declined from 32 per cent in 1996 to 25 per cent in 1999. In 1999, a plurality of Ukrainian voters thought multiparty competition was 'somewhat important' (IFES, 1999).

A sample survey conducted by the author and colleagues immediately prior to the 1998 parliamentary elections found similar results. When asked whether they agreed or disagreed with the statement 'Competition among political parties will make the political system stronger', 44.1 per cent disagreed, while only 42.0 per cent agreed.[2] The question obviously arises as to what characteristics those most opposed to party competition have. Multivariate analysis (not reported here) does not reveal many striking similarities among those most averse to multipartism; they do not appear to be significantly older or poorer than average; there is little indication that they are concentrated in any particular geographical location, settlement type, or gender group (once political affiliation is taken into consideration); nor do employment type or status appear to be relevant factors. The only significant sociological determinant of support for multiparty competition is higher education: those who have received education beyond the secondary level are a third again as likely to fully support the institution as those with lower education levels. There also appears to be a partisan bias in support for competitive politics; 44.8 per cent of who intended to vote for a party list from the right of the political spectrum in 1998 fully agreed with the statement on party competition, as against only 30.5 per cent of their fellow voters from the left, with centrists in between (see Table 2.3).

Table 2.3 Support for multipartism by party camp, 1998

Attitude	Party Camp (defined in terms of vote intention the party list) *			
	Left	Centre	Right	All
Strongly disagree	126 (31.0%)	66 (20.6%)	26 (19.4%)	218 (25.3%)
Disagree	53 (13.1%)	67 (20.9%)	21 (15.7%)	141 (16.4%)
Agree	103 (25.4%)	74 (23.1%)	27 (20.1%)	204 (23.7%)
Strongly Agree	124 (30.5%)	114 (35.5%)	60 (44.8%)	298 (34.6%)
All	406 (100%)	321 (100%)	134 (100%)	861 (100%)

* For definitions of party camp, see Table 2.2.
Source: Project on the Quality of Democratic Representation in Ukraine.

Table 2.3 breaks down party supporters for multipartism by party and party camp and Table 2.4 provides a similar categorization of individual party identifiers, who constitute 23.5 per cent of the total sample.[3] Among the party identifiers, 92.4 per cent indicated that they intended to vote. The figure among non-identifiers was 76.5 per cent, or 60.7 per cent of the sample as a whole. Thus a full three-fifths of the sample were 'floating voters' available for mobilization by parties. How did these voters make up their minds? There is evidence to suggest that intimidation, bribery and coercion has played an increasing role in Ukrainian electoral politics (OSCE, 1999; Wilson, 2000; Darden, 2001). The difficulty of gathering evidence on this type of determinant goes without saying. But, corrupt practices are not likely to tell the whole story; in any competitive situation such tactics are relatively expensive, especially when parties are competing to employ them. We can therefore expect that more traditional campaign tactics will also have had an important role in determining electoral outcomes. Two such factors can be expected to have been particularly important in influencing the vote decisions: media coverage of the election and campaign advertising by parties. These will be examined in turn.

Table 2.4 The distribution of party identification by party camp, 1998

Party	Strong Identifiers		Weak Identifiers		All Identifiers	
Communist Party	162	51.1%	24	28.2%	186	46.3%
Socialist/Rural bloc	41	12.9%	13	15.3%	54	13.4%
Progressive Socialist Party	1	0.3%	2	2.4%	3	0.7%
Working Ukraine bloc	8	2.5%	2	2.4%	10	2.5%
Total left	**212**	**66.9%**	**41**	**48.2%**	**253**	**62.9%**
Party of Greens	14	4.4%	4	4.7%	18	4.5%
Popular Democratic Party	18	5.7%	9	10.6%	27	6.7%
Hromada	11	3.5%			11	2.7%
Social Democratic Party (United)	7	2.2%	4	4.7%	11	2.7%
Agrarian Party	2	0.6%	1	1.2%	3	0.7%
Together bloc	1	0.3%	0	--	1	0.2%
NEP bloc	1	0.3%	0	--	1	0.2%
Party of National Economic Development	1	0.3%	0	--	1	0.2%
Inter-regional Reform Party (Part of the SLOn bloc.)	0	--	0	--	0	--
Constitutional Democ. Party (Part of the SLOn bloc.)	0	--	0	--	0	--
Party of Regional Revival	1	0.3%	0	--	1	0.2%
Women's Initiatives	2	0.6%			2	0.5%
Social Democratic Party	3	0.9%	1	1.2%	4	1.0%
Party of Spiritual, Economic, and Social Progress	1	0.3%	0	--	1	0.2%
European Choice bloc	1	0.3%	1	1.2%	2	0.5%
Total Centre	**63**	**19.9%**	**20**	**23.5%**	**83**	**20.7%**
Rukh	28	8.8%	15	17.6%	43	10.7%
Reforms and Order	1	0.3%	1	1.2%	2	0.5%
National Front bloc	3	0.9%	4	4.7%	7	1.7%
Forward Ukraine! bloc	0	--	1	1.2%	1	0.2%
Christian Democratic Party	1	0.3%	1	1.2%	2	0.5%
Republican Christian Party	0	--	1	1.2%	1	0.2%
Ukrainian National Assembly	9	2.8%	1	1.2%	10	2.5%
Fewer Words bloc	0	--	0	--	0	00
Total Right	**42**	**13.3%**	**24**	**28.3%**	**66**	**16.3%**
All identifiers	**317**	**100%**	**85**	**100%**	**402**	**100%**

Source: Project on the Quality of Democratic Representation in Ukraine.

Media Coverage of Parties:

Tables 2.5 and 2.6 present data on media coverage during the 1998 election campaign compiled by the Ukrainian Monitor project. The most striking aspect of these data is the extent to which the Communists (and the left in general) were under-covered in relation to their support among the electorate. This is true for both broadcast and print media. It must be noted, however, that the Socialists nearly broke even in print coverage, and that the phenomenon of under-reporting was one that affected the Communists more than any other major party. The second most striking aspect is the over-coverage of the centrist parties, especially the government-supporting Popular Democratic Party (NDP).

National Print Media

In proportional terms the left received less than two-fifths as much of the national print media coverage as they won list votes (see Table 2.5). Centrist parties, by contrast, enjoyed almost twice as much coverage in the national press as the proportion of the list vote they eventually won. The rightist parties fell somewhere in between: they received nearly half again as much coverage as they did electoral support. Beneath these overall patterns there are some interesting features of individual party support. The lack of reporting of Communist party activities is perhaps the most noteworthy of all: the Communist share of the vote is eight times greater than its share of national newspaper coverage. The Greens - a very different party - suffered a similar print media eclipse, which did not prevent them from an impressive result. In media terms, the Greens appear to have been a true dark horse party, which may not actually have sought the limelight of investigative journalism and analytic reporting.

At the other end of the spectrum, the Popular Democratic Party was allocated four times as much newspaper space as it garnered votes. The Social Democratic Party (united) (SDP(u)) did nearly as well, with a ratio of three and a half between newspaper space and list vote share. Despite its claims of media discrimination, former Prime Minister Pavlo Lazarenko's *Hromada* party actually got twice as much coverage in the national press as it received votes. Though it cannot be denied that there was a strenuous effort on the part of the government and the presidential administration to limit the media outlets available to Lazarenko and his party, these data suggest that this campaign was not overly successful (it may have even had the reverse effect, creating news for other papers to cover). These three 'prime ministerial' parties (parties headed by former and current prime ministers) evidently benefited from the networks of media patronage established by their leaders during their respective terms in office.

Table 2.5: National newspapers: Percentage of political news space (Percentage of political news items)*

Party/Bloc	23/2- 1/4	2/3- 8/3	9/3- 15/3	16/3- 22/3	Avr.	List Vote (%)	Ratio avr./L V
Left							
Communists	11 (5)	2 (2)	1 (1)	2 (2)	4 (3)	25	.16
Soc./Rural	5 (10)	---	18 (16)	9 (11)	8 (9)	9	.89
Prog. Soc.	6 (10)	1 (2)	---	1 (2)	2 (4)	4	.50
Working Uk.	---	3 (4)	---	1 (1)	1 (1)	3	.33
Defenders	2 (1)	---	---	---	1 (0)	0	*
Workers	---	2 (2)	---	---	1 (1)	1	1.00
	_24(26)_	_8(10)_	_19 (17)_	_13 (16)_	_16 (17)_	_42_	_.38_
Centre							
Greens	2 (1)	---	2 (3)	1 (1)	1 (1)	5	.20
Pop. Dem.	21 (21)	21 (28)	17 (16)	22 (28)	20 (23)	5	4.00
Hromada	11 (13)	11 (12)	8 (12)	8 (5)	10 (11)	5	2.00
SDP (U)	6 (14)	15 (12)	13 (16)	21 (18)	14 (15)	4	3.50
Agrarians	---	1 (2)	4 (3)	2 (1)	2 (2)	4	.50
Together	---	5 (4)	1 (1)	---	2 (1)	2	1.00
NEP	---	2 (3)	---	---	1 (1)	1	1.00
Nat. Econ. Dev't	5 (1)	---	1 (1)	4 (4)	3 (2)	1	3.00
SLOn	2 (1)	---	---	2 (3)	1 (1)	1	1.00
Reg. Revival	---	2 (2)	---	---	1 (1)	1	1.00
Soyuz	---	2 (2)	4 (2)	---	2 (1)	1	2.00
Women	1 (3)	---	---	---	0 (1)	1	.00
Soc. Dem.	---	---	3 (3)	1 (1)	1 (1)	0	*
Muslims	---	---	---	1 (1)	0 (0)	0	*
Spirital, Econ. Prog.	---	---	---	1 (1)	0 (0)	0	*
Euro. Choice	4 (3)	---	---	---	1 (1)	0	*
	_52(57)_	_59(65)_	_53(57)_	_63(63)_	_57(61)_	_31_	_1.84_
Right							
Rukh	11 (3)	18 (13)	15 (14)	13 (14)	14 (11)	9	1.56
Reforms	1 (1)	7 (8)	2 (2)	1 (3)	3 (4)	3	1.00
Nat. Front	3 (2)	4 (3)	---	---	2 (1)	3	.66
Forward Ukraine!	---	1 (2)	---	2 (3)	1 (1)	2	.50
Christ. Dem.	11 (5)	2 (2)	5 (4)	---	5 (3)	1	5.00
Rep. Christ.		---	1 (1)	---	0 (0)	1	.00
Uk. Nat. Ass.	---	2 (2)	4 (4)	---	2 (2)	0	*
Fewer Words	---	---	1 (1)	---	0 (0)	0	*
	_26 (11)_	_34 (30)_	_28 (26)_	_16 (20)_	_26 (22)_	_19_	_1.37_

* Newspapers covered include: _Holos Ukrainy, Uryadovyi kur"yer, Robitnycha hazeta, Sils'ki Visti, Ukraina moloda, Molod' Ukrainy, Vseukrainske vedomosti, Den', Nezavisimost, Region, Fakty, Zerkala nedeli, Sehodnya, Chas/Time._ The other major national newspaper, Pravda Ukrainy, was not being published during this period due to a government ban.

NB: Parties that cleared the four per cent threshold necessary to win seats in parliament are indicated in bold font. Party camp totals are in italics. Not all columns sum to one hundred per cent due to rounding error.

Sources: Calculated from data reported in the _Ukrainian Monitor_, 1998, No: 7-10.; _Uryadovyi kur"yer_, 1998, 9 April, p. 5.

On the right of the spectrum, *Rukh* also appears to have had a media advantage (undoubtedly partly because of the assiduous coverage of *Rukh*-supporting newspaper *Chas/Time*), though it was the Christian Democrats who had the greatest proportional success in attracting media attention (unfortunately for them, the proportions were in both cases relatively small).

National Television

A number of the tendencies evident in the print media are found in magnified form in television coverage figures: the leftist parties were at an even greater disadvantage in television time than was the case for newspaper space, and again, this was especially true of the Communists, who received an average of only four per cent of television coverage between 23 February and 22 March (see Table 2.6). The advantage enjoyed by the centrist parties, and most especially the Popular Democrats was also more pronounced in the distribution of air time. The party received on average thirty per cent of air time during this period, despite only having approximately five per cent support among the electorate - a ratio of six to one. The centrist parties as a group clearly monopolized television, gobbling up nearly two-thirds of the time allotted to party coverage. Once again, the rightist parties received moderately more coverage than their proportion of the list vote, but the discrepancy was less for television than it was for newspapers. Coverage of this camp most closely matched its popular strength.

Analysis of individual party coverage reveals that *Hromada* was at no particular television disadvantage in comparison with the proportion of the votes it took on polling day (at least when calculated in terms of the simple quantity of time devoted to its activities). But, whereas the print space it received was double its vote, the proportion of air time it was allocated was about the same as its proportion of the vote.

There are some other interesting differences in the distributions between the two media. First, the SDP(u) does not seem to have been nearly as fortunate in attracting television news as it was in securing print coverage. *Rukh* also received a lower proportion of air time than it did newspaper print; indeed the considerable advantage it enjoyed in the press corresponded with a distinct disadvantage on the airwaves. The Green party, on the other hand, appears to have experienced much less of a problem with television than with newspapers. Though the proportion of coverage it received was still less than its share of the list vote, the two figures are not very different.

Three main conclusions can be drawn from these findings. First, the media clearly favoured the centrist parties closest to the government (and former governments) - possibly because of lack of independence in the media, possibly because people in positions of institutional power have more opportunity to do things that command media attention, probably for

Table 2.6: National television: Percentage of political news time (Percentage of political news items)*

Party/Bloc	23/2-1/4	2/3-8/3	9/3-15/3	16/3-22/3	Avr.	List Vote	Ratio
Left							
Communists	1 (1)	4 (1)	1 (2)	9 (3)	4 (2)	25	.16
Soc./Rural	5 (12)	5 (14)	---	---	3 (7)	9	.33
Prog. Soc.	1 (4)	8 (3)	---	---	2 (2)	4	.50
Working Uk.	1 (1)	---	3 (2)	---	1 (1)	3	.33
Defenders	---	---	---	9 (2)	2 (1)	0	*
Workers	---	8 (1)	---	---		1	
	8 (18)	*25 (19)*	*4 (4)*	*18 (5)*	*14 (12)*	*42*	*.33*
Centre							
Greens	8 (4)	3 (4)	1 (2)	3 (7)	4 (4)	5	.8
Pop. Dem.	44 (48)	10 (22)	38 (33)	28 (30)	30 (33)	5	6.00
Hromada	1 (5)	1 (3)	7 (11)	9 (13)	5 (8)	5	1.00
SDP (u)	4 (7)	6 (10)	2 (11)	2 (12)	4 (10)	4	1.00
Agrarians	---	1 (1)	0 (2)	1 (2)	1 (1)	4	.25
Together	---	1 (3)	11 (7)	1 (2)	3 (3)	2	1.50
NEP	1 (1)	---	1 (2)	2 (2)	1 (1)	1	1.00
Nat. Econ. Dev't	3 (1)	23 (7)	7 (7)	2 (2)	9 (4)	1	9.00
SLOn	---	---	---	9 (2)	2 (1)	1	2.00
Reg. Revival	---	---	---	1 (2)	0 (1)	1	.00
Soyuz	---	---	---	9 (2)	2 (1)	1	2.00
Women	---	---	---	---	---	1	.00
Soc. Dem.	1 (1)	8 (3)	---	1 (2)	3 (2)	0	3.00
Muslims	6 (1)	---	---	---	2 (0)	0	2.00
Spiritual, Econ. Prog.	---	---	---	---	---	0	*
Euro. Choice	---	---	9 (4)	---	2 (1)	0	2.00
	68 (68)	*53 (53)*	*76 (79)*	*68 (78)*	*66 (70)*	*31*	*2.13*
Right							
Rukh	6 (1)	5 (3)	0 (4)	1 (5)	3 (3)	9	.33
Reforms	2 (1)	8 (11)	7 (7)	9 (7)	7 (7)	3	2.33
Nat. Front	2 (3)	---	---	1 (2)	1 (1)	3	.33
Forward Ukraine!	1 (4)	4 (8)	2 (4)	---	2 (4)	2	1.00
Christ. Dem.	6 (6)	3 (3)	9 (2)	4 (7)	6 (5)	1	6.00
Rep. Christ.	6 (1)	---	---	---	2 (0)	1	2.00
Uk. Nat. Ass.	6 (1)	---	---	---	2 (0)	0	*
Fewer Words	---	---	---	---	---	0	.00
	29 (17)	*20 (25)*	*18 (17)*	*15 (21)*	*21 (20)*	*19*	*1.11*

* Includes the following national television channels: UT-1, 1+1, TV-Tabachuk, ISTV, Inter, STB, NTU.

<u>Source</u>: Calculated from data reported in the *Ukrainian Monitor*, 1998, No: 7-10.

a combination of reasons. Secondly, the left did not need to rely on the (national) media to win votes. Thirdly, patterns in the distribution of print space were in most cases reflected in patterns of distribution of air time, with the exceptions noted above.

There were also several anomalies among the smaller parties. The Christian Democrats' coverage was again massively in excess of their electoral performance. The Party of National Economic Development was also remarkably successful in attracting the attention of the cameras, especially considering its ultimate demise at the ballot box.

Media coverage was thus most pronounced in the portion of the political spectrum where party identification was weakest. This meant that centrist parties could be expected to compensate for their lack of identifiers through their prominence in the press and on television. Indeed, this factor may have been one of the main reasons for the dramatic rise in centrist party support between 1994 and 1998.

Campaign Financing
According to Article 37 of the 1998 electoral law,[4] campaign financing takes two forms: state financing and private financing. The law stipulates that the central and constituency candidates are to pay for the printing of a limited number of campaign posters for parties and candidates in single-member constituencies, for the publication of programs in the press, and for air time for parties/candidates on state radio and television. The electoral commissions also have an obligation to arrange and fund meetings between party representatives/candidates and voters. According to the law, a second source of campaign finance is the individual accounts set up by parties for this purpose. Contributions to such funds can be made by the parties themselves, as well as by Ukrainian citizens and corporate bodies (*yurydychni osobi*), but not by foreign, international, or anonymous donors. State organizations (including state enterprises) are also banned from making donations to campaign funds. Details of all donations must be provided to the relevant electoral commissions. Any sums that remain on an account at the close of the campaign revert to the state budget (except under certain circumstances when an election must be repeated or re-held). No later than seven days before the elections, parties and candidates must provide the Central Electoral Commission with written declarations of the sources of the funds in their campaign accounts; information on the sums involved must be made public no later than two days before the elections.

These procedures were designed to introduce a degree of transparency into the process of campaign funding, yet they did not prove entirely effective. One of the reasons for this is a fault in the law, which does not explicitly prohibit the use of alternative sources of campaign financing. A statement on the campaign funding of the thirty parties and blocs that contested the elections was published in the state press on 26 March

(*Uryadovyi kur"yer*, 1998, p. 4-6). Seven parties, including *Rukh* and the Progressive Socialists, managed to circumvent the scrutiny of the electoral commission by simply declining to open special election accounts altogether.[5] In other cases the roundness of the figures involved strain credibility; the Party of National Economic Development, for example, appears to have raised exactly 700,000.00 *hryvnyas* for its campaign. Moreover, the Ukrainian state budget was not one kopeck better off from this fund-raising exercise, as no party declared any money left in its account at the time of the elections.

The declared figures do, however, provide some indication of the nature of the fund-raising capacity of many of the parties, both in terms of the sums involved and their sources (see Table 2.7). The way in which they used (or failed to use) their campaign accounts also provides insight into the parties' tactics and, indirectly, the nature of their support bases. The parties that declared the greatest expenditures were, unsurprisingly those allied most closely with government on the one hand (the Popular Democratic Party) and banking interests on the other (most notably the Green party).

It is also interesting to compare the amount spent with the number of votes gained. If it can be assumed that parties would have had little incentive to over-declare money spent, it is obvious that a number of parties in the campaign spent a good deal to little effect. The Party of Regional Revival (PVRU) came top in this category, spending over three *hryvnyas* from its campaign account for every list vote it won. The next most costly votes appear to have been those of by the Party of National and Economic Rebirth (PNERU), NEP bloc, and the NDP. From the point of view of the eventual distribution of seats the considerable sums spent by the PNERU, the PVRU were entirely in vain, while the single seats (all in single-member constituencies by candidates with their own separate accounts) won by NEP, the Together bloc, Working Ukraine, and Social Liberal Union (SLOn) were costly indeed, even if the only money spent on the campaign was in each case that declared to the Central Electoral Commission.

The parties on the extreme of the political spectrum, appear, on the other hand, to have been able to mobilize votes in the most cost-effective way. The Communists spent only 0.4 kopecks from their account per list vote won; though the Socialists admit to having spent ten times this, the amount involved is still minute in comparison to some of the centrist parties. Likewise, the far-right National Front and Fewer Words blocs declared having spent 1.6 and 1.0 *kopecks* respectively for every list vote. But it is the Party of Muslims that seems to have taken frugality to the extreme in these elections; although the party opened an account in accordance with the law, no money ever went in or out of it. It is difficult to believe the party relied only on state financing to manage its campaign, but ethnic solidarity among its target sector of the electorate makes a very low-cost campaign not implausible.[6]

Table 2.7: Campaign financing

Party	Declared campaign Funds (*hryvnyas*)	Sources of declared campaign funds, as proportion of total			% of the list vote won	*Hryvnyas* raised per list vote won
		Party	Individ. Donors	Corporate Donors		
<u>Left</u>						
Com. Party of Ukraine	**24,935**	**0.00%**	**90.01%**	**9.99%**	**24.65%**	**0.004**
Socialist-Rural blo	**106,967**	**0.00%**	**81.30%**	**18.70%**	**8.56%**	**0.05**
Working Ukraine	406,600	0.00%	4.92%	95.08%	3.06%	0.50
All-Ukrainian Party of Workers	56,558	0.39%	0.00%	99.61%	0.79%	0.27
<u>Centre</u>						
Green Party	**1,128,488**	**0.00%**	**0.09%**	**99.91%**	**5.44%**	**0.78**
Popular Dem. Party	**1,915,936**	**0.05%**	**0.00%**	**99.95%**	**5.01%**	**1.44**
Hromada	**190,132**	**100.00%**	**0.00%**	**0.00%**	**4.68%**	**0.15**
Social Dem. Party (United)	**529,900**	**0.00%**	**0.00%**	**100.00%**	**4.01%**	**0.50**
Agrarian Party	125,000	8.80%	10.40%	80.80%	3.68%	0.13
Together	705,935	0.00%	0.00%	100.00%	1.89%	1.40
NEP	742,000	12.40%	0.00%	87.60%	1.23%	2.27
Party of National Econ. Dev.	700,000	0.00%	0.00%	100.00%	0.94%	2.79
Social-Liberal Ass. (SLOn)	131,483	0.00%	90.10%	9.90%	0.91%	0.54
Party of Regional Revival	793,569	0.00%	4.89%	95.12%	0.91%	3.29
Women's Initiatives	28,240	0.00%	0.00%	100.00%	0.58%	0.18
Social Dem. Party o Ukraine	5,522	100.00%	0.00%	0.00%	0.32%	0.06
Party of Spiritual, Econ., Social Progress	3,772	0.00%	0.00%	100.00%	0.20%	0.07
<u>Right</u>						
National Front	**7,401**	**0.00%**	**100.00%**	**0.00%**	**2.72%**	**0.01**
Forward Ukraine!	35,000	57.14%	0.00%	42.86%	1.74%	0.08
Christian Dem. Part	217,062	0.00%	13.39%	86.61%	1.30%	0.63
Ukrainian National Assembly	30,400	0.00%	68.75%	31.25%	0.40%	0.29
Fewer Words	728	0.00%	100.00%	0.00%	0.17%	0.02

<u>NB:</u> Parties that cleared the four per cent threshold necessary to win seats in parliament are indicated in bold font. The second to last column does not sum to one hundred, as it excluded votes for those parties which did not open electoral accounts (18.27 per cent), as well as invalid votes (5.25 per cent) and votes against all parties (3.05 per cent).

<u>Sources:</u> *Uryadovyi Kur''yer* 26 March 1998, pp. 4-6; 9 April, 1998, p. 5.

It is also instructive to examine the break-down of electoral account funds by type of donor. Two parties, *Hromada* and the Social Democratic Party of Ukraine, placed funds in their accounts directly from their party coffers; in neither case did money come from any other source. Forward Ukraine! also relied mostly on its own funds to fill its account, but only seven parties deposited any of their own money. In most cases donations came either from individual citizens or from corporate bodies, and the break-down of parties according to these two types of source may tell us something about the character of these parties. The extremely modest sums that accumulated in the accounts of the far-right National Front and Fewer Words came entirely from individual donors, as did two-thirds of that declared by the Ukrainian National Assembly. The vast majority of the money declared by the Socialists and Communists also came from individual donations. Though there are reasons to suspect that all these parties used means other than their official electoral accounts to finance their campaigns, none of these parties ran visibly expensive campaigns, and there is every reason to believe that all of them rely extensively on grass-roots support networks that do not require public monetary expenditure for mobilization. A number of the centrist parties, on the other hand, were quite open about receiving large sums of corporate sponsorship. Most notable in this respect were the NDP, the Greens, PRVU, Together, PNERU, NEP, and the SDP(o), all of which declared at least half a million *hryvnyas* and at least four-fifths of their declared funds from corporate sources (though with differing results, as mentioned above). Some of these parties are well-known as parties of bankers - the Greens, the SDP(o), and the PNERU - while the SDP(o) and Together are known to have links with industry.

Though these figures are subject to doubt on a number of counts, they may suggest the following tentative interpretation: parties at the opposite ends of the political spectrum (including *Rukh* and the Progressive Socialists) continued to rely more on ideological identification to mobilize their constituencies. This type of support is cheap in monetary terms, or at least the costs involved are not readily visible ones. (It may also not have been in the interests of the anti-capitalist parties to have been seen to be spending large sums of money). In other words, the parties that have been most consistently successful and have the highest levels of party identification operate largely in the shadow electoral economy. Many of the centrist parties, on the other hand, relied on more 'modern' electoral tactics; raising and spending large amounts of money on lavish advertising campaigns which aim to sway Ukraine's large number of floating voters. Though no one of them proved particularly successful, together they cornered much of the centrist market and as a group they constituted a significant proportion of the list vote.

Patterns of media coverage and campaign spending clearly complement party identification, suggesting that campaign strategies have been used extensively to sway floating voters in Ukraine. But it is noteworthy that the parties which have been most successful are those that have managed to combine good campaign coverage with liberal spending and prominent candidates who are current or previous linked to government. This suggests that the combination of economic and political power that is vested in Ukraine's centrist parties represents a potent electoral weapon which is able to overcome popular cynicism and aversion of party politics. In fact, cynicism may be a significant factor in releasing voters from the constraints of principle and facilitating their attraction by parties based on economic power.

Conclusion

The development of party politics in Ukraine suggests that a successful campaign via media coverage and advertising can enable a political organization to maintain its access to state resources in the absence of a committed group of supporters. Recognizing this, a number of political leaders have used party labels as fronts for state penetration. This is a depressing story for those committed to the democratic process. The only encouraging aspect of this type of political manipulation is that it is difficult to sustain. The party machinations which took place in the run-up to the March 2002 parliamentary elections pointed to the transient nature of the party platforms that had launched the successful political bids of the main actors in 1998. The period leading up to the elections again witnessed a rush of party formation and an extensive reconfiguration of the party constellation, and it was clear that the outcome of next year's contest would be rather different from that of 1998.

The desire for political power in the absence of effective representative mechanisms has led in Ukraine to a situation in which the party system is the site of constant churn. The existence of relatively stable left and right wings is in this sense deceptive, for political outcomes are not decided in this portion of the political spectrum. They are decided by the centre, which is precisely the area in which voters are least attached to parties and most available to be swayed by slick advertising and the promise of selective benefits to supporters. This is, to an extent, true of most competitive political systems, but in Ukraine the consequence is a political elite that views the state largely as a source of wealth and the electorate as mere pawns in the process of securing access to state resources. The severe underdevelopment of independent civil society in Ukraine allows politicians to gravitate to the state, as there is virtually no organized pressure on them from 'below'.

In this context, the role of political parties is ambiguous. On the one hand, mobilization of the vote through party labels requires politicians to make broad appeals. On the other hand, it also allows party leaders to hide behind their party name, rather than accounting for their actions as individuals. Under these circumstances, we cannot say that there is true representative democracy. When the parties whose parliamentary factions swing votes do not exist for more than once election, accountability is all but absent. Few political parties in Ukraine can be said to be acting as channels of genuine interest inter-mediation; instead, they are vehicles through which existing elites can maintain positions of economic and political power. The Ukrainian case demonstrates that though political parties may be necessary to a vibrant democracy, their mere existence in the electoral arena is certainly not sufficient to bring democracy to life. When parties act as mechanisms for personal financial gain, they may be doing more harm to civil society than good.

References

Bilous, A. (1997). *Polityko-pravovi systemi: svit i Ukraïna* [Politico-legal systems of the world and Ukraine] Kiev: Amupp.

Birch, S. (1997). Nomenklatura democratization: Electoral clientelism in Post-Soviet Ukraine. *Democratization*, 4(4), 40-62.

Birch, S. (2000). *Elections and democratization in Ukraine*. Basingstoke: Macmillan.

Birch, S. & Wilson, A. (in press). Political parties in Ukraine: Virtual and representational. In P. Webb, S. White and D. Stansfield (Eds.), *Party politics in transitional democracies*. Oxford: Oxford University Press.

Darden, K. A. (2001). Blackmail as a tool of state domination: Ukraine under Kuchma. *East European Constitutional Review*, 10(2)/3, 67-71.

Demokratychni initsiatyvy. [Democratic initiatives] (1998a). *Politychnyi portret Ukraïny* 20 [Political portrait of Ukraine].

Demokratychni initsiatyvy. [Democratic initiatives] (1998b). *Politychnyi portret Ukraïny* 21 [Political portrait of Ukraine].

Evans, G. & Whitefield, S. (2000). *Partisanship and the social and ideological bases of the party system in Ukraine: 1993-1998*. Paper presented at the 96th Annual Meeting of the American Political Science Association, Washington, D.C.

Hamilton, A., Madison, J. & Jay, J. (1961). *The federalist papers*. (C. Rossiter, Ed.). New York: New American Library.

Harasymiw, B. (1990). Political patronage and Perestroika: Changes in Communist Party leadership in Ukraine under Gorbachev and Shcherbytsky. In R. N. Bahry (Ed.), *Echoes of Glasnost in Soviet Ukraine* (pp. 28-39). Ontario: Captus University Publications.

Hesli, V., Reisinger, W. & Miller, A. (1998). Political party development in divided societies: The case of Ukraine. *Electoral Studies*, 17(2), 235-256.

Holos Ukraïny [Voice of Ukraine]. April 18, 1998, pp. 3-9.

Holos Ukraïny [Voice of Ukraine]. April 28, 1998, p. 3.

Holos Ukraïny [Voice of Ukraine]. August 18, 1998, p. 2.

International Foundation for Electoral Systems [IFES]. (1999). Public opinion in 1999 [Electronic version]. Kyïv: International Foundation for Electoral Systems. Retrieved June 1999 from eng-www.ifes.kiev.ua/ Surveys/.

Katz, R. & Mair, P. (1995). Changing models of party organization and party democracy: The emergence of the Cartel Party. *Party Politics,* 1(1), 5-28.

KIS. (1995). Khto ye khto v ukraïns'kii politytsi [Who's Who in Ukrainian Politics], Kiev: KIS.

Kubicek, P. (2000). *Unbroken ties: The state, interest associations, and corporatism in Post-Soviet Ukraine.* Ann Arbor, Michigan: University of Michigan Press.

Kuzio, T. & Wilson, A. (1994). *Ukraine: Perestroika to independence.* Basingstoke: Macmillan.

Miller, W., White, S. & Heywood, P. (1998). *Values and political change in post-communist Europe.* Basingstoke: Macmillan.

Miller, A., Erb, G., Reisinger, W. & Hesli, V. (2000). Emerging party systems in Post-Soviet states: Fact or fiction?. *The Journal of Politics,* 62(2), 455-490.

Organization for Security and Cooperation in Europe [OSCE], (1999). *Ukraine: Presidential elections 31 October and 14 November 1999: Final report* [Electronic version]. Warsaw: OSCE. Retrieved April 1999 from www.osce.org/odhir/.

Panebianco, A. (1988). *Political parties: Organization and power.* Cambridge: Cambridge University Press.

Project on the Quality of Democratic Representation in Ukraine.

Ukrainian Monitor, 1998, No: 7-10.

Uryadovyi Kur"yer [Government Courier]. March 26, 1998, pp. 4-6.

Uryadovyi Kur"yer [Government Courier]. April 9, 1998, p. 5.

Uryadovyi Kur"yer [Government Courier]. April 21, 1998, pp. 4-10.

Vybory-94 database: Petro Mohyla Society of Kiev. (1995).

Willerton, J. P. Jr. (1988). Elite mobility in the locales: Towards a modified patronage model. In D. Lane (Ed.), *Elites and political power in the USSR* (pp. 99-126). Aldershot: Edward Elgar.

Wilson, A. (2000). *The Ukrainians: Unexpected nation.* New Haven, CT and London: Yale University Press.

TRANSITIONAL POLITICS, POLITICAL MARKETING AND CIVIC SOCIETY:

THE CASE OF THE 2000 ELECTIONS IN ROMANIA[7]

Luciana Maria SALAGEAN & Stephen BLACKWELL

The past four years were largely wasted in Romania, most commentators would agree. A five-party coalition government, which came to power in 1996 promising to privatise the economy and reveal the truth about the Communist past, failed to do either, and exhausted its energies on internal squabbles. As a punishment, the electorate failed to grant the Christian Democrats who led it a single seat in the new parliament. Instead, the election has two winners: the left-wing Party of Social Democracy, closely followed by Corneliu Vadim Tudor and his Greater Romania Party. They could best be described as 'national Communist'. Mr. Tudor, the Greater Romania leader, is fond of presenting visiting journalists with a chunky hardback volume of his own poems - in eight languages. Printed in Italy, on quality paper. And the first shock is that the poems are not bad. Many are melancholy, and refer to the poet's relationship to his mother and his sadness as she grows old and eventually leaves him. His knowledge of world literature may not be deep, but it is encyclopaedic. 'Yes, I am a nationalist,' he told one interviewer on election night. 'Jonathan Swift was a nationalist. William Shakespeare was a nationalist. There is nothing wrong with being a nationalist. It means to love your country. What is wrong is to be an extremist, a chauvinist, a xenophobe.' But his political enemies fear that he is just that (Thorpe, 2000, 5-13).

The gloomy tone of the reports filed from Bucharest by foreign correspondents in late 2000 reflected the deep disillusionment felt at the failure of the reformist government four years previously. The Romanian Presidential election was seen both as a decisive rejection of the failed reformist political and economic agenda of the Constantinescu regime and the rise of a crude form of populism that was embodied by the spectacular success of Corneliu Vadim Tudor and his nationalist Greater Romania Party (PRM) (Mungiu-Pippidi, 2001, pp. 230-252; for background see Stan, 1997; Gallagher, 1995; Light & Phinnemore, 2001). Tudor eventually finished second behind former President Ion Iliescu, leader of the Romanian Social Democracy Party (PDSR) and also previously a high-ranking communist bureaucrat until he fell from favour in the early 1980s. The success of the extreme nationalists was nevertheless a considerable shock both within Romania and among interested foreign powers. Given Tudor's almost complete lack of a concrete alternative to the existing regime and his reliance on hysterical xenophobia and conspiracy theories, most observers explained the vote as an angry cry from the poor and disaffected (BBC Online, 2000). It remains to be seen, however, whether the success of PRM represents merely a freak protest or a more permanent extremist trend in Romanian political life.

The results of the 2000 presidential elections in Romania have significant consequences for the future of the country. A distinguishing mark for any civil society is that it encompasses pluralism and diversity. To the extent that an organization, such as a religious fundamentalist, ethnic chauvinist, revolutionary, or millenarian movement, seeks to monopolize a functional or political space in society, claiming that it represents the only path, it contradicts the pluralistic and market-oriented nature of civil society (Diamond, 1994, p. 6). If parties like Vadim's Greater Romania Party become more prominent and present in Romania, the civil society risks to be transformed into an *uncivil society*, defined by the myriad of organizations with non-democratic or (right-wing) extremist ideas (Kopecky, 2003, p. 11). Nationalism has the potential to block the process of liberal democratic evolution and to revive the traditional nationalist conflicts in the region. This is best prevented by the evolution of civil society in the liberal democratic direction, characterized by the principle of tolerance. Liberally oriented civil society, as well as well as the neutral state that it generates, offers alternatives to national conflicts; unlike nationalism, in the liberally oriented civil society, cultural, national and political dimensions are not identical and as such can be separated from one another (Rau, 1998, pp. 138-148).

It is arguable that an over-emphasis on the reasons behind success of the opposition parties in the Romania 2000 election can lead us to ignore why the governing party lost so spectacularly. This paper argues that the campaign devised by the Romanian Democratic Convention (CDR), the governing political alliance, was central to the poor performance of the alliance in the elections. As well as seeking to provide an explanation of the failure of the CDR marketing strategy, we will also examine the way in which marketing techniques play an increasingly important part in Romanian electoral politics. This in turn will, hopefully, also suggest conclusions that may be applicable to other former communist countries undergoing a period of transitional reform. The Romanian analyst Andrei Stoiciu has concluded that 'political marketing [in the post-communist countries] is neither just a simple imitation of successful methods used in the West…nor only an unclear and improvised science that lacks a solid base' (2000, p. 13). The following will seek to explain how the Americanized marketing methods used so successfully by CDR in 1996 actually contributed to the alliance's downfall four years afterwards.

Political Marketing and Romanian Politics

In an era of advertising and image, politics has tended to become more and more the sum of the images and messages transmitted to the public. Thus, we arguably live in what the French theorist Guy Debord (1992) calls the 'society of spectacle'. Increasingly, specialists in political communication try to 'sell' to the electorate not a *politician*, but rather the *virtual image of a politician* filtered by both publicity and the media. Political marketing is a product of the steadily more sophisticated marketing strategies used during the last few decades and can be best described as a new form of publicity within a political context. Through political marketing, the reality of political life exists alongside a parallel *world of symbols and senses,* a world in which all possibilities can be realized. If in reality not everything is possible, this parallel world produced through publicity transforms the real politicians into *political objects* that can be manipulated (in the sense of being 'modified') according to the demands of image and communication. (See Negrine, 1996; Atkinson, 1996; Kavanagh, 1995)

The concept of marketing is self-evidently derived from economics, where *marketing* represents the point in a product's economic cycle when its image is being conceived, constructed and promoted. Even though political marketing finds both its semantic and content origin in commercial marketing, the former nevertheless differs from the latter through a 'particularization' of the promoted product, from which derive other particularities. Above all, political marketing is the marketing of the symbolic product, a product that looses its substance, its essence and its meaning. As high-profile publicity agents and media specialists now orchestrate political campaigns in Western countries, we have seen a clear replacement of the old forms of aggressive ideological debate by a new form of propaganda with a commercial heritage. The final goal of political marketing is to create for a politician an image than can be sold, an image that can be best characterized by simplicity, sincerity and intimacy. In addition to this, political poster advertisements have undergone a complete metamorphosis by means of *publicity appeal* as heavy symbolism and the serious image are replaced by a smile and spontaneity. Political slogans thus increasingly use an affective and emotional tone, an example being the description of Romanian President Ion Iliescu as *Un om pentru linistea noastra* ('A man for our peace') (Dancu, 1999, p. 41).

It is often claimed that politics as 'show business' is nothing more than a distortion of democracy that transforms citizens into a passive public and therefore hides real problems and trivializes criticism and thoughtful discussion. The media is complicit in this in that they pay more attention to the politician's personality at the expense of their actual policies. Critics of 'show business' politics claim that due to the media political discourse has become more dissolute, homogenized and neutral. However, though these critiques raise important issues other factors in favour also have to be considered. First, publicity, when perceived as the art of presenting an offer and the possibility of a free choice, constitutes an important factor in the preservation and strengthening of democracy. Secondly, we cannot easily claim that advertisements have replaced information, as it is extremely difficult to establish the exact border between information providing and advertising. Additionally, we can argue that politics as a 'show' is nothing more than a continuation of the process of 'de-sacralization' of politics, a process that originated as long ago as the seventeenth century (Dancu, 1999, pp. 41-42). The new 'easy' politics and the attendant de-mystification process thus arguably create self-discipline within political discourse and respect for democratic institutions.

The Western experience proves that a sophisticated political marketing strategy can win elections purely through succeeding in changing the way a politician is perceived. The marketing process self-evidently needs to achieve better 'sales' than the competitors. Whether seeking to project an image of morality or seriousness or emphasising youth and dynamism, the most important objective for a political candidate is to present a clear image that can be easily identified by the electorate. This objective is paramount even if the presentation is open to attack by political adversaries (Stoiciu, 2000, pp. 16-17). There is always, of course, a degree of 'creative tension' inside a political party between the politicians themselves and the media advisors paid by the party (Watts, 1997, p. 123). Even if they share the common objective of transmitting a certain message, the form of transmission they choose differs radically. This does not mean that politicians do not admit the importance of contemporary communication skills and presentation techniques: they would rather wish they could, in an ideal world, ignore all of these. Politicians as a rule do not instinctively think in marketing terms but rather would like to think that it is their charisma or their speeches both on a one-to-one basis and before assembled audiences that decide elections. In contrast, advertising people, aware that the skills of the politicians are not so unique or special as the politicians believe, objectify the whole process: they ask what the objective is and then how it can be achieved (Kavanagh, 1995, p. 169).

Post-revolutionary Romania and the CDR Campaign of 1996

Politically, the aftermath of the Romanian revolution in 1989 saw a paradoxical combination of both a public and permanent denial of old political values combined with little real change in both the personnel and attitudes of the governing elite. Political partisanship became a feature of the early months of post-revolutionary political activity in Romania, but with the notable characteristic that the dominance of the National Salvation Front (FSN) confined political discourse to either sustaining or criticising the government without any consideration of other alternatives on the political scene. The FSN was, from one point of view, a direct product of the Revolution, and for other electors a continuation of the old communist regime opposed to fundamental reform and change. Nevertheless, many were in favour of the FSN simply because it was the party organically connected to the Revolution and also because it was considered a left wing party that wished to safeguard the more positive aspects of the communist tradition that many people were still scared to renounce (Bulai, 1999, p. 139).

Though Ion Iliescu won the 1992 elections and his party, PDSR, occupied the majority of Parliamentary seats, four years later saw a resounding *right wing* victory for the newly formed CDR and its Presidential candidate, Emil Constantinescu. As well as a significant advance for the reformist tendency, the election also apparently marked the normalization of the political atmosphere in terms of the creation of a situation where right and left parties alternated in government. Above all, the election appeared to signal the introduction of modern political marketing techniques into Romanian electoral politics. For example, an electoral video clip of Emil Constantinescu, presented during the 1996 campaign, represented the utilization of symbolic identification in political marketing. The central message of this film was the idea of continuity and tradition represented by the National Peasant Party (PNT) and the idea of unity and the unifying leader. The force of the message derived from the very favourable facial resemblance between Constantinescu and Alexandru Ioan Cuza, the historic Romanian prince who helped to unite the Romanian territories in the Nineteenth Century (Electoral Campaign Broadcast, 1996; for the centrality of the past to current Romanian political discourse, see Boia, 1997).

Despite this, an analysis of the political outcome of the 1996 result as an expression of the electorate's attitudes leads to a paradoxical conclusion: the opposition's victory in 1996 was made possible by the fact that the majority of electorate had the same *voting attitude* as they had in 1992. This is explained by the difference between political communication and political action as adopted by the major Romanian political parties. During the 1992 campaign, PDSR promoted a clear left-wing message, in which social protection and the idea of maintaining the State's role in society were the key elements of a successful electoral campaign. In its actual period of government, the party (including a significant number of its allies) was not perceived as fulfilling the promises of the electoral campaign. Furthermore, during the 1996 campaign right wing and centrist parties started to court the left wing sections of the electorate, consequently destabilising those parties who were supposed to have a monopoly on such an appeal. In these circumstances, the left had no other choice other than to either try to outmatch its rivals in making promises of benevolent government intervention or propose a totally different agenda. Eventually, however, the chosen strategies proved to be ineffective. The left-wing parties were beaten by a left-orientated campaign (Bulai, 1999, p. 140; see also Hollis, 1999, pp. 449-462, 501-509.).

During the 1996 elections, the winning coalition defined a particular style of managing the campaign. The previously reactive and aggressive tactics used in structuring the message was successfully combined with one in which the party's own policies were prominent. Therefore, even though the campaign was still centred around ideological ideas that focused on the occasionally aggressive criticism of the governing party, another powerful element was included in the form of a 'contract' with the electorate. In cases where the CDR campaign directly attacked the PDSR government, the latter followed the same style as that adopted during 1992 on the assumption that it was a winning formula. The PDSR preferred, therefore, an aggressive campaign, full of criticism of the opposition and centred on important ideological ideas, yet was seen as being too pretentious and inclined to use 'scare-mongering' tactics on the electorate. The ruling party focused on a litany of the negative consequences entailed by voting for the CDR, such as the restoration of the discredited Romanian monarchy, the loss of national suzerainty and the expropriation of goods acquired by people through honest work during the communist regime (*Evenimentul Zilei*, September 26 & October 15-17, 1996).

Apart from problems related to the negative content of PDSR's electoral message, more subtle discrepancies connected to each party's conduct of the style of the campaign emerged. In 1992, PDSR was seen by many electors as a new party which had its origins in the FSN but which was also leading a legitimate fight against those who 'had betrayed' the revolution as well as against the traditional enemies represented by the CDR. 1996 also saw the first significant impact of one of the still small political movements, the PRM. The nationalists chose a very simple campaign focused on a single personality, its leader Corneliu Vadim Tudor, and with a thin substance message centred only on corruption and the fight against it. During the electoral campaign, Tudor proved himself to be an exceptional orator. Yet his success subsequent to 1996 is also the result of a previous well-thought divorce of the PRM leader from a previous coalition with the PDSR government, an action that allowed Vadim Tudor to adopt the posture of 'victim of the government' and appeal for the electorate's sympathy. The result was an enormous increase in the popularity of the extreme nationalists (Baleanu, 2001, pp. 32-40).

The Decline of the CDR Government and the Rise of a 'New Opposition', 1996-2000

In 1996, CDR found itself in the clear position of a winner and had considerable support from a broad range of the electorate. Unfortunately, the government was far from ready to initiate decisive action and soon ran into difficulties. Unfulfilled promises, Romania's failure to join the main Western institutions, visible corruption and continuing economic difficulties led to a gradual collapse of support for the CDR government and President Constantinescu (Phinnemore, 2001, pp. 245-269). Constantinescu began his 'presidential career' as the first leader of the non-communist opposition to have won the elections after 1989 and was expected to be the strong man who would finally pull the country through the painful period of post-totalitarianism, transition and economic instability. On the contrary, his public persona became increasingly weaker and uncertain. Within less than a year, President Constantinescu had very little in common with Presidential Candidate Constantinescu, the man who in 1996 confronted and won against Ion Iliescu. Even his 'legendary' goatee beard, which in 1996 represented the trans-historical connection with *Cuza*, became nothing more than the source of a derogatory nickname, 'the Goat'.

Even the young electorate, many of whom voted for the first time in 1996 and had chosen 'the change', felt betrayed and disillusioned as a result of administration's performance.[8] While the CDR argued that the inefficiency of its own government stemmed from the problems inherited during the six years of Iliescu government, many Romanians had become tired of transitional promises. The outcome in electoral terms was again paradoxical. Ion Iliescu, still the CDR's main opponent, represented *a past* of problems and disappointments, but a past that like all pasts tended to fade away in the collective memory. Constantinescu represented *the present*, a present that was not only dominated by mistakes and corruption, but also a preoccupation with certain problematic issues. After 1996, *the future* seemed uncertain and the electorate feared a situation in which it would be forced to choose between the same 'old' alternatives.

Against this background, Corneliu Vadim Tudor and the Romanian extreme nationalists became more prominent. Besides his own qualities, Tudor's party was boosted by the defection to his party of another prominent political personality, Gheorghe Funar. Elected Mayor of the Transylvanian city of Cluj-Napoca in 1992, Funar was the former leader of the Party of Romanian National Unity (PUNR) and was famous for extreme nationalist attitudes and discrimination towards the Hungarian minority. After jumping ship from PUNR (which had gone into rapid decline after 1996), Funar seemed to be the perfect 'match' for Vadim. Together they acted in a sense as a 'dream team', a team that appealed to mythical 'traditional' Romanian values and promised the punishment of those found guilty of corruption and other crimes. The improved performance of PRM and the decline in support for the CDR government should also be understood in the broader context of the Romanian inner conflict between progress and tradition. The allure of 'Westernization' was juxtaposed to an increasingly rigid social stratification. After 40 years of 'equality', even if that were only a *symbolic* form of equality, the Romanian found themselves in a condition of total and exposed inequality. Using economic criteria, quite a few specialists have noted that Romania is gradually becoming a 'bi-polar' society, with no real middle class between a comparatively wealthy upper class and a large and poor lower class (Gallagher, 2000, pp. 185-201).

The Electoral Campaign of 2000: the Marketing of the CDR

In 1996, the creation of the successful CDR alliance of centre and right parties was designed to 'counter-attack a new accession of the left' (*Adevarul*, June 17, 1996) The decision of the Union of Right Forces (UFD) to leave the government in the run-up to the 2000 elections was a severe shock to the CDR and was rapidly followed by UFD attacks on what remained of the governing coalition. This constituted the first significant indication of the CDR's bankrupt legitimacy as a ruling authority. Continued weak and indecisive government led to widespread criticism that was skilfully exploited by PDSR. In view of the considerable disillusionment with the government, the utilization of a professional political marketing during the 2000 electoral campaign might have been the only practical way of improving the negative image of CDR. What the 'CDR 2000' campaign managers did not appreciate was that 'professional political marketing' did not mean the simple 'copy and paste' of the Western models, but rather the adaptation of these models to the political, social and economic context of Romania. Unfortunately, the political marketing strategy adopted by CDR for its 2000 electoral campaign was, at best, disorganized and lacking in focus.

At the national level, the main campaign slogan adopted by CDR 2000 was totally uninspired. In seeking to appeal to the emotional side of Romanians, the message transmitted nothing more than a sentiment of marginalization and exclusion in the face of overwhelming difficulties. '*Singuri in fata Europei*', due to the ambiguous nature of the word '*singuri*' could very well be read as either 'alone facing Europe', 'the only ones facing Europe' or 'on our own in front of Europe'. Probably the original idea was to transmit that Romanians were on their own in front of the gates of Europe and that it was up to the nation to build a strong Romania that deserved to be integrated within the EU. Unfortunately, the effect produced by this slogan was a diametrical opposite because to the fact that during the period of Constantinescu's presidency the CDR government had made little progress in securing Romania's accession to the EU. '*Singuri in fata Europei*', despite the numerous potential interpretations, was far from being an optimistic message and rather conveyed a sentiment of abandonment, disappointment and even despair. The second political slogan launched by CDR 2000 as a central theme of its electoral campaign, '*Singuri importiva stangi?* likewise read as 'alone against the left'. CDR 2000 thus automatically positioned itself as fighting a political left that many electors had ceased to identify with bad policies or a dubious historical legacy (Rompres News Agency, 2000).

We can also quote here as a further example a fragment from a radio advertisement for the CDR 2000 campaign. *'Am adus Romania la usile Europei. Nu putem ramane afara. Pentru Europa, votaţi Conventia Democrata Romana, CDR 2000!'* ('We brought Romania to the gates of Europe. We must not remain outside. For Europe, vote for Romanian Democrat Convention, CRD 2000!'). Once again the image of 'the gates of Europe' (probably being closed) with Romania being left 'outside' and the use of the negative structure 'we must not' had obvious connotations of isolation and rejection. Further attempts to create apprehension of a PDSR victory also backfired, in that Romanians in 2000 had fonder memories of the previous PDSR government than the incumbent CDR administration. It should also be noted that the nostalgia factor even extended back beyond 1989 to the Ceausescu regime, which was perhaps the most significant indictment of the economic failure of the reformist government and the acute sense of poverty felt by most Romanians.[9]

The Electoral Campaign of 2000: Ion Iliescu, The Return of the Man from the 'Political Twilight Zone'

Throughout the whole period of the 2000 electoral campaign Ion Iliescu, the Presidential candidate of PDSR, adopted a detached and remote attitude that in many senses marginalized him from the intense debates of the mainstream electoral campaign. Occupying a 'twilight zone' permitted Iliescu to remain aloof from political controversy, and also conferred on him an aura of mystery. As an astute politician, Ion Iliescu was facing an additional enemy apart from the opposing parties. Iliescu was relatively old and, more so, was looking his age of 71 in 2000. He certainly was aware of the not very endearing nickname 'the granny' and was well aware of the judgement that 'in Romania life expectancy for women is under 80 and for men is under 70: therefore, Iliescu is either dead or an old woman.' More than that Iliescu knew very well that he did not have any chance in competing with the youth of his counter-candidates and therefore he adopted a strategy that can be summed up by the phrase 'don't go public'.

In addition to this, Iliescu's campaign managers were well aware of the appeal of the mysterious and of the likelihood that their candidate would be idealised and to an extent abstracted. Iliescu's specialist advisers knew very well how to exploit and increase the growing positive reaction of the government by hiding the object of their 'contemplation'. By positioning himself inside a political twilight zone, Iliescu personally appropriated the role of the experienced campaigner who was confident of victory. Calm and detached, his position clearly suggested the attitude of a father who was indulgently allowing his (political) children to play. Iliescu's campaign is a clear example of a careful assessment of both the weak and strong points of the candidate and the skilful management of the image presented to the voters (Mungiu-Pippidi, 2000, pp. 248-251). CDR's attitude, in contrast, showed an insufficient appreciation of a political marketing strategy. Beginning with the final period of its government, CDR presented itself as a victim that was overwhelmed by opposition attacks and by the difficulty of ruling Romania. Through effective political marketing, CDR might have succeeded in persuading the population about both the good and the bad aspects of government, and to explain that under the given economic conditions their achievements were truly significant.

The Electoral Campaign of 2000: The Failure of the CDR's 'Visual' Political Marketing Strategy

Another important reason behind the fall of CDR was the fragmentation of the alliance due to internal conflicts among the component parties. If Iliescu preferred to occupy the *political twilight zone*, then CDR ultimately would not have a single leadership candidate to present. The compromise solution was to sustain an 'independent' who was also clearly 'one of their own', Mugur Isarescu. Once this had been resolved, both CDR and Isarescu resolved to pursue a strategy of 'open political marketing'. Unfortunately, the uninspired content of election advertisements compounded the poor image presented by the alliance and its candidate. Examples of the serious errors made were as follows:

The elitist video message: One television clip designed for the promotion of Mugur Isarescu presented a group of children sharing with the public their hopes for the future. Their thoughts presented a pessimistic picture: 'when I grow up I want to be a student and get beaten by the miners' and 'when I grow up I want to be a pensioner and not have enough money.' Clearly, this type of electoral clip was addressed to people who appreciated irony and sarcasm. The problem was that intellectuals and educated professionals were the basis of CDR support. CDR and Isarescu's goal should have been to attract other sections of Romanian society and not merely present messages that appealed to a select, literate audience.

The incongruent video clip: One of CDR's major problems was the absence of their own clear candidate for the presidency. For a political structure as big as CDR, the lack of an easily identifiable leader figure proved to be lethal. The moment Constantinescu announced that he would not run again for the presidency CDR was at a loss. Isarescu, Constantinescu's Prime Minister, announced his candidature but as an independent separate from the main CDR 2000 campaign. People from the campaign staff of CDR 2000 claimed that they tried on several occasions to adopt a common front of the CDR and the independent Isarescu but without success. Certain analysts argued that Isarescu's attitude towards CDR 2000 reflected the attitude of a chauvinist husband towards an ugly wife who was good for home cooking but unfit to be seen with in public. Looking from a different perspective, Isarescu's desire to be an independent candidate and to distance himself from the CDR was perfectly understandable. CDR 2000 was a dying party, a sinking ship and Isarescu was trying to at least save himself after the captain had already abandoned the ship. Nevertheless, despite the attempt to distance Isarescu from CDR, one of the most frequently broadcast TV clips showed pictures of Constantinescu and Isarescu holding hands together in recognition of the victory in 1996, which obviously created a strong association between CDR and the 'independent' candidate. In a world dominated by the image, an image can change everything: 'I believe it because I've seen it at the television' undermines the most carefully worked out political marketing strategy.

A lack of presence in the regions: The result of a poll conducted by CDR 2000 in several rural areas in October 2000 revealed that more than 50 per cent of the population in these districts still thought that Emil Constantinescu was going to run for the Presidency. This was despite the fact that Constantinescu had made a highly publicized decision to stand down several months previously. In addition to this, local journalists from several of the larger Romanian towns complained that they were completely ignored by Isarescu, who preferred to give interviews to the Bucharest journalists who travelled with him on the campaign trail. Even if Isarescu wanted to be seen and heard, he favoured certain people and regions, a fact that consequently damaged his popularity and image.

Divide and lose: Isarescu's chances were also diminished by the decision of Teodor Stolojan, a former prime minister during the period of the first Iliescu Presidency, to run as the candidate of PNL. The result was, predictably, the splitting of the centrist and right wing votes between two candidates whose aptitudes, proposals and qualifications were almost identical. Taking advantage of the opportunity for *divide et impera*, PDSR found that its efforts to promote Iliescu were made considerably easier. If the two parties could have agreed on a single joint candidate, most analysts concur that he would have succeeded in taking the presidential elections to a second round with every possibility of defeating Iliescu in the final vote.[10]

The Electoral Campaign of 2000: Television Debates and the Rise of Corneliu Vadim Tudor

For many observers the success of Corneliu Vadim Tudor, a charismatic demagogue who was able to push the extreme nationalist vote beyond the 'safety threshold' of ten per cent, was the most striking and disturbing outcome of the 2000 elections in Romania.[11] Vadim's success also confirmed that television debates have increasingly allowed the candidates in Romanian elections to confront the public directly and thus have become the most powerful mass medium in the country. In the majority of countries with a democratic tradition, television debates or talk shows constitute an important medium through which a politician can promote his/her own image and provide opportunities to demonstrate spontaneity, oratorical gifts and charisma. Generally, during such debates, the politician has the perfect chance to present his ideas in front of a large audience and to criticize the proposals of other candidates (Mickievicz & Firestone, 1996, p. 59). In the particular case of the 2000 Romanian elections, the television debates provided the means by which most of the participants seriously damaged their own images.

The only significant exception in this respect was Vadim Tudor. Apart from the fact that Vadim's technique involved talking until everyone had either forgotten the original point or were tired of trying (and failing) to interject, the PRM leader was the only participant that kept a constant attitude and image within the television debates. On the contrary, his rival party leaders reacted badly to the accusatory and violent style of Vadim and tried to counter-attack in the same vulgar and brutal style. Unfortunately, none of them was a serious adversary for Vadim and by trying to be offensive, they instead looked ridiculous and childish. For example, when Vadim attacked Petre Roman (president of PD) by naming his father a traitor, Roman lost his well-known calm and reacted by shouting 'Leave my father alone! Don't say nasty things about my father!', a reaction quite inappropriate for a Minister of Foreign Affairs. The only major party leader who was astute enough to avoid a direct confrontation was Ion Iliescu who refused to participate in almost any television debate that involved only himself and Vadim. In general, the television electoral debates in the 2000 electoral campaign, marked as they were by endless quarrels with personal attack and very little political substance, did great harm to the image of the Romanian democratic process (BBC, 2000).

In some senses, Vadim's campaign was made more interesting by the fact that, apart from appealing to an older conservative electorate that was attracted to extreme nationalism, PRM also had a significant impact in terms of attracting the young electorate. The reasons behind this were several, though it is worth noting that PRM's appeal was enhanced by the fact that it presented a third party alternative. If in 1996 the young electorate 'voted with the change', in that they voted against PDSR and memories of the old communist structures, in 2000 they could not do a 180 degree turn and vote again for Iliescu even though CDR had proved to be a major disappointment. PRM and Vadim also gained from being the only party that emphasized a crude form of social justice, a particular message that had a great deal of resonance among ordinary Romanians tired of austerity measures. During the last months of the electoral campaign, the PRM discourse actually largely abandoned its traditional xenophobic content and started to imitate the CDR message seen in 1996 (*Adevarul*, October 16, 2000). Consequently, Vadim became the country's champion of justice and strong anti-corruption measures. Even if Vadim's message was far from being coherent, it offered attractive and simple solutions to the pressing issues of poverty and social collapse.

Conclusion

The electoral campaign of 2000 was the year when techniques of political marketing were more clearly applied in Romania than at any time previously. At the same time, these elections were the concrete proof of the disastrous consequences of an ill-conceived political marketing campaign. Messages that were constructed in a hurry, images not correctly defined and other factors all resulted in significant losses for those parties who neglected their political communication strategy. Winning a political campaign through new techniques of political marketing is as much a question of advertising as it is of a political program. In contemporary societies, political doctrine needs the support of the economic and psychological methods used for promoting products. More efficient political publicity, in theory, will help to diminish those elements within Romanian political culture that seek to exploit extremism and fanatical nationalism. Better presentation will also 'demystify' the political process and undermine the authoritarian tendencies within Romanian politics.

Measuring the quality of a Romanian election campaign such as the one seen in 2000 is an inexact process. Like any other democratic country, a Romanian political campaign is ultimately good or bad according to its results and not the quality of the message or the professionalism of the communication techniques used. More than ten years after the fall of communism, Romania is still searching for its own distinctive civic and political values. The potential for a shift from nationalism to liberalism originates in the consciousness of the individual members of civil society and it is fully accomplished when tolerance prevails in their attitudes towards one another. Hopefully, the lesson drawn from the 2000 presidential is how quickly an emerging democratic society could be transformed over night into an undemocratic one.

Assuming that a key element in the development of civic society is effective communication between the political parties and the electorate, the result of the 2000 election campaign was a cause for concern. A former leader of PDSR stated that the result marked the 'end of the myth of a political right that could bring salvation'.[12] Though this was undoubtedly true, the use of terminology such as 'myth' and 'salvation' is revealing. The tendency of the Romanian electorate to put their faith in seemingly benign 'father figures' only to see their unrealistic hopes banished by yet another false dawn shows the limitations of political communication within the country. Both the Romanian media and politicians need to combine the increasing influence of Western political marketing techniques with more informed discussion of the real issues affecting the ordinary people.

List of Abbreviations:

CDR (later CDR 2000)	Romanian Democratic Convention
FSN	National Salvation Front
PD	Democratic Party
PDSR	The Romanian Party of Social Democracy
PNL	National Liberal Party
PNTCD/PNT	National Peasant, Christian and Democratic Party/National Peasant Party
PRM	Greater Romania Party
PS	Socialist Party
PSM	Socialist Party of Labour
PUNR	Party of Romanian National Unity
UDMR	Democratic Union of Hungarians from Romania
UFD	Union of Right Forces
USD	Social-Democratic Union

References

Adevarul [The Truth], Bucharest Daily Newspaper, June 17, 1996, p. 2.

Adevarul [The Truth], Bucharest Daily Newspaper, October 16, 2000, p. 9.

Atkinson, M. (1996). *Our masters' voices: The language and body language of politics.* London & New York: Routledge.

BBC Online. (December 10, 2000). *World News.* Retrieved from http://news.bbc. co.uk/hi/english/world/europe/437281.stm

BBC. (November 8, 2000). *World News.* Retrieved from http://www.bbc. co.uk/hi/english/world/europe/482347.stm

Baleanu, V. G. (2001). *The dark side of politics in post-communist Romania* (Paper G92). Sandhurst: Conflict Studies Research Centre, Royal Military Academy.

Boia, L. (1997). *History and myth in Romanian consciousness.* Bucharest: Humanitas.

Bulai, A. (1999). *Mecanismele electorale ale societatii romanesti* [The Electoral Process in Romanian Society]. Bucharest: Editura Paideia.

Conventia Democrata Romana [Romanian Democratic Convention]. (October 13, 1996). *Electoral Campaign* [Television Broadcast]. Romania: PRO TV.

Dancu, V. S. (1999). *Comunicarea simbolica: Arhitectura discursului publicitar* [Symbolic Communication: the Architecture of Advertising Discourse]. Cluj-Napoca: Editura Dacia.

Debord, G. (1992). *La societe du spectacle* [The society of spectacle]. Paris: Gallimard.

Diamond, L. (1994). Rethinking civil society: Toward democratic consolidation. *Journal of Democracy, 5*(3), 6.

Evenimentul Zilei [The Daily Event], September 26, 1996, p. 1.

Evenimentul Zilei [The Daily Event], October 15-17, 1996, p. 3.

Gallagher, T. (1995). *Romania after Ceausescu: The politics of intolerance.* Edinburgh: Edinburgh University Press.

Gallagher, T. (2000). Romania: Nationalism defines democracy. In W. Kostecki, K. Zukrowska & B. J. Góralczyk. (Eds.). *Transformations of post-communist states* (pp. 185-201). Basingstoke: Macmillan.

Hollis, W. (1999). *Democratic consolidation in Eastern Europe: The influence of the communist legacy in Hungary, the Czech Republic and Romania.* New York: Columbia University Press.

Kavanagh, D. (1995). *Election campaigning: The new marketing politics.* Oxford: Blackwell Publishing.

Kopecky, P. (2003). Civil society, uncivil society and contentious politics in post-communist Europe. In P. Kopecky & C. Mudde. (Eds.). *Uncivil society? Contentious politics in post-communist Europe.* London & New York: Routledge.

Light, D. & Phinnemore, D. (Eds.). (2001). *Post-communist Romania: Coming to terms with transition.* Basingstoke: Palgrave.

Mickievicz, E. and Firestone, C. (1996). *Televiziunea si alegerile* [Television and Elections]. Bucharest: Stiinta si tehnica.

Mungiu-Pippidi, A. (2001). The return of populism – The 2000 Romanian elections. *Government and Opposition,* 36(2/Spring), 230-52.

Negrine, R. (1996). *The communication of politics.* Aldershot: Sage Books.

Phinnemore, D. (2001). Romania and Euro-Atlantic integration since 1989: a Decade of Frustration?. In D. Light & D. Phinnemore, (Eds.), *Post-Communist Romania: Coming to Terms with Transition* (pp. 245-269). Wilthshire: Palgrave Macmillan.

Rau, Z. (1998). *From communism to liberalism: Essays on the individual and civil society.* Lodz: Wydawnictwi Uniwersytetu Lodzkiego.

Rompres News Agency. (August 11, 2000·). Retrieved from http://www.rompres.ro/stiri/archiva/081100.

Siani-Davies, P. (2001). The revolution after the Revolution. In D. Light & D. Phinnemore, (Eds.), *Post-communist Romania: Coming to terms with transition* (pp. 15-34). Wilthshire: Palgrave Macmillan.

Stan, L. (Ed.). (1997). *Romania in transition.* London: Dartmouth Publishing Company.

Stoiciu, A. (2000). *Comunicarea politica: Cum se vand idei si oameni* [Political Communication: Selling People and Ideas]. Bucharest: Humanitas-Libra.

Thorpe, N. (December 3, 2000). *Romanians gamble with their future.* BBC News Online. Retrieved from http://news.bbc.co.uk/1/hi/programmes/from_our_own_correspondent/1052551.stm

Watts, D. (1997). *Political communication today.* Manchester: Manchester University Press.

THE EVOLUTION OF THE MULTIPARTY SYSTEM IN UKRAINE:

PRELUDE TO A ROBUST DEMOCRACY?

Olga KESARCHUK

As a former Soviet republic, Ukraine did not operate as a multiparty political system but instead was governed by a local branch of the Communist Party of the Soviet Union (CPSU), which was in turn subordinated to the centre. Article 6 of the USSR's Constitution stated that the Communist Party would be the only party recognized by the state. It was not until the introduction of *perestroika* that the undemocratic and totalitarian nature of the system was questioned and subsequently revised.

The formation of political parties in Ukraine occurred partly as a result of the popular movements during the Gorbachov era. After the collapse of the Soviet Union, Ukraine was able to legally assure the rights of its citizens 'for uniting into parties … for exercising and protecting their rights and freedoms, and for satisfying their political, economic, social, cultural and other interests' (Ukrainian Constitution, Article 36, 1996). However, lacking the experience of a strong political culture, legalising political parties *per se* did not result in a smooth transition to a multiparty system. The Ukrainian party system that emerged was hypertrophied, fragmented and inefficient. Additionally, the very nature of the parties raised concerns; they did not conform to the generally accepted Western standards applicable to parties.

The purpose of this paper is to critically examine the evolution of the Ukrainian party system since 1991. Given that the multiparty system is in place, one could argue that democracy is working in Ukraine. While the parties represent the various interests of Ukrainian citizens, the aim of this paper is to investigate the validity of this claim. Some of the findings in this paper may also be applicable to other post-Soviet countries; however this is beyond the scope of this paper. In this paper, I briefly discuss the relationship between the multiparty system in Ukraine and democracy. I consider the multiparty system in Ukraine offering a brief historical overview of its formation. I then discuss certain issues particular to the Ukrainian party system that I view as problematic, including the issue of 'party of power'. In conclusion, I evaluate the influence of the 2002 parliamentary elections on the development of parties in Ukraine.

The Multiparty System as a Constituent of Democracy

The political party system in its modern sense is closely connected with the development of representative democracy. Thus, in the majority of Western democracies, political parties emerged with the spread of suffrage. Parties articulated society's interests into specific programs, giving greater legitimacy to the state government and stimulating competition for power.

In his book, *Political Parties: Their Organization and Activity in the Modern State,* Maurice Duverger (1959) calls modern political parties, 'children of democracy'. For him, a 'modern party' is one that is able to realize the general voting right and win a parliamentary majority through the use of democratic institutions and mechanisms. Duverger (1959) also contributes to the development of the field by analysing systems of parties and forms of realization of power, such as the alternation and domination of parties. He draws the conclusion that political parties are simply necessary, constituting one of the main attributes and bases of modern democracy: 'A regime without parties is a regime without democracy.'

Many other organizations besides political parties try to obtain political power, and primarily seek to influence government. Some 'think tanks', research groups and quasi-educational interest groups produce articles and papers that are slanted to support one political point of view over another. Trade unions, by definition, take a partisan position. Special interest groups attempt to influence legislation in order to benefit their group at the expense of the public. Lobbyists for individual corporations meet with members of the legislature and their staff in order to gain legislative preferences for their clients, such as tax brakes or government subsidies. No matter how problematic this trend may be, it is practically impossible to stop this development when a country institutionalizes freedom of association and speech (Pilon, 2001). However, these organizations cannot and should not replace political parties and take upon themselves the role of parties in a democratic society.

What then are the main features that distinguish a political party from an interest group? First of all, a party unites its members according to their voluntary will, which rests primarily on publicly declared *common goals and interests, and only using political means in order to reach these goals.* Thus, special interest groups that try to influence the decision-making process via non-political means are excluded. Secondly, a party expresses the political interests of its members and the people who are directly involved in its work as well as a certain *social group*, or, at least it claims to do so. This excludes club-sect type organizations. Thirdly, the interests expressed by a party should be of a *national character* rather than narrowly corporate. Parties present their ideological views and political platforms to the public, necessitating that a party should have a distinctly formulated program. Without this, it would be a corporate organization or a lobby group. Finally, a fully developed party should have *a branch-type structure* in which the relationships between the parts are strictly defined. The party should have a number of activists, a network of regional organizations and elected central organs. Thus, small organizations that claim to be active participants in political life but are not recognized as real subjects of public politics cannot be called 'parties'. All the above conditions are premised upon a level of political maturity in society and the state. Society should not consist of closed communities, but be civil, which means it should have a differentiated social structure and a certain degree of independence from the state. The state in turn should represent an open system, which functions under society's control. It should provide the mechanisms that enable society to influence the state and ensure the adequate exercise of popular will through different forms of social institutions (Korgunuk & Zaslavskiy, 1996).

A state that allows the existence of many parties competing for power within its political system is conceived to be democratic. Party competition is an important factor in strengthening the democratic nature of the state and in protecting citizens' rights and freedoms. Parties can favour certain social groups, sectors or issues. However, parties in a democratic society should not try to monopolize the 'truth'. When competing alongside other parties, they target as many co-thinkers among the population as possible using persuasion and agitation, but not via force or by using money.

Parties also serve as essential agencies of mass mobilization and as such help to integrate local communities into a nation. In competitive party systems, this process of integration can be analysed at two levels. On the one level, each party establishes a network of cross-local communication channels that help to strengthen national identities. On the other, their very competitiveness creates a national system of government, which should, in theory, be above any particular set of officeholders. Lipset and Rokkan (1967) refer to a political party as an 'agent of conflict and [an] instrument of integration.'

At present democracy exists predominantly in its representative form. In order to implement democracy it is necessary to unite the diffused political will of its sovereign owners (the people) into politically strong and active blocs. It is through political parties that the will of different social groups is included best into the decision-making process. Thus, parties become the most effective instrument of realizing group interests in the sphere of politics.

A representative democracy typically combines certain institutional features that at first glance appear to be conflicting. On the one hand, representative democracy integrates into the political process unresolved and crucial political issues. Thus, it reflects political choice, guaranteeing that practically all interests are represented in the political process. On the other hand, the complexities of decision-making and the potential of ever-changing social preferences place certain constraints on those who participate in the political process. In order to remain competitive, parties must collectively maintain certain moral, ideological and organizational standards, and appeal to the electorate. Parties operating in a democratic multiparty system cannot ignore the interests of the people. Indeed, if they do, they risk being voted out of power.

The Multiparty System of Ukraine

Having discussed the relationship between a multiparty system and democracy, we can now analyze it in the Ukrainian context.

The Formation of the Multiparty System in Ukraine

In Ukraine, the ground for the formation of political parties was paved by M. Gorbachov's *perestroika*, particularly through its emphasis on *glasnost* and pluralism. By the end of the 1980s, many clubs, unions and movements appeared in Ukraine, such as 'Memorial' and 'The Green World'. Although the vast majority of parties did not have a broad political agenda, their appearance heralded the beginning of the Ukrainian society's politicization.

The emergence of the People's Movement of Ukraine (*Rukh*) in 1989 constitutes a turning point in Ukraine's political history. To a great extent, it symbolized the legalization of political pluralism in the republic (Haran', 1991). Representatives from all sides of the political spectrum created *Rukh*. *Rukh* was conceptualized as standing for economic, political and ideological pluralism. Initially, its declared aim was to aid *perestroika* to take root in Ukraine, as well as to promote economic, political and cultural development of the Republic. Gradually, *Rukh* escalated its goals and started to campaign for an independent and democratic Ukraine.[13] Even though *Rukh* was legally not a party at this point (Article 6 was still valid), one could argue that it was carrying out the functions of a political party, i.e., participating in the struggle for power.

It was not until 1990 that a multiparty system was established in Ukraine that would include parties from different political orientations. In October of that year, the *Verkhovna Rada* of the Ukrainian SSR adopted laws on political parties and elections that structured the country's multipartism. At this point, Article 6 of the Soviet Constitution ceased to be implemented.

Ukraine's proclamation of independence on 24 August 1991 represents a watershed in terms of its transition towards a liberal democratic society. On the one hand, the revolutionary leap helped the opposition forces achieve their goals of dismantling the Soviet state and liquidating the monopoly on power of the CPSU. On the other hand, after eliminating the external enemy the newly formed parties and movements entered into a state of confusion when confronted with the need to adjust their positions to the new reality.[14.]

The Ukrainian Party System: Its Character, Evolution and Problems

If one were to judge the Ukrainian political system by the sheer number of parties, an impression of a truly democratic state appears. Indeed, the Ministry of Justice registered 127 political parties by December 2001.[15] However, this impression is deceptive. A number of factors hinder Ukraine's advancement towards liberal democracy. In the section below, I discuss the Ukrainian party system and its characteristics that I view as problematic.

Shallow Social Roots

Ukraine's history – i.e., part of a colonial-feudal empire followed by seventy years of communist rule – has given birth to an extremely 'etatized' society. The totalitarian regime was characterized by hypertrophied domination of the state/the Communist Party, with the nearly total absence of non-governmental democratic institutions. The parties that emerged in post-Soviet Ukraine had no historic roots in the pre-Soviet era. Those parties that existed in Ukraine in the beginning of the 20th century were eliminated when the *Bolsheviks* came to power. *Afterwards, the independence parties appeared prior to the crystallization of the new social stratification*; therefore, they could not clearly articulate the interests of social groups that they were to represent.

In Ukraine, the building of grass root foundations of political parties had to be compressed in time between the collapse of the USSR and the first truly democratic elections. Under such circumstances, politically savvy elites could completely dominate the political process. In Ukraine there was only a little circulation of communist elites in power. Parties were 'thrown together' by aspiring politicians instead of the masses, which were yet unorganised (Klobucar & Miller, 2002). The nationally conscious Ukrainian elites were unsuccessful in shaping the evolving rhetorical foundations of debates. While the 'top down' method of party building was acceptable for some time, it should have been replaced by the 'bottom up' method. This has yet to happen in Ukraine.

Small Membership and Party Instability

Ukrainian parties have a comparatively small number of registered members. Although almost two million Ukrainians, or four per cent of the population, are estimated to belong to parties, this figure does not seem reliable, and the number of paid membership is probably much smaller. Only a handful of parties are mass- membership based, including the Communist Party (around 140,000 members), the Socialist Party (around 60,000 members) and the *Rukh* Party (60,000 members before its split). The pro-Kuchma Party of Regions claims to have 460,000 members, the Social Democratic Party (united) claims 300,000 and the Agrarian Party claims more than 200,000, but these figures are doubtful (Nations in Transit, 2002). The majority of

Ukrainians are not affiliated with any particular party or ideology. Thus, most parties rely on fluctuating preferences of the electorate that makes decisions spontaneously right before the elections. Similarly, the lack of funds results in the absence of continual involvement of people in policy formulation and decision-making. Parties try to concentrate their efforts on achieving the final goal, namely acquiring power. They radically increase their political activity before elections, but avoid everyday contact and co-operation with the masses.

A popular view on political party identification in Ukraine maintains that the only true partisans in the post-Soviet society are those who identify themselves with the Communist Party. In their research on partisan development in Ukraine, Miller and Klobucar (2001) found no supportive evidence of this. They maintain that the emergence of party identification in Ukraine cannot be viewed as a result of democratization *per se*. In their view, party identification in post-Soviet societies appears to be emerging, not as a result of social cleavages as predicted by traditional theories of party development, but from a cognitive process: as citizens learn about the different policies and political orientations of various parties, they begin to develop an attachment to a particular party that best reflects their own preferences and interests.

Instability is another problem facing the Ukrainian party system. Sarah Birch (2001) provides a detailed description of party stability, including the concepts of party volatility and replacement. Birch argues that despite the potential benefits of flexibility in the party system, excessive instability undermines the basis for political representation. This applies to the Ukrainian case, where parties generally have a short political life. After a while they disappear from the political arena for good, or get reorganized depending on whether the interests of their founders have been realized. This reduces the accountability of parties and party leaders before the voters.

Regional and Issue Divisions

The Ukrainian parties usually target the electorate that concentrates in specific regions and tends to live in big cities. Indeed, rural population is not involved in party activities and remains highly apolitical. Limited access to the mass media impedes parties reach to the masses. Regional divisions have been salient for the Ukrainian party system. The left and the centre-left parties enjoy a high level of support in the East and the South, where the predominantly Russian-speaking population lives. The right and the centre-right parties have their major pull of supporters in Western Ukraine, where the predominant Ukrainian-speaking population lives. However, with time these regional divisions have been losing their significance. As the 1998 parliamentary elections illustrated, party preference and party strength were still regionally concentrated, but the boundaries of party support no longer coincided exactly with the region (Hesli et al., 1998). Over time, differentiations on the basis of particular issues have become more defined and diverse.

Ineffective Legal Provisions

For a long period of time, Ukrainian parties operated without a proper legal framework. During the first few years of Ukraine's independence, their activities were regulated by the *Law on Civil Organizations* adopted on 16 June, 1992. It quickly became clear that this law had to be revised and supplemented as it gave too much power to the executive. For example, the law allowed state organs to determine whether a particular association was a political party or a civic organization, in turn compromising the freedom of citizens to unite into associations and to choose their activities independently. The mechanism for prohibiting a party's activities also lacked sufficient legal safeguards.

Ukraine agreed to adopt the 'Law on Political Parties in Ukraine' at the time of its accession to the Council of Europe in 1995 as one of the conditions this organization had put before the country. It was only in December 1999 that the *Verkhovna Rada* of Ukraine adopted it. However, the content of the law did not satisfy the President of Ukraine, Leonid Kuchma. He vetoed the bill twice, but the Parliament was able to override the veto. On 5 April 2001, the *Verkhovna Rada* finally adopted the Law with some modifications suggested by the president. This is a significant event that merits more detailed consideration.

The newly adopted law was quite progressive in many respects. The complete control of the executive branch of government over internal party life was omitted. The president had suggested the re-registering of the already existing parties and their regional organizations with the Ministry of Justice before the 2002 parliamentary elections, but it was not accepted. The procedures of party registration, as well as their reorganization, liquidation or self-dismissal, were now set more clearly. An increase in the number of signatures - from 1,000 to 10,000 - necessary for having a party registered is another example of the positive aspects of the Law.

However, the Law also has some major drawbacks. Given the strong positions the oligarchs occupy in the political system, the requirement of 10,000 signatures is easily met. The issue of party financing from the state budget is not resolved. The list of persons who cannot be members of parties lacks clarity. The vague expression 'the employees of internal state bodies' leaves much room for manoeuvre. As a result, Mykola Azarov, the Head of the State Tax Administration at that time, was able to become the head of the Party of Regions of Ukraine (PRU),[16] which was registered in March 2001(*Politychnyy Kalendar*, 2001, No.3).

The Impact of the Mixed Electoral System on Party Development

The Ukrainian party system during the first period of independence can be classified as 'atomized' due to the overabundance and heterogeneity of parties, and their inability to unify into more or less weighty political organizations. The majoritarian electoral system for the *Verkhovna Rada*, the state's supreme legislative body, hindered the establishment of a multiparty system in Ukraine. It added significantly to the degree of atomization among the Ukrainian parties in the Parliament of 1994-1998. The law mediated against the election of extremists and the polarising effect of their campaign rhetoric. However, it significantly stalled the development of the party system in Ukraine. During the 1994 campaign, the decision for electing a deputy was only loosely connected with the party affiliations of the candidates and the voters (Hesli et al., 1998). As a result, of the 450 deputies in Parliament, only 168 were party members. In 1994, the Ukrainian electorate tended to prefer candidates who were not affiliated with any party, in part due to the confusion with the overabundance of parties that were hardly distinguishable from each other.

Table 2.8 Parties/blocs that surpassed the four per cent barrier in the 1998 parliamentary elections

	The Winning Party/Bloc of Parties	% According to the Proportional Lists	Number of Mandates through the Proportional Lists	Number of Deputies Winning the Single Majority Districts
1.	The Communist Party of Ukraine	24.65%	84	38
2.	The Popular *Rukh* of Ukraine	9.40%	32	13
3.	The Election Bloc "For Truth, for People, for Ukraine!" (the Socialist Party of Ukraine; the Peasants' Party of Ukraine)	8.56%	29	3 2
4.	The Green Party of Ukraine	5.44%	19	-
5.	The Popular-Democratic Party	5.01%	17	11
6.	The All-Ukrainian Association "*Hromada*"	4.68%	16	7
7.	The Progressive Socialist Party of Ukraine	4.05%	14	2
8.	The Social-Democratic Party of Ukraine (united)	4.01%	14	3

Source: Central Electoral Commission (www.cvk.gov.ua).

In the next parliamentary election of 1998, a mixed system was introduced: 50 per cent (225) of the popular deputies were elected via the majoritarian system, while 50 per cent were elected through the proportional system. Parties that overcame the four per cent threshold got into parliament receiving a proportion of the 225 seats according to the number of votes they got. Many political forces welcomed the introduction of the mixed electoral system. The national democratic parties particularly favoured it, hoping to develop a significant hold in constituencies in the East, a position not attainable under the majoritarian system. The well-organized Communists and Socialists believed that their ability to transcend regional power bases would also help them to succeed in the proportional system (Craumer et al., 1999).

Changing the electoral system proved to be a positive step that paved the way for the subsequent formation of a majority coalition in Parliament (in spite of the nature of this coalition to be discussed later), thereby structuring the parliament to some extent. Of the 30 parties/blocs on the voting list, only eight were able to overcome the barrier. As Craumer and Clem (1999) note in their study, applying Tagepera's and Shugart's formula for estimating the theoretical number of effective parties, the number of parties in an equivalent election would be nine. As we can see, the actual results were very close to this number [Table 2.8].

Table 2.9 The voting results for approving the appointment of V. Yushchenko as the prime-minister of Ukraine (December 22, 1999)

NO.	Factions and Groups	For	Against	Abstained	Did not Vote	Absent	% For	% Against
1	CPU	0	0	0	1	114	0	0
2	The *Rukh*/U	16	0	0	0	0	100	0
3	The *Rukh*/K	27	0	0	0	0	100	0
4	SPU	10	1	4	1	7	43.5	4.3
5	PZU (the Greens)	17	0	0	0	0	100	0
6	NDP (National Democrats)	28	0	0	0	0	100	0
7	*Hromada*	12	1	0	0	1	85.7	7.1
8	PSPU	4	10	0	0	0	28.6	71.4
9	SDPU (united)	36	0	0	0	0	100	0
10	SelPU	8	0	0	1	6	53.3	0
11	'Independent'	13	0	0	0	0	100	0
12	"*Reformy-Kongress*"	15	0	0	0	0	100	0
13	*DemSouz*	33	0	0	0	0	100	0
14	'Fatherland'	31	0	0	0	1	96.6	0
15	'Labour Ukraine'	28	0	0	0	0	100	0
16	'Solidarity'	-	-	-	-	-	-	-
17	'*Yabluko*'	-	-	-	-	-	-	-
18	'Regions of Ukraine'	-	-	-	-	-	-	-
	Non-Faction Deputies	18	0	0	1	0	94.7	0
	Total	296	12	4	4	129	66.2	2.7

<u>Source:</u> www.tomenko.kiev.ua

The formation of the majority coalition in the *Verkhovna Rada* in 1999, its short history and its disintegration are significant events in Ukrainian parliamentary development. The coalition that was formed out of non-Left parties declared political support for the President of Ukraine, L. Kuchma, as well as for the legislative provisions for continuing reforms advocated by the newly formed government of Victor Yushchenko. The unofficial goal was to take power away from the leftist majority in the *Verkhovna Rada* and to demonstrate loyalty to the President in order to avoid the dismissal of the parliament. The coalition was founded on a political agreement, without the formal participation of parties (*Politychnyy Kalendar*, 2001, No.9). However, the notorious 'tapegate scandal', in which the President was the main defendant, and the ensuing crisis in the executive branch, soon split the majority coalition into pro- and anti-presidential parts. Thus, this majority coalition can be characterized as 'situational', as parties reached only a temporary consensus on a number of issues. As the circumstances changed, they found it too difficult to be in one bloc and collapsed after Victor Yushchenko's government received a no-confidence vote in the *Verkhovna Rada*. The 'situational' character of the majority coalition is especially evident when viewing the voting results of the pro-presidential factions (SDPU (united), 'Labour Ukraine', so forth) on the subject of approving or dismissing V. Yushchenko's government [Tables 2.9 and 2.10]. The pro-presidential parties that rubberstamped the appointment of Yushchenko government in 1999 by President Kuchma voted it out of office in 2001.

Table 2.10 The voting results for dismissing V. Yushchenko as the prime-minister of Ukraine (April 26, 2001)

No.	Factions And Groups	For	Against	Ab-stained	Did Not Vote	Ab-sent	% For	% Against
1	CPU	105	0	0	0	7	93.8	0
2	The *Rukh*/U	0	11	0	4	1	0	68.8
3	The *Rukh*/K	0	11	0	12	0	0	47.8
4	SPU	2	0	14	0	0	12.5	0
5	PZU (the Greens)	9	2	0	2	4	52.9	11.8
6	NDP (National Democrats)	8	1	1	2	5	47.1	5.9
7	*Hromada*	-	-	-	-	-	-	-
8	PSPU	-	-	-	-	-	-	-
9	SDPU (united)	31	1	1	0	2	88.6	2.9
10	SelPU	-	-	-	-	-	-	-
11	'Independent'	-	-	-	-	-	-	-
12	*'Reformy-Kongress'*	0	13	0	0	1	0	92.9
13	*DemSouz*	20	3	0	3	3	68.9	10.3
14	'Fatherland'	0	5	0	17	3	0	20
15	'Labor Ukraine'	41	2	2	0	1	89.1	4.3
16	'Solidarity'	1	7	2	8	3	4.8	33.3
17	"Yabluko"	13	0	1	0	1	86.7	0
18	'Regions of Ukraine'	14	3	1	1	1	70.0	15.0
	Non-Faction Deputies	19	10	2	4	8	44.2	23.3
	Total	263	69	24	53	40	58.6	15.4

<u>Source:</u> *Politychnyy Kalendar* 4 (40), 2001.

Ideological Escape and Ideology Discredited

One of the generally accepted ways of party classification is to group them according to the ideologies they represent. In the case of Ukraine, it is difficult to do so due to the vagueness of party programs and the absence of ideologically determined principles underlying them. The difference among parties is not determined by ideology, but by the loyalty or opposition they harbour for the President of Ukraine. Generally, parties formed for protecting the interests of their leaders or certain financial groups tend to have a centrist outlook. Indeed, the vast majority of centrist parties in Ukraine represent a multitude of business interests and personal political machines (Craumer et al., 1999). In general, when writing their programs, parties focus primarily on winning votes rather than ability and intentions to realize the propositions in the future.

Herbert Kitschelt (1995) classifies parties into three major groups: clientelistic, charisma-based, and programmatic parties. He argues that, while programmatic parties are harder to forge than charismatic or clientelistic parties, they are more likely to reinforce, consolidate and stabilize the democratic system than the other two alternatives. In Ukraine, most parties are clientelistic in nature, particularly the centrist ones. They avoid the high co-ordination costs of consensus building among their activists, and followers since affiliation and continuing loyalty are based on selective material and solidarity incentives. They work around rather than through the stated rules of democratic competition.

Olexiy Haran' (2001) applies Herbert Kitschelt's classification system to the Ukrainian left in the following manner: Peasants' Party of Ukraine (SelPU) as a clientelistic party, Progressive Socialist Party of Ukraine (PSPU) as a 'one leader party', and the Communist Party of Ukraine (CPU), that is, both the ideological (party of the 'program') and clientelistic. However, despite the vocal and visible presence of the CPU in the new parliament, the party is gradually losing its ideological moorings. It now has an amorphous structure that does not carry much weight in the present political process. The CPU failed to become a real oppositional force when it did not challenge the president's idea of holding a referendum on the 'popular initiative.' The referendum of 2000 originated in the presidential administration with the view to introduce substantial changes to the Ukrainian Constitution. Thus, the CPU appears to be more a spectator than a player in the Ukrainian political field. While this cannot be separated from the general crisis of the communist ideology, it is also the product of disagreements among the leadership about the future tactics and strategies for the communist movement in Ukraine. It was only in 2002 that the Communists identified themselves as oppositional to Leonid Kuchma's regime.

With regards to the rightist parties, the situation is also complicated. The People's Movement of Ukraine (*Rukh*) achieved 9.4 per cent of the vote in the parliamentary election of 1998, second only to the Communists.

However, after a serious conflict in the wake of the upcoming presidential elections of 1999, the party split into the Ukrainian People's Movement (the *Rukh*/K), led by Yuriy Kostenko, and the People's Movement of Ukraine (the *Rukh*/U), led by Gennadiy Udovenko. The split of the *Rukh* party as a result of minor disagreements played into the hands of the pro-presidential oligarchic parties. The attempts of the right-oriented parties to consolidate themselves were only successful in 2001 when the *Rukhs* grouped with other right and centre-right parties into one election bloc (to be discussed in detail further).

The Party of Power in Ukraine

In Western politics, we frequently encounter the term 'the party *in* power'. It typically refers to a party that received the majority of electoral votes and holds leadership position in government and/or in parliament, or has formed the government entirely with its own members. This party has the responsibility of framing and implementing the policies for the country until the next election. In the Ukrainian case, however, we come across the notion of 'the party *of* power'. The mere substitution of a preposition is of enormous significance in this case.[17]

The appearance of the 'party of power' in Ukraine is closely connected with the particularities of the country's post-communist transformation. Parliamentarism and the multiparty system arrived on the Ukrainian political scene only after independence in 1991. Given the relatively short experience of party development, Western notions have acquired a distorted meaning in the Ukrainian political environment. Half-feudal patronage-clientele associations, the successors of the former nomenclature or patriarchal clans, have been using the party camouflage for realization of their private goals. Providing legislative support to their economic interests is the primary concern for such associations. Administrative and economic clans dominate the country's political system. It is clans, and not parties or other civil associations that form and defend the interests of certain social groups. These politically active social groups represent the relatively narrow social strata of wealthy citizens ignoring the interests of the population at large. The Popular Democratic Party under the leadership of the former prime-minister, Valeriy Pustovoytenko, that was formed in 1996 is considered to be Ukraine's first 'party of power.'

The three main oligarchic groups in Ukraine today include:

• ***The Donetsk group***, which controls the main Donbas metallurgy plants, coal mines, the newspaper *Segodnya*, and the football club *Shakhtar* (Donetsk). It created the Party of Regions of Ukraine. The Head of Donetsk's regional administration, Viktor Yanukovych, became prime minister in November 2002.

• ***The group of Surkis and Medvedchuk***, which controls the metallurgy consortium *Metallurgiya*, the corporation *Slavutych*, one-fourth of the Ukrainian *oblenergos* (energy distribution companies), numerous off-shore companies, the TV-channels *1+1* and *Inter*, the newspapers *Kievskie vedomosti* and *Komanda*, as well as the football club *Dynamo* (Kyiv). Its political wing is the oligarchic Social Democratic Party of Ukraine (SDPU united). Victor Medvedchuk is currently the head of the Presidential Administration.

• **_The group of Viktor Pinchuk_** (Investment and Industrial Group 'Interpipe'), which includes five huge pipe plants, the political party 'Labour Ukraine' (with around 40 members in parliament), the newspaper *Fakty,* and the TV channel ICTV. Viktor Pinchuk is a member of parliament and the husband of the President's daughter, Olena Kuchma (Haran', 2002).

One of the main characteristics of a 'party of power' is having a permanent hold on power. However, at different times, the 'party of power' may include different political parties. Irrespective of this, Ukraine's 'party of power' has been always identified with the President. Although the economic interests of oligarchic clans may conflict, they are united in their loyalty to the head of state.

One of the key strategic goals of any 'party of power' is to limit political competition as much as possible. While the 'party of power' in itself constitutes a minority, the rest of parliament is, ironically, called 'the opposition'. Another characteristic feature of the 'party of power' is its non-ideological nature. Once again, the centrist position is considered as the safest means for retaining power. For this reason, 'parties of power' in Ukraine have party names that include broad and vague terms, such as 'democratic', 'popular', etc.

The SDPU (united) is the only 'party of power' that clearly states its ideological affiliation in its name. However, in this case, the social-democratic ideology has been hijacked by the Social Democrats (united), discrediting the very idea of social democracy. In fact, in their work on left-oriented parties in Ukraine, Olexiy Haran's and Olexander Mayboroda (2000) do not discuss the SDPU (united). They claim that the present SDPU (united) 'has little to do with social democracy.' At a time when the Communist party is losing its ideological moorings, social democracy appears to be quite attractive. The national and regional leaders of the SDPU (united) are actively involved in entrepreneurial activities instead of defending workers rights as prescribed by the social-democratic ideology. Social-democratic values, such as internationalism, social equity and pragmatism can reap huge political dividends for parties. The SDPU (united) is not considered to be representative of the beliefs of its rank-and-file members. For example, according to a poll conducted in spring 2001, 67.7 per cent of the party electorate positively evaluated the party, and were in favour of extending the Cabinet's term in power. However, almost 90 per cent of the party voted 'for' the resignation of the Government [See Table 2.10]. The voting results are demonstrative of how the 'party of power' sacrifices ideology in order to protect its corporate interests.

The Ukrainian Party System after the 2002 Parliamentary Elections

In March 2002, Ukraine held its third parliamentary elections since its independence. The growing authoritarian tendencies of President Leonid Kuchma, a highly unbalanced system of power and the growing citizen mistrust in the major power institutions, preceded these elections. As the famous 'Gonganzegate/Kuchmagate' scandal – which accused President Kuchma of ordering the murder of an opposition journalist, Heorhij Gongadze in September 2001 - lost its momentum, the *Verkhovna Rada* elections represented a legitimate opportunity for settling the dispute between the power holders and the opposition. By focusing on the results of the 2002 parliamentary elections, I aim to assess their influence on the development of Ukrainian party system.

Similar to previous parliamentary elections of 1998, the elections of 2002 were held according to the proportional/majoritarian electoral system that was in place. President Kuchma vetoed a legislative draft on the electoral system five times. This draft initially attempted to introduce an entirely proportional electoral system, and then moved to a partly PR system. The introduction of this system would encourage the structuring of Parliament along party lines producing a positive impact on the Ukrainian politics. The authorities in their turn feared that the Ukrainian Communists could repeat the Moldavian Communist Party's victory in 2001 after the PR system was introduced there. The majoritarian system was viewed as favourable to parties associated with Leonid Kuchma. Indeed, these parties performed worse under the PR system compared to elections in the single-member districts that can be controlled more easily.

The bloc of political parties, '*Nasha Ukrayina*' (Our Ukraine), headed by the former pro-reform Prime Minister Victor Yushchenko represented the most promising challenger to the pro-presidential parties. It consisted of ten parties, mainly of a centre-right political orientation: including the Popular *Rukh* of Ukraine and the Ukrainian Popular *Rukh*, which re-unified before the election, as well as the Party of Reform and Order, the Liberal Party of Ukraine, and the Congress of Ukrainian Nationalists. The more radical opposition formed the bloc of parties led by Yuliya Tymoshenko. It consisted of Tymoshenko's Association '*Bat'kivshchyna*' (Fatherland), the '*Sobor*' party, the Ukrainian Republican party headed by Levko Lukyanenko, a former Soviet dissident, and the Social-Democratic party.

The parties of the left and centre-left political orientation were primarily represented by the Communist (the CPU) and Socialist (the SPU) parties. In 2002, the Communists avoided using the ethnic divisions for political purposes to the extent of the previous elections, especially when compared to previous elections. As Olexiy Haran' (2002) notes, the CPU had already transformed itself into a 'system' party, softening its rhetoric considerably. As for the Socialists, they had drifted towards the centre of the political spectrum, becoming increasingly more social-democratic in their beliefs. However, given that the oligarchic Social-Democratic Party of Ukraine (united) had effectively positioned itself as social democratic, the Socialists were somewhat 'forced' to retain their socialist ideology.

Table 2.11 Proportional list results

	The party (Election bloc of parties)	Overall number of national votes	%
1	The Election Bloc of Political Parties: The Bloc of Victor Yushchenko 'Our Ukraine'	6 108 088	23,57
2	The Communist Party of Ukraine	5 178 074	19,98
3	The Election Bloc of Political Parties: For A United Ukraine!	3 051 056	11,77
4	The Election Bloc of Political Parties: The Election Bloc of Yuliya Tymoshenko	1 882 087	7,26
5	The Socialist Party of Ukraine	1 780 642	6,87
6	The Social-Democratic Party of Ukraine (united)	1 626 721	6,27
7	The Election Bloc of Political Parties: The Bloc of Nataliya Vitrenko	836 198	3,22
8	'Women for the Future' The All-Ukrainian Political Association	547 916	2,11
9	The Election Bloc of Political Parties 'The Winter Crop Team'	525 025	2,02
10	The Communist Party of Ukraine (renewed)	362 712	1,39
11	The Green Party of Ukraine	338 252	1,30
12	The Political Party *Yabluko* ('The Apple')	299 764	1,15
13	The Election Bloc of Political Parties *'Yednist'* ('Unity')	282 491	1,09
14	The Election Bloc of Political Parties: The Democratic Party of Ukraine – 'The Democratic Union' Party	227 393	0,87
15	'The New Generation of Ukraine' Party	201 157	0,77
16	The Election Bloc of Political Parties: *Rus'kyy Blok* (The Russian Bloc)	190 839	0,73
17	The Election Bloc of Political Parties: 'ZUBR' ("For Ukraine, Bilorus, Russia")	112 259	0,43
18	The Communist Party of Workers and Peasants	106 904	0,41
19	The Peasant's Party of Ukraine	98 428	0,37
20	The Party of Rehabilitation of the Heavily Ill of Ukraine	91 098	0,35
21	The All-Ukrainian Party of Workers	88 842	0,34
22	'The All-Ukrainian Association of Christians' Political Party	75 174	0,29
23	The Social-Democratic Party of Ukraine	68 664	0,26
24	The Election Bloc of Political Parties *'Narodnyy Rukh Ukrayiny'* (The People's Movement of Ukraine)	41 730	0,16
25	The Election Bloc of Political Parties 'Against All'	29 665	0,11
26	The Ukrainian Naval Party	29 025	0,11
27	The People's Party of Investors and Social Protection	27 273	0,10
28	The All-Ukrainian Party 'The New Power'	26 299	0,10
29	The Ukrainian Political Party 'The Christian Movement'	23 591	0,09
30	The All-Ukrainian Association of the Left Party 'The Justice'	21 957	0,08
31	The Ukrainian National Assembly	11 839	0,04
32	The Election Bloc of Political Parties, The Ukrainian Party and the All-Ukrainian Party of Inter-National Understanding 'The New World'	11 048	0,04
33	The Liberal Party of Ukraine (renewed)	8 535	0,03

Source: *Politychnyy Kalendar* 4 (51) 2002.

The most ambitious contestant of the 2002 parliamentary elections was the bloc of pro-presidential parties '*Za Yedynu Ukrayinu*!' ('For a United Ukraine', shortened by the public to '*Za Yedu*!' – 'For Food!' (ZYU!)). From the very start, this bloc associated itself with Leonid Kuchma.[18] The 'Labour Ukraine' party (headed by S. Tygypko), the Party of Regions (at that time headed by M. Azarov), the Head of the Tax Administration, the Popular Democratic Party (led by ex- prime minister V. Pustovoytenko), the Agrarian Party of M.Gladiy, and the Party of Manufacturers and Entrepreneurs (led by the then prime minister A. Kinakh) formed the bloc. They hoped to achieve as high as 25 per cent of votes on the proportional lists. While many independent polls placed the popularity of 'ZYU!' at no more than four per cent, Leonid Kuchma ordered all state officials from the rayon level upward to work to ensure that the bloc obtained 30 per cent of the votes (Kuzio, 2002a). The bloc positioned itself as centrist and its amorphous and vague program emphasized stability, and the need for the corporatist status quo. Leonid Kuchma deserves credit for successfully uniting powerful political forces for the duration of the elections. Indeed, many members of the coalition were fierce business rivals. Only the Social Democrats (united), who were also close to the presidential apparatus, ran independently.

The nature of the 2002 election campaign warrants discussion. Aggressive, intensive and extensive use of financial, media and administrative resources marked the pre-election period. Despite the limitations by law of the amount of money available for election campaign, numerous parties exceeded this figure many times over. The mass media was dominated by the 'power bloc' ZYU!, ignoring the opposition candidates. At all levels, government officials were directed to use their position and resources to promote the ZYU! Bloc (this phenomenon is called 'administrative resource' in Ukraine).

The election result was quite unexpected for both the ruling party and the opposition. The massive negative campaign against the opposition forces did not prevent them from entering the Parliament. Furthermore, the 'ZYU!' and the SDPU (united) polled a low result, particularly considering their enormous administrative and financial investments. Six contestants passed the four per cent threshold barrier [Table 2.11]. 'Our Ukraine' bloc proved to be the winner, with the Communists and 'ZYU!' trailing behind. Olexiy Haran' (2002) called the results of the parliamentary elections based on party lists, 'a victory for democracy'. Moreover, many parties, whose formation was unofficially inspired by the Presidential Administration in order to draw votes away from the opposition (e.g., the Winter Crop Team, the 'New Generation' Party, 'Women For the Future'), did not enter the Parliament.

In contrast to the PR results, the single majority districts demonstrated a clear 'loss of democracy'. It is in the SMDs that the 'ZYU!' bloc appeared as a confident winner [Tables 2.12]. With 66 of 'ZYU!' nominated candidates and 20 self-nominated members of its parties winning in the SMDs, the

Table 2.12 The majoritarian elections results

The Party (Election Bloc of Parties)	The Number of Districts Where the Party/Bloc Lists Won	The Number of Districts Where the Candidates Nominated by Parties/Blocs Won
The Election Bloc of Political Parties: The Bloc of Victor Yushchenko 'Our Ukraine'	94	41
The Communist Party of Ukraine	100	6
The Election Bloc of Political Parties 'For A United Ukraine!'	18	66
The Election Bloc of Political Parties: The Election Bloc of Yuliya Tymoshenko	1	–
The Socialist Party of Ukraine	12	2
The Social-Democratic Party of Ukraine (united)	–	5

Table 2.13 The party affiliation of deputies in the Verkhovna Rada (Election blocs)

№ p/p	The Party (Election Bloc of Parties)	Multi-Mandate District	Single-Mandate Districts		Total
			Nominated by a party/bloc	Self-Nominated Who Also Belong to a Party/Bloc by Party Membership	
1.	The Election Bloc of Political Parties: The Bloc of Victor Yushchenko 'Our Ukraine'	70	41	1	112
2.	The Communist Party of Ukraine	59	6		65
3.	The Election Bloc of Political Parties 'For A United Ukraine!'	35	66	20	121
4.	The Election Bloc of Political Parties: The Election Bloc of Yuliya Tymoshenko	22			22
5.	The Socialist Party of Ukraine	20	2		22
6.	The Social-Democratic Party of Ukraine (united)	19	5	3	27
7.	The Election Bloc of Political Parties: The Democratic Party of Ukraine – 'The Democratic Union'		4	1	5
8.	The Election Bloc of Political Parties 'Yednist' ('Unity')		3	1	4
9.	The Party of National-Economic Development of Ukraine		1		1
10.	The Ukrainian Naval Party		1		1
11.	The Ukrainian National Assembly			1	1
	Total by Parties and Blocs	225	129	27	381
	Non-Party Deputies from Single-Mandate Districts, Self-Nominated			66	66

majoritarian elections brought the 'bloc of power' 2.5 times as many deputies as the proportional part. With 56 more deputies, who initially positioned themselves as non-party candidates but joined the 'ZYU!' after entering Parliament, the bloc was able to form the biggest faction in the *Verkhovna Rada*. However, soon afterwards the bloc disunited. The temporary electoral alliance proved insufficient in creating permanent unification.

The 2002 Parliamentary Elections: Lessons about Ukraine's Democracy

With reference to their influence on the evolution of the Ukrainian party system, the lessons 2002 parliamentary elections can be briefly summarized as follows:

1.   The results of the elections demonstrated that the East–West division has become less evident and can no longer be effectively manipulated as an electoral tool.[19] One can still regionally identify the most supportive electorate for the main electoral contestants. However, there are no longer "parties of one region" in the present parliament. This is in contrast to the previous parliament where the Progressive Socialist Party of Ukraine and the *Hromada* draw their electorate exclusively from a particular region. This suggests that parties will have to develop a more constructive approach in the future when developing their political programs, as well as concentrate on unifying rather than separating issues. This is especially the case for the Communist Party of Ukraine.

2.   The elections once again demonstrated that the Ukrainian multiparty system is not particularly effective and consists of a few real political players. Of the thirty-three parties/blocs registered to participate in the elections, twenty did not even poll one per cent of the votes, while seven parties polled between one per cent and four per cent. However, their participation in the election was beneficial for the Presidential Administration by 'burning' votes that could have gone to the opposition. Six of those that did not pass the four per cent barrier, had the phrase 'all-Ukrainian' in their name. This suggests that there was an element of populism and 'wishful thinking' in choosing such a party name, and instead these parties were formed around narrow social groups. They qualify better to be considered political associations - which is what they are in reality - rather than parties.

3.   The election results demonstrated why Ukrainian authorities were eager to maintain the majoritarian part of the electoral system, as it allowed to compensate the pro-presidential parties for the disastrous results in the PR part of the elections. Indeed, the 2002 parliamentary elections illustrated the evident mistrust of society in the current power institutions. However, as a result of the majoritarian part of the elections, the 'ZYU!' bloc were able to present itself as the winner of the elections, perhaps, at the expense of forming a true multiparty system in Ukraine. In this sense, the elections were

not an expression of the popular will but a means of legitimating the 'parties of power' in power.

4.   Another notable feature of the 2002 parliamentary elections was the appearance of a more politically conscious and politically educated Ukrainian electorate. In general, the Ukrainian voters were not swayed by the parties whose name or leader were associated the major players (i.e., the so-called 'political tweedledees'). As a result, the bloc of '*Narodnyy Rukh Ukrayiny*', led by B. Boyko, only polled 0.16 per cent of the votes,[20] the Communist Party of Workers and Peasants obtained 0.41 per cent, the All-Ukrainian Party of Workers, headed by Olexander Moroz (the politically unknown double of the Socialist leader), got 0.34 per cent, and the Communist Party of Ukraine (renewed) obtained 1.39 per cent of the votes. Furthermore, the well-paid Russian political strategists and image-makers (spin-doctors) were unable to compensate for the lack of ideology in certain parties, such as the Winter Crop Generation, funded by an oligarch and L. Kuchma's son-in-law, V. Pinchuk, of 'Labour Ukraine'. Taras Kuzio (2002b) states that the Winter Crop Team represents 'the culmination of the oligarch take-over of the political centre in Ukraine'. Despite the large sums of money invested in the campaign, the oligarchic SDPU (united) was the last group to cross the threshold on the party lists. The strategy to entice the "apolitical" section of the Ukrainian electorate was also not effective. One of the biggest surprises of the 2002 elections was the failure of the 'Women for the Future', associated with the wife of Leonid Kuchma and the pro-presidential Party of Greens of Ukraine (PGU) to pass the four per cent threshold. It has also become apparent that the Ukrainian electorate is not entirely indifferent to ideology as it had been expected earlier. Indeed, there has been a visible shift towards pro-market forces and parties. For the first time in the history of an independent Ukraine, the Communist party did not make up the largest faction in Parliament.

5.   Another tendency observed during the 2002 elections in stark contrast to the 1998 elections, was the creation of political blocs involving several parties. Of the six winners in the 2002 elections, three were blocs of parties, and of the 33 participating contestants, 12 were blocs. In the 1998 parliamentary elections, only one winner (out of eight) was represented by a bloc of parties (the Socialists grouped with the Peasants' party), and nine of the 30 contestants were blocs. Only six parties took part in both the 1998 and the 2002 parliamentary elections as independent parties.[21] If gathering into blocs implies consolidating and unifying the position of parties and thus strengthening them, this electoral trend should be viewed positively. However, if we recall that the bloc of 'ZYU!' split into eight factions immediately after electing the parliamentary leadership, the optimism about party system development may appear to be premature.

6.   Mykola Tomenko has called the 2002 Ukrainian elections to the *Verhovna Rada* a 'noticeable step towards the development of the party system of Ukraine'. Despite that the ratio between members of parties and

non-members changed minimally (68 per cent in 1998 and 67 per cent in 2002), he views the lack of self-nominated candidates in 2002 as evidence that sustains his thesis. Forty percent of self-nominees were among the elected deputies in the 2002 Parliament, compared to 57 per cent in the parliament of 1998 (*Politychnyy Kalendar*, 2002, No.3). The number of party-affiliated deputies has also increased at the local level. After the 1998 elections, party members accounted for only 8 per cent of local, rayon and oblast' deputies (among the heads of *raion* and *oblast radas* this figure increased to 20 per cent). After the 2002 local elections, party members already accounted for 22 per cent of local, rayon, and oblast' deputies. In December 2001, the *Verkhovna Rada* passed a bill on local elections that hoped to introduce a majoritarian electoral system for local and mayoral elections, and an equal mix of majoritarian and proportional voting for the rayon and oblast' elections. However, President Kuchma vetoed it (Haran', 2002).

Since the 2002 elections, Ukrainian democracy appears to be losing ground, evidenced by the newly elected leadership of the *Verkhovna Rada*: Volodymyr Lytvyn, former Head of the Presidential Administration and number one on the 'ZYU!' bloc list, was elected Speaker, Henadiy Vasyliev, who represents the Donetsk wing of 'For a United Ukraine' became first deputy, and Oleksandr Zinchenko, who was one of the leaders of the Social Democrats (united), was elected deputy speaker. The parties that won the majority of the popular votes were prevented access to the Parliament's leadership from the outset.

Another strategic loss of the Ukrainian opposition parties to the 'parties of power' occurred during the formation of pro-presidential majority in October 2002. The parties of the former 'ZYU!' bloc formed the basis of the majority, and the Social Democrats (united) joined them. Perplexingly, this majority was based not on support from the Ukrainian electorate, but on the parties' support of the current President (*Politychnyy Kalendar*, 2002, No.9). A number of opposition deputies left their original factions and joined the majority. While the reasons differed, many were attracted by opportunities of career advancement and the unofficial financial rewards. The creation of such a majority in the Ukrainian Parliament was a premature act, which went beyond the constitutional provisions, and could be a hindrance to the development of Ukrainian parliamentarism and the party system. The vast majority of positions (such as heads of commissions and committees) that were occupied by members of opposition parties were now in the hands of the parties of power. In this sense, it would be correct to argue that Ukraine has reached a deadlock *vis-à-vis* the advancement of reforms. An unintended consequence of legislative and more broadly state-power monopolisation by the parties of power along with the President Kuchma has led the Ukrainian opposition to become more united. September 16, 2002 marks yet another turning point in Ukrainian history: four ideologically close yet politically distant forces (the CPU, the SPU, 'Our Ukraine' and Yuliya Tymoshenko's bloc) jointly protested against the Ukraine's president and the system of power that has been assembled. The outcome of this act of protest and the subsequent struggle between the two opposing forces remains uncertain.

Table 2.14 Changes in the political factions in the 2002 Verkhovna Rada

	Factions	Number of Seats at the Time of the Faction's Creation	Seats (as of 30 Nov. 2002)	Seats (as of 10 Jan. 2003)
1	'Our Ukraine'	119	108	102
2	The Communist Party of Ukraine	64	60	60
3	Yuliya Tymoshenko's Bloc	23	18	18
4	The Socialist Party of Ukraine	22	20	20
	Total	**228**	**206**	**200**
	Pro-Presidential Factions:			
5	The Social Democratic Party of Ukraine (United)	31	39	40
	Factions on the basis of 'For a United Ukraine'			
6	The Party of Industrialists and Entrepreneurs – The 'Labour Ukraine' Party	38	42	42
7	'Regions of Ukraine'	35	38	42
8	The People's Democratic Party	17	16	16
9	Agrarian Party	16	16	16
10	'European Choice'	15	20	18
11	'Democratic Initiatives'	16	22	22
12	'Sovereignty of the People'	17	16	20
13	'People's Choice'	15	15	15
14	**Total**	**200**	**224**	**231**
	Non-affiliated		19	19
	Total in Parliament		**449**	**450**

Conclusion

This paper traced the evolution of the multiparty system in Ukraine from a critical perspective. I analysed how the multiparty system works in Ukraine, and why the Ukrainian parties do not carry out the functions typically ascribed to political parties in Western democracies. I addressed the concept of the 'party of power' as a phenomenon characteristic of the Ukrainian party system. Other features of an underdeveloped party system in Ukraine noted in the paper include: shallow social roots and weak ties between the masses and the elites, the limited membership and short political life of parties, regional and issue divisions, ineffective legal provisions, inability/lack of political will to adopt a fully proportional electoral system, which would foster structuring the Ukrainian party system, and the diverse attempts of parties to refrain from defining themselves ideologically, or the 'hijacking' of parties by oligarchs for their own ends.

By focusing on the parliamentary elections of 2002, I attempted to assess the impact of the elections on the development of the Ukrainian multiparty system. One can detect a dialectical process at work here: the monopolising tendency of the parties of power in the Parliament has given rise to its own antithesis, a united Ukrainian opposition. Although one cannot say for certain, the synthesis of this dialectical process may hold a great deal of promise for the future of democracy in Ukraine.

References

Bilous, A. (2000). *Polityko-pravovi systemy: Svit I Ukrayina* [The Political and Legal Systems: the World and Ukraine]. Kyiv: AMUPP.

Birch, S. (August 30– September 2, 2001). *Electoral systems and party system stability in post-communist Europe.* Paper presented at the 97th annual meeting of the American Political Science Association, San Francisco.

Central Electoral Commission Data. Retrieved from www.cvk.gov.ua.

Craumer, P. R. & Clem, J. I. (1999). Ukraine's emerging electoral geography: A regional analysis of the 1998 parliamentary elections. *Post-Soviet Geography and Economics*, 40(1), 1-26.

Duverger, M. (1959). *Political parties: Their organization and activity in the modern state.* New York: Wiley.

Haran', O. (1991). *Ukrayina Bagatopartiyna* [Multiparty Ukraine]. Kyiv: Pamyatky Ukrayiny.

Haran', O. (1993). *Ubyty drakona. Z istoriyi Rukhu ta novykh partiy Ukrayiny* [To kill a dragon: From the history of the Rukh and new parties of Ukraine]. Kyiv: Lybid.

Haran', O. & Mayboroda, O. (2000). *Ukrayins'ki livi: Mizh Leninismom I social-demokratieu* [The Ukrainian left: Between the Leninism and social democracy]. Kyiv: KM Academia.

Haran', O. (2001). Can Ukrainian communists and socialists evolve to social democracy?. *Demokratizatsiya*, 9(4/Fall), 570-587.

Haran', O. (2002). *Politics and society in independent Ukraine.* Paper presented at the joint seminar of European Forum: Stefan Batory Foundation.

Herron, E. S. (2001, August 30-September 2). *The causes and consequences of fluid factional membership in Ukraine.* Paper presented at the annual American Political Science Association Conference, San Francisco.

Hesli, V. L., Reisinger, W. M. & Miller, A. H. (1998). Political party development in divided societies: The case of Ukraine. *Electoral Studies,* 17 (2), 235-256.

Karatnycky, A., Motyl, A. & Schnetzer, A. (Eds.). (2002). *Nations in transit 2002.* Freedom House, Inc.: Transaction Publishers.

Kitschelt, H. (1995). Formation of party cleavages in post-communist democracies. *Party Politics*, 1(4), 447-472.

Klobucar, T. & Miller, A. (August 28-September 1, 2002). *Party activists and party development in Post Soviet democracies.* Paper presented at the annual meeting of the American Political Science Association, Boston, Massachusetts.

Korgunuk Y. & Zaslavskiy S. (1996). *Rossiyskaya mnogopartiynost': Stanovleniye, funktsionirovaniye, razvitiye* [The Russian multipartiness: Establishment, functioning, development] [Electronic version]. Moscow: INDEM. Retrieved September 11, 2001 from www.partinform.ru.

Kuzio, T. (November 20, 2001). Endnote: Ukraine's approaching elections and fractured multiparty system. *RFE/RL Newsline,* 5 (220/Part II) Retrieved December 20, 2001 from http://www.utoronto.ca/crees/faculty/kuzio.htm.

Kuzio, T. (March 4, 2002a). Strong and weak 'Parties of Power' in Russia and Ukraine. *RFE/RL Newsline.* Retrieved April 15, 2002 from www.uanews.co.uk/rferl/ukraine/ua29a.htm

Kuzio, T. (March 26, 2002b). Endnote: Winter-crop generation: First oligarch-backed center-right party. *RFE/RL Newsline* 6(57/Part II). Retrieved April 15, 2002 from http://www.utoronto.ca/~crees/faculty/kuzio15.htm

Kuzio, T. & Wilson, A. (1994). *Ukraine: From perestroika to independence.* New York: St. Martin's Press.

Lipset, S. M. & Rokkan, S. (1967). Cleavage structures, party systems and voter alignments: An introduction. In S.M. Lipset, & S. Rokkan. (Eds.), *Party systems and voter alignments,* (pp. 1-64). New York: Free Press.

Miller, A. H. & Klobucar, T. F. (August, 2001). *Partisan development in Post-Soviet Ukraine.* Paper presented at the annual American Political Science Association Conference, San Francisco.

Mostovaya, Y. (November 17-23, 2001). The party of power exists. And exist it will. *Dzerkalo Tyzhnya,* 45(369).

Parlaments'ka bil'shist': Politychne strukturuvannya chy krok do samorozpusku Verkhovnoyi Rady? [The parliamentary majority: Political structuring or a step towards self-dissolution of the Verkhovna Rada?]. (2002). *Politychnyy Kalendar,* 9(55).

Pidsumky Parlaments'kykh Vyboriv 2002 Roku [The Results of the 2002 Parliamentary Elections]. (2002). *Politychnyy Kalendar,* 3 (50).

Pilon, J. G. (2001). Civic education: A primer / Democratic citizenship. In D. Lawrence, S. Riabov & O. Demyanchuk (Eds.), *Conceptual-Methodological Issues of Civic Education.* Kyiv.

Politychnyy Kalendar, 4 (40), 2001.

Politychnyy Kalendar, 4 (51) 2002.

Tomenko, M. & Protsenko, O. (1998). *Pravo vyboru: Politychni partiyi ta vyborchi bloky* [The right to chose: The political parties and electoral blocs]. Kyiv: Vybory do VRU.

Tomenko, M. & Oliynyk, V. (2000). *Partiyna elita Ukrayiny 2000* [The party elite of Ukraine 2000]. Kyiv: Logos.

Ukrainian Constitution, Article 36, 1996.

Ukrayins'ki partiyi naperedodni vyboriv: Stanovlennya Ukrayins'koyi bagatopartiynosti [The Ukrainian parties before the elections: The establishment of Ukrainian multipartyness]. (2001). *Politychnyy Kalendar,* 9(44).

Veto prezydenta na zakon Ukrayiny pro vybory narodnykh deputativ Ukrayiny: Pravovi ta politychni aspekty [The presidential veto on the law of Ukraine on the elections of people's deputies of Ukraine: Legal and political Aspects]. (2001). *Politychnyy Kalendar,* 2(38).

Vidstavka uryadu: Suspil'no-politychni aspekty [The government dismissal: Social and political aspects]. (2001). *Politychnyy Kalendar*, 4(40).

Voting Results. Retrieved from www.tomenko.kiev.ua.

Zamnius, V., Kovryzhenko, D., Kotlyar, D., et al. (2002). *Orientyry vybortsya 2002: Dovidnyk* [The electorate's orientations: A guide]. Kyiv: Millennium.

Zakon pro politychni partiyi v konteksti evolutsiyi politychnoyi systemy v Ukrayini [The law on the political parties in the context of evolution of the political system in Ukraine]. (2001). *Politychnyy Kalendar*, 3(39).

PART III

CIVIL SOCIETY
AND ITS ORGANIZATIONS

DEMOCRATIZATION FROM BELOW:

THE ROLE OF CIVIL SOCIETY IN AZERBAIJAN

Ayça ERGUN

Post-Soviet democratization is a non-linear process within which the shift from authoritarian rule to democracy has been shaped by the Soviet historical, social and political heritage. It contains features of liberalization and democratization as well as authoritarian practices, and can thus be characterized as a process where old and new formations compete. In this sense, the path of post-Soviet democratization is determined by the co-existence of patterns of continuity and of change. Continuity can be seen in the old Communist *nomenklatura* and their authoritarian and semi-authoritarian practices, clientelistic networks, the lack of democratic institutions and the dominance of regionalism. Whereas new institution-building, national law-making, the formation of political parties, the establishment of social organizations, the shift to a market economy, the rule of law and a free press represent patterns of change.

In an environment of conflicting co-existence between continuity and change and simultaneity and uncertainty, new actors – distinct from the political elite – become initiators of democratization. In the post-Soviet era, the old elite, accustomed to the previous ruling practices, resisted further democratization and continued to embrace authoritarianism. However, change created a situation whereby a restoration of the old regime was no longer possible. Resistance from the opposition and the increasing influence of international agencies further hindered the opportunity to restore the old regime. Instead there emerged a hybrid form of political transformation where *new* and *old* competed and co-existed. As the regime was unwilling to democratize, the dynamics of democratization were shaped by society. Such a configuration in transition should not be overlooked: a new hybrid regime

– incorporating the legacies of the old regime and the imperatives of transformation – and society (as opposed to political institutions) represent the fora for democratization.

The literature on post-communist transition to democracy primarily focuses on the role of state actors rather than societal non-elite and non-state actors. In studies investigating the role of civil society in democratic transitions in post-Soviet countries, (see for example Bermeo, 1992; Ekiert, 1996; Fish, 1995; Gill, 2000; Rose, Mishler & Haerpfer, 1998; Rueschemeyer, D., Rueschemeyer, M. & Wittrick, 1998; Ruffin & Waugh, 1999; Tishmaneanu, 1995) the importance of civil society is recognized only after procedural requirements have been met and democracy has been consolidated. However, discovering the type of civil society being forged is frequently overlooked. Indeed, there are very few studies that address state-society relation with regards to the post-soviet peculiarities. (For example Ekiert, 1995; 1996; Ekiert, & Rubik, 1999; Fish, 1995)

This article investigates the society element of democratization, focusing on the dynamics that are taking place in the sphere of non-governmental organizations (NGO) in post-Soviet Azerbaijan. In the first section, I consider the nature of civil society, particularly paying attention to the aims and activities of social organizations and their role in the democratization process. In the second section, the article describes and discusses the relationship between the state and civil society in Azerbaijan.

Ekiert and Rubik (1999) stated that 'if there is such a thing as "democracy by design", many non-elite actors were among the designers' (p. 7) while also acknowledging that 'little is known about the activities of non-elite actors and the ways in which their activities shape the process of democratization' (p. 9). All definitions of civil society refer to the organized activities of social organizations, umbrella groups, movements and professional unions acting outside and independent of the state yet sharing common aims and beliefs. (For a detailed analysis and discussion, see Diamond, 1999; Gill, 2000; Linz & Stepan, 1996; Keane, 1988) L. Diamond (1999) defines civil society as 'the realm of organized social life that is open, voluntary, self-generating, at least partially self-supporting, autonomous from the state, and bound by a legal order or a set of shared values' (p. 221). The state is considered fundamental, in providing the legal arrangements for civil society and civil society is believed to contribute to further democratization. In this sense, an ideal relationship between the state and civil society is one in which civil society plays an intermediary role between the state and society and the state protects and promotes civil society by legal recognition and guarantee (Keane, 1998, p. 3). Linz and Stepan (1996) consider 'civil society' as one of the interacting areas for consolidating democracy, an 'arena of the polity where self-organizing groups, movements, and individuals, relatively autonomous from the state, attempt to articulate values, create associations and solidarities, and advance their interests' (p. 7). They highlight the fact that civil society is 'the celebrity of democratic resistance and transition' (p. 9). In transitions where the state is in opposition to civil society, 'a real civil society does not eventuate' and state-society relations are better explained with reference to 'the growth of civil society forces, [that is] organizations that will be the nucleus of civil society' (Gill, 2000, p. 118).

The attempt to apply the term 'civil society' – a term derived from Western European experience – to the post-Soviet context is highly problematic; indeed, pre-defined categories oblige readers to view the post-communist reality through the eyes of another's experience. The lack of a tradition of including societal forces in political transformation, the attempts to transform all spheres of society simultaneously (i.e., political, economic and civil) and the inexperience of local organizations illustrate some of the difficulties in applying pre-defined categories and notions to the post-soviet world.

What may have been called 'civil society' under Soviet rule was in fact a collection of social organizations formed under the guidance, initiative and control of the Party. These organizations did not constitute the base of civil society as they lacked autonomy. Further, it is dubious to describe the participants of the national independence movements of the Southern Caucasus as civil society forces; their organizational foundation derived from the context rather than clearly defined actions and agendas. It was only after the achievement of independence that political parties and non-governmental organizations outside of the state emerged. Given that independent social and political activity outside of the party and the state was new, most NGO's were incorporated into political parties or subjected to the influence of international organizations.

The new institution-building, the reforms to the market economy and the re-defining of the nation are still presently on-going, as a result newly established local organizations have yet to achieve their potential of acting as an intermediary between the state and society. Moreover, under the present semi-authoritarian circumstances – inherited from the previous regime type and consolidated by the old elite now in power – societal actors are either excluded from the political transformation or captured by the pro-government or pro-opposition political parties.

In the post-Soviet political transformation of Azerbaijan there is strong evidence of 'civil society forces' operating. In the Southern Caucasus in general and in Azerbaijan in particular, the emergence of civil society forces is not a product of the declarations of independence and/or the liberalizing or part democratizing of states. In fact, the formation of civil society precedes the independence period.

The period 1988-1991 was marked by the introduction of *glasnost* (openness) and *perestroika* (restructuring). *Glasnost* and *perestroika* introduced changes in Azerbaijan, the consequences of which affected independence and the political transformation that followed. *Glasnost* and *perestroika* provided the political opportunity for 'society' to play a role in the political transformation. They paved the way for the formation of social organizations independent of the Communist Party of Azerbaijan (CPAz) and revived collective action. Social organizations were formed to 'implement the principles of *glasnost* and *perestroika*' (Varliq's programme, 1988). They later were crucial in initiating political socialization and activism.

The primary set of changes introduced by *glasnost* and *perestroika* affected two main processes in Azerbaijan democratization and state-building. They led to the formation of social organizations, primarily small literary unions, where the intellectual elite gathered to discuss the possibilities for action within the confines of *glasnost* and *perestroika*. The formation of these unions expanded the boundaries of organizational activity and paved the way for the emergence of alternatives to the CPAz. However, they did not directly challenge the existing structure of the Soviet Union and the CPAz until after the emergence of the national question.

The first progenitor organizations of civil society initiated openness and restructuring and were led by the intellectual elite of that time with the goals of independence and democracy. These organizations had the explicit aims of (re)discovering the cultural and historical origins of the Azerbaijani people and restoring sovereignty. By late 1987 and early 1988, new organizations were established, such as the Organization for the Defence of Azerbaijan's Sovereignty, *Varlik* (Wealth), *Birlik* (Unity),[1] *Chenlibel* Scientific Literary Union[2] and Baku Alimler Klubü (Baku Intellectuals Club). These groups were not affiliated to the CPAz, indicative of a period of creating 'civil society' outside the confines of the CPAz. Their formation was interpreted as representative of the 'necessity to take action to form a social-political organization that could lead a large mass-movement given that the Party was not taking the necessary precautions to guarantee the territorial integrity and real sovereignty of the country' (Balayev & Mirze, 2000, p. 13). They were formed under the banner of literary unions, with intellectuals and young students discussing the works of poets and writers on Azerbaijani historical and cultural life. Rather than being structured organizations with clearly defined aims and actions, they were more akin to discussion groups where key social, cultural and political issues were debated by publicly known academics, writers and poets. They were raising democratic consciousness without referring to any explicit political issues.[3] Given that their programs had a developed political content and were aimed at collective action, their establishment represents the first challenge to the regime.

The second set of changes affected nation-building. The emergence of national issues in Azerbaijan – such as national identity, national consciousness, national defence and nationhood – was accelerated by Armenian demands on the Nagorno-Karabagh Autonomous Region *Oblast* (NKAO), a mountainous enclave approximately forty-four hundred square kilometres wide and located in the Azerbaijan SSR. The region was under the territorial jurisdiction of the Azerbaijan SSR but was populated largely by Armenians. The Karabagh Armenians demands for secession of the *oblast* to Armenian jurisdiction motivated the Azerbaijanis' national identity aspirations (Altstadt, 1994, p. 105; Dragadze, 1989, p. 55). As a result, the broad, diversified and culturally oriented organizational activity altered its direction, turning into a politicized protest-based movement (Freedom Square Movement) that would later pave the way for the formation of the People's Front of Azerbaijan.

1988 coincides with the introduction of *glasnost* and *perestroika* and represents a crucial turning point. It signifies the emergence of organizational activity and the raising of national consciousness in Azerbaijan. The combination *glasnost* and *perestroika* caused a national and a political awakening, which would be concretized by the subsequent events. By 1988 both the Soviet regime and the CPAz were subjected to severe criticism as a result of their inefficiency in handling the Nagorno-Karabagh issue, their half-hearted implementation of *glasnost* and *perestroika* and their confrontations with the newly emerged politico-intellectual elite and organized activity. It was via *glasnost* and *perestroika* that the intellectual elite shifted from universities and the Academy of Sciences to unions and organizations, thus creating a nationalist counter elite.

From the inception of the movement, nationhood went hand in hand with democratization since the Karabagh issue was significant both for statehood and nationhood. The Karabagh conflict determined the discourses of the new regime as well as questions regarding national identity and statehood. The pre-independence organizations, then, were the birthplace of national consciousness, discovering the ethnic, cultural and social origins of the nation under new and relatively liberal conditions. These organizations re-articulated national consciousness in new circumstances. These literary unions moved from expressing their relatively timid political views to becoming increasingly politically oriented, in part because of developments in NKAO and the perceived aggressiveness of Armenians.

In fact, the literary unions shifted from cultural, intellectual and literary issues to politically oriented and nationalistic ones. While many Karabagh focused organizations – e.g., The Karabagh Veterans' Union, the *Gaghy* (Concern), The People's Aid Committee to Karabagh, *Birlik*, *Dirchelish* (Azerbaijan Resurgence Party), *Kizilbash* People's Front, the Karabagh's Relief Committee, the Social Democrat Organization of Azerbaijan – were established, they were short-lived (Altstadt, 1992, pp. 204-205; Swietochowski, 1995, p. 196). Nonetheless, these organizations demonstrate the centrality of the Karabagh issue for stimulating their creation.[4] The shift from cultural issues to political/nationalistic ones, new organizational capacity as well as popular support led to the establishment of the PFA.

Stimulated by the Karabagh Armenians' demands on the Nagorno-Karabagh Autonomous Region, these organizations led to the formation of a mass movement engaged in open political action, such as rallies, meetings and strikes. Initially, they protested against Soviet rule and then against their two 'brother' nationalities, the Armenians and Russians. The reluctance of the Communist Party of Azerbaijan to implement *glasnost* and *perestroika* and to deal with the Karabagh problem accelerated the formation of a nationalist independence movement. The People's Front Movement of Azerbaijan was established, with the twin goals of sovereignty and independence. It was initially a nation-wide organization challenging the party elite, but soon appeared as a potential candidate to rule the independent Republic of Azerbaijan.

The People's Front rule (1992-1993) under the presidency of Ebulfez Elcibey signalled a new phase in the political transformation of Azerbaijan. Its coming to power symbolised the introduction of the new system in which independence, democracy and national identity would be the main concerns. However, the new regime challenged the legacies of the past. While trying to reshape the existing structures with new institution-building, democratic principles and the replacement of the old cadres, the People's Front Government was also affected by the legacies of the clientelistic networks, regionalism and more importantly by the old elite which were not as yet insignificant.

The patterns of continuity surfaced after the overthrow of the People's Front Government and its replacement with the former communist party secretary, ex-politburo member and head of the Nakhchivan Autonomous Republic of Azerbaijan, Heydar Aliyev. Aliyev's coming to power in 1993 indicated the victory of past legacies. After his coming to power, Azerbaijan's political transformation faced numerous hurdles due to anti-democratic practices in elections, repression of the opposition, consolidation of one-man rule, bribery, corruption and regionalism. The change of regime and its replacement by Aliyev signified a step back towards the past. Nevertheless, it did not lead to a restoration of Soviet-type authoritarianism.

Azerbaijan's route to democratization has been shaped by historical and political legacies as well as newly introduced concepts, such as: democracy, nation-statehood and a market economy. The democratization process was initiated by the overthrowing of an authoritarian regime by the independence movement. Yet the transition to democracy remained incomplete due to the impact of patterns of continuity derived from the prior regime type; the patterns of change did not produce a consolidated democracy. It is a country where the *old* and *new*, represented by government and opposition elites respectively, compete. In this respect, the government versus opposition divide is the main dichotomy that affects political transformation in Azerbaijan. The binary divide determines not only the path of democratization in Azerbaijan but also the nature of the future regime. The regime and the opposition represent distinctively different points of view on each issue related to domestic and international politics.

In this sense, they are the 'other' of each other. It is this tension between the two groups (with different political backgrounds, agendas and prospects for democratization) that determines the current political transformation. In this context, the formation of new political parties and increasing the number of NGOs encourage agreements between political parties and social organizations. Although the government elite was reluctant to introduce change, the galvanized society element demanded change, the democratization of society and the widening of representation.

The mass movement between 1988-1991 was the embryonic form of the civil society. It questioned the Soviet regime and argued for independence, which invariably entailed breaking the dependency ties with the Soviet Union. It also promoted a revival of national identity. The slogans of 'freedom', 'democracy', 'resignation' and 'Karabagh' also dominated the post-independence period's organizational activity. However, independence did not bring real change as the representatives of the old regime were still in power. After the replacement of the PFA by Aliyev's government, a new phase of post-Soviet political transformation began.

Civil Society: The Sphere of Non-Governmental Organizations

There were around 1,500 NGOs in Azerbaijan by late 2003 (UNDP, 2003). This number includes both the re-registered social organizations established during the Soviet period and those established after the achievement of independence. However, there are also quite a large number of organizations that are currently very active but not yet registered.[5]

Their main areas of activities include: human rights, democratization, electoral reforms, environmental issues, gender, migration/refugees rights, education, disabled people, children and youth. (Hasanov, 1999, pp. 2-3; Nelson, 1999) There are also professional organizations, including trade unions, most of which are re-registered organizations formerly affiliated to the CPAz. The law of November 1992, 'The Law of Azerbaijan Republic on Public Associations' (for the full text of the law, see *Azerbaycan*, 12 November 1992), regulated the activities of civil society until a new law, 'The Law on Non-Governmental Organizations', was issued in November 2000.

In the 1992 law, social organizations were defined as 'a voluntary association based on the mutual interests of citizens and the expression of their free will' (Law of the Republic of Azerbaijan on Public Associations, Article 1, 1992). It was based on the principles of voluntary participation, equality of their members, law and publicity (Law of the Republic of Azerbaijan on Public Associations, Article 2). The state ensured rights, public associations and legitimate interests, creating the conditions for organizational activities in accordance with the Constitution and the laws of the Republic of Azerbaijan (Law of the Republic of Azerbaijan on Public Associations, Article 9). However, 'public associations have no right to interfere in the activities of state bodies and executives' (Law of the Republic of Azerbaijan on Public Associations, Article 8).

In 1999, the parliament developed a new draft, making changes to and additions to the existing legislation. In the draft law, a 'social union' (*ictimai birlik*) was defined as 'a non-commercial voluntary association created as a result of the expression of the will of citizens with mutual interests' (Draft Law on Changes to and Addition to the Law of the Republic of Azerbaijan on Social Organizations, Article 1). These voluntary organizations could take the form of social organizations, religious institutions, foundations, associations, social movements and federations (Draft Law on Changes to and Addition to the Law of the Republic of Azerbaijan on Social Organizations, Article 1). The state assigns the following duties to social organizations:

'-to act in accordance with the legislation of the Republic of Azerbaijan and the aims stated in their programs.

-to inform the body responsible for state registration about the continuity of its activities.

-to present their decisions and financial statements when the registration body asks for them

-to assure the participation of the representative of the registration body in any activities.

-to create conditions for the officials and state bodies responsible for the supervision of the social organizations' activities to realise their duties' (Draft Law on Changes to and Addition to the Law of the Republic of Azerbaijan on Social Organizations, Article 8, Section 1).

After the discussion and ratification, a new law on non-governmental organizations was issued on 13 June 2000.[6] The new law defines an NGO as a 'social union and foundation': '[A] social union is a non-governmental organization founded on the initiative of a legal personality on the basis of a voluntary act and does not aim to make a profit' (Law on Non-Governmental Organizations, Article 2, Section 1); a foundation is 'an NGO that does not have members, founded by one or more legal personality dealing with social, cultural, educational issues' (Law on Non-Governmental Organizations, Article 2, Section 1).

Each organization must be registered with the Ministry of Justice in order to act legally. The requirements for registration involve: applying for recognition via an authorized representative of the social organization within a month of holding their first meeting, describing the programme of the organization, providing information on the founders of the organization (name, occupation, passport number and place of birth) as well as providing a list of members and five copies of the programme. The registration mechanism, which will be discussed below, is tantamount to the regime controlling civil societal activity.

The aims of local NGOs can be summarised as: achieving improvements in the democratization of society, protecting human rights and disabled people, bettering the conditions of refugees, providing humanitarian aid and contributing to conflict resolution. Most NGOs conduct their activities on a project basis ranging in time from the short to medium term. These projects involve: researching the violation of human rights; conducting democratic assessments; monitoring activities, particularly in pre-election; organising seminars, conferences, round tables and workshops; and publishing leaflets, brochures and books.

Through these activities NGOs contribute to the re-definition of state-society relations. NGOs play a vital role in consciousness raising and in increasing public awareness on a wide range of issues from civil and political rights to election procedures, from children rights to gender issues, from protection of journalists to defence of political prisoners. Such activities are also a learning process for the members of social organizations. They train people as well as becoming centres for training trainers. However, their previous lack of experience alongside the reluctance of the regime to include the society element in the political transformation hinder the development of civil society in Azerbaijan.

Most of the NGOs do not have many members and are run by three to ten people who define and conduct its activities. Within the local NGOs one can observe a personalistic network. One can be the chair of one NGO, vice-president of another and a member of another one. In some cases, the chairs are also members of the administrative bodies of political parties. This makes some organizations work like a chain and their inter-relationship and cooperation make activity more realistic and feasible.[7] Given their financial difficulties, some NGOs require support from political parties in order to benefit from parties' technical assistance, e.g., office support, computer and fax machine facilities and occasionally even staff.[8] Political parties pay great attention to the existence and activities of social organizations in establishing democratic society. They are also considering 'friendly' organizations as tools for support, especially in election periods.

Civil society in a broader sense organises itself on the basis of the funding provided by international organizations. Training and seminars create a milieu of interaction between them and others. Some organizations operating in the same sphere have regular meetings.[9] However, tend not to collaborate on a project basis, but rather facilitate the creation of personal networks. In terms of the interrelationship among the organizations, those who work in the same field have regular contact.[10] These meetings primarily take place in the premises of international organizations, e.g., ISAR and the UN Resource and Training Centre.

The formation of civil society is predominately initiated by new organizations established after independence. However, in the organizational domain, there are a considerable number of re-registered old unions formerly affiliated to the CPAz. These old unions do not efficiently and actively take part in the creation of civil society. The interrelationship between the old organizations, which were established during the Soviet period and new ones, is rather limited. Representatives of new organizations argue that, although they have respect for older (regime-affiliated) organizations, they find them 'old', not adapting to 'global changes' and not effectively representing the interests of their members.[11] The old unions, such as the Writers' and the Journalists' Unions, acknowledge that they do not have a constant relationship with newly established unions. They confess however that they were prestigious and influential in society and fundamental in protecting the rights of journalists and writers. Nevertheless, after independence, they lack state-sponsored resources to promote their organizations and are reluctant and unable to forge relationships with the international community.[12]

The considerable gap between the old and new organizations demonstrates the dominance of patterns of change in civil society. Change is predominantly initiated by new organizations, which are the products of pre-independence activity and the liberalization policies of post-independence. Their activity centres on the foundation of an organization, preparing its programme and articulating it in different spheres, such as the polity, health, migration, refugees and human rights.

There are also other problems, common to all organizations, which undermine their effectiveness. A survey suggests that local NGOs' lack of equipment (fax, telephone, computer and office space) and access to technology (e-mail and internet) creates a lack of awareness regarding their work in forming civil society.[13] Similarly, they have an inability to expand their projects to the regions, lack good relations with the state and the business community, have insufficient training and lack contacts with other NGOs, especially international NGOs (Nelson, 1999, p. 9).

Yet the activities of most NGOs are limited to the capital. Although a few conducted seminars and conferences in the regions, the scope of consciousness raising is limited to Baku and its surrounding areas, primarily because of intolerance and the arbitrary practices of local authorities.[14] One argued that 'whenever we organise a conference or a seminar in the regions, if we invite people from the state, they [local authorities] do not cause any trouble. But whenever we invite a representative from the opposition, they do not give us permission'.[15] This is one of the main reasons why many NGOs do not have any regional branches. However, the problems related to material resources, expanding the scope and the range of activities constitute minor obstacles for civil society development. In the process of political transformation what becomes more important is the relationship between NGOs and the state and how they conceive of each other.

Civil Society and State

The relationship between the regime and local organizations is complex and multi-dimensional. It contains two contradictory features: encouragement and antagonism. By 1998, as a result of the growing number and activity of local NGOs as well as the influence, advice and guidance of international NGOs, the state-building project of late Aliyev's government incorporated 'civil society' (or the citizens' community) into the political transformation. New units and departments were established within the presidential apparatus and parliament. In the presidential apparatus, a new unit for NGOs was created working closely with the Directorate of Social and Political Affairs. The head of the Directorate argued that government policy was to 'involve NGOs in the process of state-building and in all aspects of the society'.[16] This unit collaborated with the UN Resource and Training Centre for NGOs and encouraged the formation of an umbrella group for NGOs, the NGO Forum on 11 July 1999. The Forum was established with the approval of the government. By August 2000, the number of NGOs with the Forum increased to 218 members.

Its programme states that the Forum aims 'to achieve the coordination of the NGOs; to initiate the regional expansion of the local organizations; and to establish the links between the local NGOs and international organizations' (The NGO Forum Foundation Document, 1999). It notes that 'the Azerbaijani state is not sufficiently keen on the development of non-governmental organizations, considering them as anti-state organizations that spread state secrets, and jealous of NGOs contacts with foreign states' (The NGO Forum Foundation Document, 1999). Although the main aim was to gather all pro-government, pro-opposition and neutral organizations in order to make coordination, collaboration and interaction between NGOs more efficient, the attempt failed.

After its first conference, some of the participant organizations left the Forum and formed another umbrella group of local NGOs in August 1999: the NGO Congress. They charged the Forum of being pro-government rather than independent. The reason for diversification was attributed to some NGOs believing that the Forum was under the control and influence of the regime and thus could not perform independent activity.[17] Some criticised the Forum for being a superior body over NGOs, arguing that equal participation and representation was impossible to achieve.

In the final programmes of both the Forum and the Congress their aims were defined as follows: 'to achieve the development of the NGO sector in Azerbaijan, to solve their problems and to coordinate their activities' (NGO Forum Programme, 1999, p. 3; NGO Congress Programme, 1999, p. 1). In order to realise these aims, the activities would require forming a modern civil sector, utilising international experience in forming NGOs' and working for the resolution of problems preventing the formation of NGOs and the running of activities. In contrast to the Congress, the Forum hopes to 'contribute to the improvement of the mutual relationship between the

Azerbaijani government and NGOs'. The establishment of these two umbrella groups in the NGO sphere and their almost identical aims further strengthens the dichotomy between government and opposition as well as demonstrates the need for unification if NGOs are be more effective, coherent and powerful.

Although the Congress has practically ceased all its activities, the Forum has been rather successful over the last couple of years, holding its second conference in June 2001 and re-electing its President, Azay Guliyev (*525ci gazet*, 17 June 2001). In its last conference, the former head of the Directorate of Social and Political Affairs in the presidential apparatus stated that 'the NGOs are a branch of Azerbaijani statehood' (Ibid., 2001). Similarly, the current head of the department suggested that Azerbaijan had chosen the route of democracy and the development of civil society and that 'the Azerbaijani government considers civil society as its ally' (Ibid., 2001).

In parliament, the Commission of Human Rights and Democratic Institution-Building considers the problems of NGOs. By late 1999, when the parliament was working on a new draft law for social organizations in order to change their legal status, the representatives of local NGOs were invited to parliamentary meetings and presented their proposals. [18] In this respect, many (though not all) social organizations played a part in state-building.

Inviting local NGOs was partially a result of the relationship between government and international agencies. The representatives of the international organizations considered late Aliyev's institution-building as a symbolic and substantial development, suggesting that the government realized the need for encouraging/creating civil society. In this respect international pressure forced the government to implement necessary changes to the legal framework and the institution-building process. This has had two positive consequences. On the one hand, government, in collaboration with the international community, has subsequently supported 'civil society formation' in Azerbaijan. On the other hand, international NGOs recognized their duty in encouraging civil society in order to promote democratization. However, the creation of the NGO Forum under the auspices of the regime affiliates 'civil society' to state institutions. This inhibits their relations with the state and society (Herzig, 1999, p. 39). The heads and representatives of state departments and commissions in the presidential apparatus and in parliament participate in meetings and conferences, organised by the NGO Forum and other pro-government organizations. However, they avoid participating in meetings organised by pro-opposition ones. Most of the pro-opposition NGOs stated that state officials declined their invitations to their organizations and events in numerous occasions.

There is then a differential treatment towards NGOs from Government: those that get approval and those labelled as the opposition. The regime encourages the establishment of pro-government organizations to create an *image* of promoting civil society. However, it is cautious *vis-à-vis* the activities of NGOs that are connected with opposition political parties and those who do not support government's policies (either established by their members or simply located in opposition parties' headquarters).[19]

In practice, the binary divide still dominates the formation of civil society: if the regime considers social organizations as 'opposition' or 'affiliated to the opposition' it becomes oppressive. Goltz notes that 'The majority (of NGOs), precisely because they are *non-governmental* are, in fact, *oppositional* organizations, and [are] seen by the government as politically charged groups interested less in building civil society in conjunction with the government than solely in changing the government and replacing it with themselves' (Goltz, 1996). When the regime does not consider NGOs as a threat, they can act freely. However, to not constitute a threat implies either being pro-government, and thus controlled by the regime, or not dealing with political issues.

The Head of the Registration Unit of the Ministry of Justice criticized NGOs' connections with political parties, arguing that they were not acting independently but 'dealing with political activities' that should not be the concern of NGOs. He stated that 'one should protect NGOs from political tendencies. If they want to be interested in politics we have many parties, they should go and participate.'[20] In other words, whenever the regime considers NGOs' as acting 'politically', arbitrary practices are more likely to apply. The definition of 'political' remains rather vague and open to any interpretation by the regime and state authorities.

In this respect, the regime attributes a *social* rather than a *political* role to NGOs. NGOs that address issues related to democratization, monitoring or human rights are subject to arbitrary practices legitimized on the basis of the refusal of registration.[21] The registration mechanism is another tool that allows the regime to control local organizations. The list of founders given to state's registration unit identifies individuals and whether they are pro- or anti-government. Many organizations that have experienced delays in their registration or have been rejected conceptualize the registration process as controlling civil society and according them with an unlawful status. One of the NGO leaders argued that state policy towards NGOs was formed on the basis of 'permission' and 'control'. He added that the regime uses the registration mechanism as a means of control over organizations perceived to be pro-opposition and as a tool to de-legitimise their activities. Many social organizations argue that state representatives consider them as 'anti-government' or 'anti-state' rather than 'non-governmental'.[22] Therefore, non-registered NGOs '…are forced to work illegally and in constant jeopardy of being closed down or harassed' (Nelson, 1999, p. 7). Thus, the perception of civil society presented in the state policies creates hostility between the regime and civil society.

The dichotomy of government versus opposition has a considerable impact on state-society relations in the organizational sphere. The local

NGOs are apprehensive of this binary divide. However, they cannot help but reproduce it. When excluded from institutionalized politics, local NGOs become affiliated to political parties or umbrella groups that are either 'government' or 'opposition'. Their inclusion into the binary divide has two contradictory consequences. On the one hand, it threatens their independent work. On the other hand, it increases their activity as a result of the support provided by political parties.

An NGOs ability to affect or to oppose the government is very limited. Pressure on the regime is realised either by international partners or through affiliated political parties or umbrella groups. Although many organizations believed that they did not have a considerable impact on government policies, some stated that they have an impact, albeit of an indirect and limited nature. One NGO leader noted that the state frequently organises a conference on a similar theme/subject immediately after their own conference. She acknowledged that this suggests that NGOs do impact on government, albeit indirectly, but added that state officials would probably deny this.[23]

Local NGOs cannot construct a civil society identity on their own. Thus, their potential for collective action or for initiating change is frequently realised through their affiliations with political parties and umbrella groups. However, the very presence of NGOs is a change within the system, constituting a new sphere of social initiative and interaction.

Local NGOs in Azerbaijan are fundamental in creating the foundations for civil society. In its current form, the organizational sphere is dispersed, under the influence of political parties (government and opposition) or captured by international organizations. The patterns of change are more dominant in civil society than in the regime. Civil society identifies itself with the discourse of change. Thus, the continuation of Soviet legacies appears more prevalent in the regime and less in civil society. The society dimension of democratization re-defines itself outside the single party and state domains. It also becomes articulated in the state and political society given that these too are both under construction. The formation of the organizational sphere also creates new leaders or would-be leaders who will (probably) play a future role in politics.

Local NGOs focus more on democratization and state-building than on nation-building. They define and contribute to the democratic transformation, but are simultaneously defined and limited by the regime. When determining whether these definitions refer to a change of regime or to organizations operating in the same regime, we should take into account the patterns of continuity and change. Local NGOs operate within a milieu where they represent a change yet are frequently confronted with the reality of continuity. The furthering of their activities is contingent on their ability to transform the regime as well as the regime's tolerance to their activities.

The difference between social organizations in the pre-independence period and those operating in the post-independence period is evident: the former were mechanisms of change and *demokratia*, whereas the latter are a part of civil society. After 1997 NGOs adopted the discourse of the 'third sphere' and the term 'citizenship community' substituted that of 'civil society'. They have recently started to express their will and conduct their activities in accordance with this new discourse, which was introduced by the international community. Learning from abroad has definitely changed the vocabulary of the democratization discourse. Increasing interaction with the international community – either via foreign countries and international governmental organizations or via international non-governmental organizations – shapes the nature of 'civil society', structuring its relations with the government and vice versa.

Considering the regime's attitudes towards other NGOs known as opposition, it can be argued that government allows civil society to act freely as long as it remains loyal to the regime, under its approval and in need of its support. In the case of Azerbaijan a large number of local organizations cooperate with a semi-authoritarian state in order to ensure their existence. This 'cooperation' has some implications. On the one hand, such cooperation facilitates the state's control over civil society. It also furthers the state's image as a 'democratizing country' in international public opinion. On the other hand, it creates an environment where some members of civil society cannot fulfil their function of mediation between the state and society.

Conclusion

In the last ten years of political transformation in Azerbaijan a civil society has developed, yet it can only be defined as a sphere of non-governmental organizations. The relationship between the state and these organizations has a remarkable character. Most of these are independent from the state and define themselves in opposition to a regime considered 'anti-democratic' or 'not democratic enough'. They are also however dependent on the state, they are formed against the regime and act through the regime's responses to their activities. In other words, it is a dialectical relationship in which real change is initiated by civil society both by democratizing themselves and directing the change towards democratization. The post-communist political transformation towards democratization takes place in civil society rather than institutional politics.

The most striking feature of Azerbaijani civil society formation is that it precedes democratization. The role attributed to civil society by the students of democratization in the consolidation of democracy phase occurs prior to consolidation, situating the activities of social organizations at the centre of democratization. Although there are violations, civil society finds ways to express its demands. Democratization takes place within the pre-defined boundaries set by government, civil society pushes the limits and in turn benefits from the patterns of liberalisation. All these render the regime less authoritarian.

NGOs introduce a change that is not internalised at the regime level. However, the regime adapts itself to the presence when making legal arrangements and initiating new institution-building as well as encouraging and supporting pro-government NGOs. Thus, civil society and the regime reform and re-articulate themselves in relation to each other.

The activities of NGOs contribute to democratization, creating a sphere for protest and demanding change. The birth of civil society fulfils the functions of consciousness raising, increasing public awareness and creating channels for participating in state-building and institution-building. They make the regime less authoritarian, but not yet more democratic. If we consider the lack of democratic experience and institutions prior to the regime change, the activities in the civic sphere have contributed to shaping the path towards democratization, a path simultaneously affected by the conflicting co-existence of continuity and change.

References

Altstadt, A. (1992). *The Azerbaijani Turks: Power and identity under the Soviet Rule*. Stanford CA: Hoover Institution Press.

Altstadt, A. (1994). Decolonization in Azerbaijan and the struggle to democratize. In D.V. Schwartz & R. Panossian. (Eds.), *Nationalism and history: The politics of nation-building in Post Soviet Armenia, Azerbaijan and Georgia* (pp. 95-125). Toronto: University of Toronto Press.

Azadliq. (July 19, 2000). Draft Law on Changes to and Addition to the Law of the Republic of Azerbaijan on Social Organizations, Article 1, pp. 4-5.

Balayev, A. & Mirze, R. (Eds.), (2000). *20 Yanvar hadiseleri, senedler, movgeler, serhler* [20 January events, documents, positions, comments]. Baki: Casioglu.

Bermeo, N. (Ed.), (1992). *Liberalization and democratization, change in the Soviet Union and Eastern Europe*. Baltimore: The Johns Hopkins University Press.

Diamond, L. (1999). *Developing democracy towards consolidation*. Baltimore: The Johns Hopkins University Press.

Dragadze, T. (1989). The Armenian-Azerbaijani conflict. *Third World Quarterly*, 11(1), 55-71.

Ekiert, G. (1995). Democratization processes in East Central Europe: A theoretical consideration. In G. Pridham. (Ed.), *Transition to democracy* (pp. 329-357). Aldershot: Dartmouth (also published in *British Journal of Political Science*, 21, 285-313).

Ekiert, G. (1996). *The state against society*. Princeton: Princeton University Press.

Ekiert, G. & Rubik, J. (1999). *The rebellious civil society*. Ann Arbor: The University of Michigan Press.

Fish, S. M. (1995). *Democracy from scratch*. New Jersey: Princeton University Press.

Gill, G. (2000). *The dynamics of democratization, elites, civil society and the transition process*. Basingstoke: Macmillan.

Goltz, T. (1996). A Montana perspective on international aid and ethnic politics in Azerbaijan. Retrieved July 1999 from http://scf.usc.edu/bagirov/azeri/goltz1.htm

Hasanov, A. (1999). Azerbaycan'da ucuncu sektorun durumu: Bir gayri hokumet teskilati gozu ile [Third sector in Azerbaijan: From the point of view of an NGO]. *Gayri Hokumet Teskilatlari Enformasya Bulleteni*.

Herzig, E. (1999). *The new Caucasus: Armenia, Azerbaijan and Georgia*. London: RIIA.

Keane, J. (1988). *Civil society and the state: European perspectives*. London: Verso.

Keane, J. (1998). *Democracy and civil society*. London: The University of Westminster Press.

Law of the Republic of Azerbaijan on Public Associations. (Baku, 1992). Unpublished manuscript.

Law on Non-Governmental Organizations. (1992). Retrieved May 1999 from http://88.88.88.15/az/az_htm/A1658.HTM

Linz, J. J. & Stepan, A. (1996). *Problems of democratic transition and consolidation*. Baltimore: The Johns Hopkins University Press.

Michaeli, M. & Reese, W. (1989, September 1). The "Birlik" Society in the Azerbaijani Democratic Movement. *RFE/RL Report on the USSR*, 30-31.

Nelson, T. (1999). *Building civil society in Azerbaijan: Overview and Needs Assessment Survey*. Baku: ISAR.

NGO Congress Programme. (Baku, 1999).

NGO Forum Foundation Document. (Baku, 1999).

NGO Forum Programme. (Baku, 1999).

Rose, R., Mishler, W. & Haerpfer, C. (1998). *Democracy and its alternatives*. London: Polity Press.

Rueschemeyer, D., Rueschemeyer, M. & Wittrick, B. (Eds.), (1998). *Participation and democracy: East and West*. New York: M.E. Sharp.

Ruffin, H. M. & Waugh, D. (Eds.), (1999). *Civil society in Central Asia*. Seattle: University of Washington Press.

Swietochowski, T. (1995). *Russia and Azerbaijan: A borderland in transition*. New York: Columbia University Press.

Tishmaneanu, V. (Ed.), (1995). *Political culture and civil society in Russia and the new states of Eurasia*. New York: M.E. Sharp.

UNDP. (2003). *Azerbaijan Human Development Report*. Retrieved June 2004 from www.un-az.org/undp/nhdr2003/45html.

Varliq's programme. (Baku, 1988). Unpublished manuscript.

CIVIL SOCIETY
– A KEY ELEMENT OF THE
POST-COLD-WAR ZEITGEIST
CIVIC SOCIETY STRUCTURE IN BULGARIA

Elena TRIFFONOVA

The fall of the Berlin Wall and the endeavours of Central and Eastern Europe countries to construct or reconstruct civil society as part of the liberation of their nations illustrates the importance attached to the idea. The global tendency towards democracy further raised the significance of civil society in the transition of post-socialist countries.

Since the 1990s, non-governmental organizations (NGOs) have emerged in every post-socialist country as an important force working to democratize the decision-making process, protect human rights and provide essential services to the most needy.

Traditionally, civil society is conceived of as an essential condition of democracy. Some arguments come close to seeing civil society and citizenship as the defining conditions of democracy. In fact, civil society is only one component of democracy, albeit an important one.

The Concept of Civil Society

In this article I will use the definition of civil society proposed by Martin Shaw. Shaw states that civil society is a 'sphere of association in society in distinction to the state, involving a network of institutions through which society and groups within it represent themselves in cultural, ideological and political senses' (Shaw, 1999, pp. 269-278).

If we consider the term historically, we encounter many different definitions of 'civil society'. For example, in the works of Cicero, other

Romans and ancient Greek philosophers equated the term with the state (Carothers, 1999-2000).

The Latin notion of *'civilis societas'* referred to communities that conformed to norms that rose above and beyond the laws of the state. But the origins of the modern concept of civil society lie in certain key stages of modernity, primarily those occurring at the end of the eighteenth and early nineteenth centuries (Shaw, 1999, pp. 269-278).

A great number of political theorists from Thomas Paine to Georg Hegel developed the concept of civil society as a domain separate from the state, where citizens affiliate according to their own interests and wishes. This new thinking reverberated changing industrial circumstances: the rise of private property, market competition and the bourgeoisie. It also grew out of the promoted exigency for liberty, as seen in the American and French revolutions (Schopflin, 1997)

The term fell into disuse in the mid-19th century as political philosophers turned their attention to the social and political consequences of the industrial revolution (Salamon, 1993). It became fashionable after World War II in the writings of the Marxist theorist Antonio Gramsci, (Cohen, 1982) who revived the term to portray civil society as a distinctive premise of independent political activity, a crucial sphere of struggle against tyranny.

Gramsci built a comparative theory of political change around the concept of civil society. He argued that in the East, where civil society was weak, revolution might have succeeded through a direct violent assault on the state (as in Russia in 1917). In the West, however, where civil society was strong, this would not be possible. The institutions of civil society formed the 'outer earthworks' of the state, through which the ruling classes maintained their 'hegemony' or dominance in society (Ekiert, 1996). It was thus necessary to transform civil society in order to create an alternative hegemony of the subordinated classes, primarily to challenge state power.

Gramsci's (1990/1977) hegemonic theory of civil society saw transformation as a cultural as well as political process and specified an important role for intellectuals. According to Gramsci (1990/1977) each class developed its own intellectual groupings. While some traditional groups, such as priests and lawyers, continued from previous phases of society, many new groups had been created 'organically' through the development of capitalism - managers, educators, social workers, etc. These groups, playing central roles in the institutions of civil society, contributed to maintaining the existing hegemony. A counter-hegemony, which Gramsci conceived of in Marxist terms, i.e., led by the working class, would require its own organic intellectuals and beliefs.

Gramsci's ideas were instrumental in the 1970s, for Western scholars and in motivating the 'Eurocommunist' strategy of the Italian and numerous other West European Communist parties (Ekiert, 1996). Another strong stimulus in the development of civil society thinking, originated in the same period from oppositional thinkers in the Socialist states of East-Central Europe. In an advance on Gramsci's ideas, many oppositionists recognised the difficulty of a direct challenge on the legitimacy of the communist regimes as a result of their authoritarian character. It would thus be easier to develop civil society around cultural institutions that made an indirect challenge to the values of the system.

In the more liberal situation of the late 1990s, however, civil society 'mushroomed' in many Socialist countries. The growth of autonomous cultural and social institutions prepared the foundations for a challenge to political power, as Gramsci had previously argued. As Communism collapsed and competitive party politics developed, key intellectual elites moved from civil society to political parties and the state, leading to a crisis in civil society practice and thinking. Nevertheless, in the late 1990s, the more advanced Central European countries were characterised by more extensive civil societies (based on voluntary associations) than was the case a decade earlier, although the political significance of these civil societies changed.

Implicit in these ideas of civil society was the notion that it was a sphere of peaceful civility in contrast to the coercion, authoritarianism and violence of non-democratic states. At the end of the twentieth century, then, the development of civil society is viewed as a significant criterion for the development of democracy. Democracy entails more than the formal establishment of certain rights, institutions and procedures, despite their importance. It similarly requires the consolidation of the social relations that support these. These supports include the development of an educated middle class and a framework of civil institutions that can support democracy. For former Socialist states and many countries of the 'Third World' democratization has advanced in the last decade of the twentieth century and the creation of civil society is widely viewed as a concomitant of democratic change. After the 1990s, civil society became a 'hub' for everyone from presidents to political scientists. The global trend towards democracy opened up a path for civil society in the former Socialist countries of South Eastern Europe.

The crash of communism also brought with it the crash of the Socialist State, which claimed to be the greatest 'aggrandizement of rationality' (Ekiert, 1996). Etatism, whether associated with the left or the right, has been increasingly rejected. Such questions, manifesting themselves with some urgency, are recent additions to the political agenda and demand a thorough reappraisal.

Likewise, the outline, contents and processes of civil society are equally shaped by its own bearings, aspirations, successes and miscarriages, not to mention traditions and rituals. The intellectual and operational range of civil society then is far from unlimited, but is bounded by other actors on the stage and by the way in which it understands its own history (See Krut, Howard, Gleckman & Pattison, 1997).

Non-Government Organizations as Organized Appearances of Civil Society: Different Categories of Non-Governmental Organizations (NGOs)

Civil society is often described as a return to reciprocity in political and social arrangements, as well as the third force through which the traditional hierarchy of state and subject can be unseated. The term is used somewhat more rigorously by political scientists to encompass all those components of society - and all those arrangements within it - that exist outside the state's reach or instigation. Presently, the most widespread understanding of civil society is as the promoter of a range of political and social goals. In short, civil society simultaneously encompasses everything that is not the state and represents a set of inherently democratic values.

The term NGO is very broad and includes many different types of organizations. In the field of development they include research institutes, churches, professional associations and lobby groups. The World Bank (2001) classifies NGOs into two categories:

a) *operational* NGOs - whose primary purpose is the design and implementation of development-related projects;

b) *advocacy* NGOs - whose primary purpose is to defend or promote a specific cause and who seek to influence policies and practices. (Below I will focus in more detail on advocacy action as opposed to policy dialogue between civil society and state institutions in Bulgaria).

It should be noted, however, that these two categories are not mutually exclusive. A growing number of NGOs engage in both operational and advocacy activities, and some advocacy groups, while not directly involved in designing and implementing projects, focus on specific project-related concerns.

There is also another group of NGOs: think tanks. Their work concentrates on reconciling the needs of citizens with the realities of politics and limited resources. Think tanks can be viewed as a type of 'invention in government' or 'islands of excellence applying full-time interdisciplinary scientific thinking to the in-depth improvement of policymaking, acting as a main bridge between power and knowledge' (Johnson, 1996). The principal customer of think tanks is government. Since their agenda focuses on the improvement of public policy, think-tanks must forge close relations with governments. Other customers include the media and business communities. In providing news and analysis focused on political risks as well as environmental and economic issues, many think tanks consider the private sector and public media as their most important constituencies.

Existing Mechanisms for the Civic Representation of Interests in Bulgaria

In societies, such as the Balkan countries, where many different historical phenomena have created a greater than usual distrust between the government and people, the gap between the two is usually filled by one of two things: either a resilient and kinship-based traditional society or a civil society. Bulgaria has both, but in a less than traditional mix. After the demolition of the former socialist regime, modern mechanisms for the civic representation of interests have attempted to find practical application in Bulgaria. Thus far, the public has been rather unsuccessful in developing an active civic approach in order to effectively and efficiently solve acute problems.

Civil society is the third sector of community alongside the state and the market. dynamic civil society represents an important counter-balance to government and business. Non-attendance to the elementary principals of a market economy, publicity and democratic state institutions as well as the absence of a civic culture based on voluntary association are the inheritance of Bulgaria's totalitarian past. (Dainov, 2000)

The gap between people wanting to participate (high) and actual participation (low) is nearly insurmountable. This perception, reinforced by donors and intermediaries seeking funding, has adverse consequences; it undervalues the many achievements of NGOs and discourages new initiatives that could further strengthen their contributions. It also ignores the reality that changing political cultures is a long-term and time-consuming process, requiring considerable time before those changes are cemented in society. (Taneva, 2002) Remarkably, changing political culture has in fact been accelerated, in part stimulated by the serious exchange occurring between European Union countries and North America, particularly the U.S., and Bulgarian participants. NGOs are recognizing that there is a vast difference between having 'connections' to influence outcomes and building relationships that flow from public and institutional responsibilities. Connections are personal (based on favouritism), not always fair and, at times extralegal, if not illegal.

The existing mechanisms for the public representation of interests in Bulgaria suffer as a result of deeply rooted insufficiencies:

- *lack of sufficient democratic traditions in civic representation*

After the collapse of communism we observe a large-scale 'regeneration' of civil action in Bulgaria. Many active citizens, intellectuals, teachers and students from universities, including some state servants, were directly involved in several NGOs (Nagle & Mahr, 1999, pp. 14-40). 1990 heralded a period of 'change' whereby the entire state administration, central plane economic principals and educational programs were 'cleaned' of outmoded rhetoric, etc. On the other hand, the process of internal transformation in state institutions had not yet been completed. Insufficient democratization and the absence of defined 'rules of the game' determined the logic of Bulgarian transition (IRIS, 2002, pp. 15-45).

The inherited and profound indifference for the development and efficiency of the state sector combined with the lack of transparent public mechanisms in the decision making process and the imitation of democratic correction, led to the creation of incapable of state institutions at the national, regional and local levels. The absence of accessible and reliable public institutions created for protecting the common civic interest reinforced existing institutions and the idea of the state as a servant 'for' and 'to' itself (Engelbrekt, 1992, p. 32).

- *resolution of problems is sought through mobilization of kinship relationships rather than reliance on modern mechanisms of civil representation*

This principal is a direct analogy of the aforementioned position. Commonly, the fervour of kinship relationships in the former socialist countries resulted in an under-developed public sector and minimal civic activity. The strength of kinship relationships, then, is a direct consequence of an undeveloped civic culture in a traditional society with a high degree of personalization of state institutions (Kabakchieva, 2001).

Current Overview of Bulgarian NGOs: The Size of the NGO Sector

By the end of 2000, Bulgaria had an adult population of 6.4 million and 4,500 registered NGOs, all of which were created after 1989. A comprehensive study conducted in 1999 indicates that 1,600 of these NGOs are active and no less than 700 are full-time organizations (IRIS, 2002, pp. 32-36).

The post-1989 NGO community attracts funding equivalent to 1.5 percent of the total GDP (IRIS, 2002, p. 39). This is equal to the total national budget for the environment and is somewhat larger than the national budget for culture.

Most NGOs are set up with help from either US or EU-based donor organizations. Further, most of the influential NGOs continue to exist as a result of EU and US-funded projects, addressing a wide range of issues but focusing primarily on citizen and community empowerment in the decision-making and problem-solving process. This fact has led some researchers to conclude that the Bulgarian NGO community is above all a 'political' one. In other words, it is dedicated to working out and pursuing, irrespective of the diverse NGO fields, agendas of civil society and empowerment as well as overcoming exclusion and discrimination.

The breakdown of data regarding the development of the NGO sector suggests that the number of functionally operating organizations[24] ranges between 350 and 500 (CID, 1999).[25] We can characterize the current situation in the following schema of configuration:

- group of interests, which are publicly protected; they could be mediated by other corporate interests or are a subject of situational mobilization;

- the institutional and technical base, which is established and developed at disproportionate levels;

- territorial representation, which is excessively uneven;

- the initial forms of introducing public relations practices in NGO activities;

- an adequate level of intensity of the dialogue with international institutions in the non-governmental sphere;

- incomplete development of skills in fundraising and especially grant-making, with particular reference to the skills for effective management of finances in the sector;

- the initial attempts of non-profit marketing and social economy;

- relatively well-developed centres, i.e., 'think tanks' with a raising influence in consulting and implementing civic initiatives.

The non-governmental sector in Bulgaria is demanding a greater intensification in terms of transfer of experience, resources, knowledge and personnel in the sphere of civic initiatives. The unbalanced development of NGOs (in terms of territoriality and with regards to the priorities of their activities) illustrates the necessity of establishing working mechanisms for overcoming the 'centre-periphery' dilemma. This outlines the first sphere in which endeavours could be modelled, aiming at influencing the development processes of NGOs.

In the early 1990s, two ascendant types of NGOs were formed. The first type encompasses those centres and institutes that are presently referred to as 'think tanks' or 'research institutes'. The second type includes all the remaining NGOs, which covers the whole range of issues with which NGOs are typically concerned, e.g., charities, professional guilds, environmental pressure groups, etc. Bulgaria's political system, the media and the early business sector were formed together during this initial structuring of NGOs. In the early stages of the transitional period, connections between the activities of some dubious businesses and some of the first NGOs resulted in a wave of public mistrust towards NGOs, which were suspected of serving not public but private interests. This led directly to the withdrawal of favourable taxation regimes for NGOs. Today, NGOs still do not have tax-exempt status, and this undermines the development of the NGO sector.

In the mid-1990s, conditions for the operation of NGOs further deteriorated as a result of a series of economic crises and of governments that were openly hostile towards NGOs. Among these the Socialist cabinet of 1995-1997 stands out as particularly hostile. It infiltrated NGO circles with its own agents, leading to the eventual break-up of the Union of Bulgarian Foundations, and appointed NGO 'superintendents', who were attached to various Ministries with the responsibility of following the organizations' activities and reporting back to Ministers and government.

At the same time, the public consensus on the need to reform society in Bulgaria fragmented. Successive governments and the public abandoned reform agendas from 1993 onwards (IRIS, 2002, pp. 35-41). It was the NGO sector that filled the now empty reformist niche by acting as 'the saviours of the democratic agenda'. In close partnership with the independent media, the leading NGOs from that period grew into a significant public force. They formed, maintained and defended reformist and democratic agendas in public debate, but also succeeded in leaving their stamp on the very manner in which the debate was conducted.

The role of the state is important in providing an overall framework for citizen participation and interaction and in mediating between different societal groups, organizations and classes. As a social space, civil society is distinct from the State sector, which may be narrowly defined as the legislative-executive-judicial system of authority and institutions. Yet it exists in co-relation to the state and views its primary relevance as antithetical to the state sector.

The central place of the state emanates from the historical nature and international functioning of a global system composed of sovereign nation-states (Krut et al., 1997). The state is seen as having specific sets of responsibilities that relate to the individual and the collective.

In recent years, the arena of NGO action has expanded from the local and national settings to the international level. The institutional transformations that are occurring in the context of globalization have resulted in international actors - such as United Nations agencies, regional organizations, finance and trade institutions and transnational corporations - as well as inter-governmental 'summits' assuming an increasingly prominent role in global governance. NGOs have been late- comers to this evolving system of global governance but are now finding ways to influence the international decision-making process associated with development issues.

Conclusion

Evidently, the political and economic changes that are underway have extended the importance of the non-profit sector and brought it to the attention of policy makers. This expanding tendency, primarily visible in Western Europe, may perhaps spread to the Eastern European countries that apply for EU membership. Privatization efforts, the use of new public management and the need for innovations in social service delivery, health care and education entail a number of major challenges for this third sector.

The governments are 'down-sizing' and are in the process of 'off-loading' (Anteier, 12 February 2002) some of their traditional tasks to private and non-profit institutions as well as to commercial providers. In an era of budget-cutting, lean management and privatization efforts, the voluntary sector is confronted with great challenges and opportunities.

There are a vast array of goods and services that are either quasi-public or quasi-private. It is with reference to these goods that most of the current disagreement regarding the meaning and culture of collective goods occurs. Importantly, new organizational forms emerge, primarily in the contested terrain it is here that the vast majority of growth in the non-profit sector has occurred. It is then important to identity the attempts of a number of European countries to modernize association and corporate laws to allow for greater flexibility in the legal forms of not-for-profit organizations. In one way or another, they are all attempts to push the boundaries of current policies and laws (Ibid., 2002).

In order to understand the relation between civil society and the state we have noted that civil society groups can be much more effective in shaping state policy if the state has coherent powers for setting and enforcing policy. Effective non-governmental advocacy work will strengthen rather than weaken state capacity.

References

Anteier, H. (February, 2002). The third sector in Europe: Five theses. *Civil Society Working Paper,* 12.

Anheier, H. K. & Toepler, S. (1998). Commerce and the muse: Are art museums becoming commercial?. In B. A. Weisbrod, (Ed.), *To profit or not to profit: The commercial transformation of the nonprofit sector* (pp. 48-59). New York: Cambridge University Press.

Behn, R. D. & Kant, P. A. (1999). Strategies for avoiding the pitfalls of performance contracting. *Public Productivity and Management Review,* 22 (4).

Carothers, T. (1999-2000). Think again: Civil society. *Foreign Policy Magazine,* (Winter). Retrieved from http://www.incommunicado.info/node/view /10.

CID (1999). *Analytical Research Report Institutional Infrastructure of The Ngo Sector: Organizations With Socio-Economic Orientation.* Sofia: CID.

Cohen, J. L. (1982). *Class and civil society: The Limits of Marxian Critical Theory.* Amherst: University of Massachusetts Press.

Carl Cuneo's Notes: "*Antonio Gramsci: Four Conceptions of the State*" Dept. of Sociology, McMaster University, Hamilton, Ontario pp. 125- 223.

Dainov, E. (2000). *Politicheskiat debat I prehodat v Balgaria* [The political debate and transition in Bulgaria]. Sofia.

Ekiert, G. (1996). *The state against society : Political crises and their aftermath in East Central Europe.* Princeton, N.J.: Princeton University Press.

Engelbrekt, K. (1992). Bulgaria. *RFE/RL Research Report,* pp. 32-39.

Fosler, R. S. (2000). *Working together to promote civil society.* Retrieved from http://www.independentsector.org/programs/leadership/three_ sector_ workingtogether.pdf.

Gramsci, A. (1990). Selections from political writings (1910-1920). Q. Hoare (Ed.). London & New York: Lawrence & Wishart; International Publishers, 1977. Pp. xxi-393. (Reprinted from 1977, University of Minnesota Press).

IRIS. (1999). *Strategy planning for the Bulgarian NGO Movement within Dem Net II Program.* Sofia.

IRIS. (2002). *Bulgaria in NATO.* Sofia.

Johnson, E. C. (1996). *How think tanks improve public policy.* Retrieved 1999 from http://www.cipe.org/publications/fs/ert/e21/priE21.htm

Kabakchieva, P. (2001). *Grazhdanskoto obshestvo sreshty darzhavata-balgarskata sityacia* [Civil society versus the state-Bulgarian situation]. Sofia.

Krut, R., Howard, K., Gleckman, H. & Pattison, D. (1997). Globalization and civil society: NGO influence in international decision-making. *Discussion Paper,* No. 83.

Lipset, S. M. (1996). *American exceptionalism: A double-edged sword.* New York: W.W. Norton.

Lipsky, M. & Smith, S. R. (1989-90). Nonprofit organizations, government, and the welfare state. *Political Science Quarterly,* 104 (4), 625–648.

Melendez, S.E. (1998). The nonprofit sector: The cornerstone of civil society. *Issues of Democracy.* Retrieved from USIA Electronic Journal: address www.921.sw.ccu.edu.tw/cd/refer.html - 18k.

Nagle, J. D. & Mahr, A. (1999). *Democracy and democratisation: Post-communist Europe in comparative perspective.* London: Sage.

Salamon, L. M. (1993). The global associational revolution: The rise of the third sector on the world scene [CCSS-WP-4]. Retrieved 1993 from http://www.jhu.edu/~ccss/pubs/ccsswork/

Salamon, L. M. (1998). Nonprofit organizations: America's invisible sector. *Issues of Democracy,* 3 (1). Retrieved 1998 from USIA Electronic Journal: http://www.usia.gov/Journals/itdr/0198/ijde/salamon.htm

Salamon, L. M. (1999). *America's nonprofit sector: A primer,* New York: The Foundation Centre.

Schopflin, G. (June 20-21, 1997). *Civil society, ethnicity and the state: A threefold relationship.* Paper presented at the conference Civil Society in Austria, Vienna.

Shaw, M. (1999). Civil society. In L. Kurtz, (Ed.), *Encyclopaedia of violence, peace and conflict.* San Diego: Academic Press.

Taneva, B. (2002). *Balgarskata politicheska kyltyra: Tradicii I savremennost* [Bulgarian political culture: The traditions and contemporary]. Sofia.

World Bank. (2001). *NGO World Bank Collaboration.* Retrieved from www.worldbank.org/publications/bgindex.htm.

THE CIVILIARCHIC* TRANSFORMATION OF CIVIL SOCIETY IN ARMENIA:

CIVILIOLOGIC** DISCOURSE

Ashot S. ALEXANYAN

Civil society is conceived here as the realm of organized social life that is voluntary, self-generating, (largely) self-supporting, autonomous from the state, and bound by a legal order or set of shared rules… Actors in civil society need the protection of an institutionalized legal order to guard their autonomy and freedom of action (Diamond, 1994, p. 5).

The institutional development of civil society in modern Armenia has been taking place according to regularities and features particular to the European civilitet. The ***civiliarchic social-political*** processes taking place in post-communist Armenian society aid in forging modern civil society, 'dynamic democracy' (Pelinka, 1974, pp. 32-34), functional possibilities and human and citizenship rights. In Michael Walzer's (1998, p. 24) definition: 'Only a democratic state can create a democratic civil society; only a democratic civil society can sustain a democratic state'.

The process of national independence and autonomy as well as the establishment of political, legal and civil-responsibility provide the political impetus for the formation of the key components of civil society. Thereafter, the NGO-alization of world politics and cooperation among international, regional and Armenian local NGOs - which creates an inter-conditioned, supervised and public-mediated system between national and global civil societies, national NGOs and the state as well as transnational NGOs and states – further encourage civil society's formation. That is, elements correspond to the criteria of the ***civil globalitet*** and ***global civilitet*** as Habermas noted in his well-known thesis and allow 'state citizenship and world citizenship build one continuum' (Habermas, 1992, p. 660).

The initial formation tendencies of the state, political regime, political elite and party system, public and religious organizations, public opinion, political culture, perception and participation as well as communication technologies lead to 'social, communicative and administrative power' (Habermas, 1992, pp. 215-217), and to a new polarization of *"Zivilitätspotentiale"* (Kleger, 1994, pp. 60-69) in civil-Armenia. However, integrating the Armenian civil transition and **civili-centralism** into the European and international civil community is not without problems.

The Civil-historical Context

The dynamics of developing **civiliarchic societies** creates public relations, civil freedoms and rights as well as laws and norms. For centuries Armenian people did not have a national state and **civiliarchic institutions** were divided into different geopolitical parts. Despite the fragmentation of the Armenian 'homo civilicus', Armenian culture retained its 'historical development continuity' (Gevorgyan, 1997, p. 23).

In the 4th century Armenia a system of laws existed (in the form of mundane and canonical legal acts) regulating the internal life of the old Armenian **civiliteia** and defining the principles of self-organization. However, until the 12th century, Armenian legal norms had a dominant religious component and were, according to K. Samuelyan (1939, p. 74), based on a foreign collection of codex ('*datastanagirq*') and foreign ideas of rights. Instead of traditional legal forms, the rules compiled in a collection of norms, i.e., *"Kanonagirq Hayots"* (Collection of Norms, Vol. VIII), David Alavkavord's canons, Mkhitar Gosh's and Smbat Sparapet's Collections of norms, etc.

Despite using canonical law and the absence of national state governance, as H. Gevorgyan (1997) stated, 'Armenian society did not become theocratic' (p. 32). The '*Ashkharhajoghov*' ('World-assembly') functioning of the old Armenian **civiliteia** and church national assemblies have been considered 'as national democratic institutions and nationally representative bodies assimilating a particular parliamentarism...' (Samuelyan, 1939, p. 45).

The absence of national state institutions in the middle of the 11th century and the end of the 14th and in the beginning of the 20th century (when the first Armenian republic was established), had a negative impact on the formation of an Armenian **civilitet** and '*homo civilicus*'. In spite of the existence of the national church and independent regional kingdoms, which fostered 'national' self-determination, the absence of state traditions resulted in a fragmentation of society.

However, it is necessary to mention that the activity of the state and public institutions in the first Armenian Republic (1918) is the best example of an Armenian *civilismus*. Thus, according to the program presented by the government of the first Armenian Republic, state policy hoped to create political stability, social welfare and legal mechanisms in all spheres of public life. In essence, these were the first tentative steps towards the creation of a democratic political system. The active work of the government in protecting the rights of various parts of Armenian society, replacing the appointed parliament with an elected one, preparing the works of the Constitutional Assembly and developing a national currency are representative of this.

The Dialectics between Totalitarian Democracy26 and Proletariat Dictatorship

Armenia was a part of a new type of state: the USSR. The ideological objective of the Soviet Union, created under the auspices of a proletariat dictatorship, was the formation of a classless society where the communist public's self-governance would be reign supreme. The totalitarian proletarocracy and democratic political regime, according to the ideologues of the international proletariat, were based on 'true democratic institutions' and the 'principle of democratic centralism'. Despite the ideal that 'power belongs to the people' in a Soviet country, the single-party system of proletariat democracy resulted in all spheres of public life becoming overwhelmingly ideologically orientated.

Taking into consideration the social-economic circumstances and geopolitical conflict after Sovietization, Armenia was the only state that managed to avoid danger. However, after Sovietization, fragmentation and 'misunderstanding' between various parts of Armenian society also developed.

Despite a common cultural system, two different social civilizations were formed. Armenian society was divided. The first was formed during the historical development of the Armenian civilitet and dominates in the worldwide Armenian Diaspora (West Diaspora Reality), while the second started chaotically during the Sovietization of the first Armenian Republic (East Soviet Armenian Reality).

During the seventy years of Soviet rule the central and local governmental structures, characteristic of state power, were formed and social welfare, living standards and the economic system were improved. These changes were caused by the social-political and economic reality of the Soviet Union to which many countries belonged or rather were under protectorate. In each case there are various displays of totalitarianism, be it in Russia, East Europe, the Baltic countries, Middle Asia and the Caucasus, or in Afghanistan, Vietnam, China, Cuba, Africa, etc. There were also many *'cult lichnosti'* (cult of personality) displays in the Soviet Union: Lenin, Stalin, Khruschev and in latter stages Andropov and Gorbachev, especially Gorbachev's *'novoe mishlenie'*. The so-called 'soviet nostalgia' and the nation-wide popularity of 'renewed' communist parties or some former communist leaders in some post-soviet countries, which at first sight appeared strange, were conditioned by this phenomenon.

Aron (1970a, pp. 217-268; 1970b, p. 52), Sartori (1997, p. 433), Przeworski (1985, pp. 15-16, 47-82), Cohen (1983, pp. 26-40), Lummis (1996, pp. 25-37) and others, considering various hybrid forms of totalitarianism, radical people-democracy and proletarocracy, developed paradoxical theses based on the political reality. For example, Sartori's (1997, pp. 433-434, 437, 452-461) 'second democracy', 'non-liberal democracy', 'non-free democracy', 'illiberal democracy', 'communist democracy', 'the theory of democratic dictatorship', 'dictatorship against dictatorship', 'democracy without demophile', etc. testify to this. Dahrendorf's (1961, p. 335) explanation is also enlightening: 'the ideas of totalitarianism without non-liberty and democracy without freedom in any circumstances are not paradoxical constructions of philosophical fantasy, but show contradictory tendencies of social and political reality'.

The Future of Civiliarchic Democracy

The reforms to the totalitarian political system of the USSR (1985-89), such as *perestroika* and *glasnost*, which were recorded in the decisions of the Congresses and Conferences of the Communist Party of the Soviet Union, led to the collapse of the Soviet Union. However, the chaotic national autonomy movements, which originated in the 1950s and 1960s in East Europe and the Baltic countries as well as in other republics of Soviet Union, including Soviet Armenia, became more radical and mass-based in the early 1980s. For example, the Solidarity Movement in Poland played a pivotal role and, according to Wesolowski (1995, p. 113): 'The Solidarity ethos focused on certain fundamental values in its social thinking. These included national independence, human dignity, social solidarity and fair industrial relations'

Initially, the Karabagh Committee organized the liberal-democratic civil movements of 1988 in Soviet Armenia, establishing nation-wide opposition and subsequently being termed an Armenian National Movement. The 'civil disobediences' (Cohen & Arato, 1992, pp. 564-604), which stemmed from the desire of national independence and in order to protect the rights of Armenians in the Nagorno Karabagh Autonomous Republic, were a struggle of Armenian *Zivilitätspotentiale* (civilitet potential) against present soviet *Zivilitätsdefizite* (civilitet deficit).

One of the most important achievements of the Armenian National Movement was the creation of a liberal-democratic base and civil public mechanisms for the development of 'human being-citizen-society-state' interrelations. In other words, the realization of all that Abraham Lincoln defined as *'government of the people, by the people, and for the people'*. Armenia's independence, similar to almost all other post-soviet countries, illustrated that the state and nation continued to be 'two principally different social organizations' (Shatski, 1997, p. 16).

Under the legislative system of the USSR and the Armenian SSR and having won the Supreme Soviet elections the liberal democrats came to power, advocating the right of self-determination for nations, universal norms for human rights and international law. Subsequently, the Supreme Soviet of Armenian SSR adopted the Declaration of the Independence of Armenia on 23 August 1990 and strived to develop 'the democratic traditions of an independent Republic of Armenia founded on 28 May 28 1918' (Collection of acting laws of the Republic of Armenia, 1995, pp. 9-10).

It is significant to note the following: 1) the nation-wide opposition party's victory, associated with the Armenian National Movement, in legitimate elections; 2) that the elections took place during the period of Soviet rule, and included there were the elections for the Supreme Soviet of Armenian SSR and the presidium of Supreme Soviet; 3) the victory of liberal democracy and the establishment of a *civiliocratic political system* and the *civiliarchic culture* of Civil Armenia (the Third Armenian Republic); and 4) the modification of direct-liberal democracy into representative-polyarchic democracy, transforming the Armenian National Movement into a liberal and party-based political force.

Thus, unavoidable in any democracy, elite features became typical in Armenian democracy, or, as Dahrendorf (2002, p. 54) defined, 'oligarchic element'. The victory of liberal democracy, in contrast to that seen in other republics of the Soviet Union, occurred 'without bloodshed' (Dahrendorf, 2003, p. 9) and was a result of the political solidarity present in Armenian society. The initial reforms after independence aimed to establish a pluralist electoral system, a deepening of public self-government as well as the adoption of laws regulating the activities of political parties, non-governmental and religious organizations and the mass media as well as the strengthening of other public mechanisms. The first presidential elections (1991) and the Constitutional referendum (1995) are examples of the political activity.

State and non-governmental bodies requested substantial and qualitative modifications. In all spheres of public life the forming relations between the state and civil society were creating new public traditions, political socializations and a civic culture. For example, opposition in the Armenian National Movement, led to the creation of a separate party (National Democratic Union) and a presidential decree to limit the activity of the Armenian Revolutionary Federation political party (1994).

The development of liberal principles and 'actual democracy' in the Armenian National Movement created the conditions for public competition among various actors in the political system, but it was necessary to have a guarantee for 'the development of a stable and effective democratic government' (Pelinka, 1976, pp. 22-26). 'The universalist tradition of cultural and political modernity' (Cohen and Arato, 1992, pp. 24-25) from a political and *civiliarchic guarantee* point of view and finding solutions to problems, such as what A. G. Almond and S. Verba (1963, p. 498) termed 'the problem of transferring the civic culture from generation to generation' further demonstrate this. In this sense, Armenian membership of the OSCE, the UN, and the Council of Europe were considered of paramount importance.

The mechanisms of nation-state power, alongside the reforms stipulated in governmental programs, transformed the political system in 1995 and provided for the evolution of political and social-economic relations. (Bulletin of National Assembly of RA, 1995, p. 5) The Program of the Armenian Government for the period of 1995-99, presented to the National Assembly on 26 July 1995, was characterized as: 'Active reforms for the Armenian political and social-economic reality, and a time of transformation of public relations.'

The reforms aimed to:

a. Aid the development of a free market economy, private property, a new bank, a fiscal and credit policy, new economic relations and partnerships as well as encourage foreign investments, etc.

b. Facilitate the transition to democracy and political pluralism, a multi-party system, decrease the state monopoly, build an effective civil service system, and enlarge the social and legal functions of the state, judicial and legal systems as well as public self-government.

Thus, in order to create the elementary economic prerequisites of civil society it was very important to adopt laws such as: the State property law (1990), Property law (1990), Agricultural and agricultural farms law (1991), law on enterprises and business activity (1992), law on privatization of state enterprises and unfinished enterprises that are under construction (1992), as well as the Land Code (1991). Yet 'the bases of privatization in Armenia' (1991), adopted by the Council of Ministers, was unable to facilitate a smooth and balanced transition from a state-centred economic system to a liberal capitalist one in spite of its positive dimensions.

It stands to reason that the institutional development of civil society and 'proportional democracy' needed a sufficiently developed legislative base (Lehmbruch, 1967, pp. 7-9, 41). However, the lack of non-governmental organizations in numerous fields of public life and the reality that existing NGOs had not established 'objective groups and a base', limited their (and civil society's) ability to influence the preparation, adoption and realization of political decisions.

The economic blockade, the collapse of the 'rouble zone', the war situation in Nagorno Karabagh and the consequences of the 1988 earthquake similarly impacted on the development of civil society. The liberalization of the economy, that is, the so called privatization of 'public property' coincided with a decline in social protection and living standards, the disintegration of the 'middle level', increased poverty and mass unemployment, decrease in the number of working places and further limitation of the rights of working collectives. The creation of a market economy, as well as a labour market and processes to regulate employment, did not result in the development of 'partner-opponent' relationships in civil society organizations, such as Trade Unions, the Association of Producers and Businessmen, the Union of Consumers, the Farmers' Union, the Union of Traders, Bank Associations, etc. The practical realization of the economic transition also resulted in insufficient provisions for working collectives to participate in the process of privatizing enterprises. Non-efficient state control in the process of public property management and distribution, as well as the absence of such control, i.e., the correlation of elements that Gellner (1995, pp. 96-101) called 'political centralization and economical decentralization' are visible in the Armenian case.

Such tendencies have been formed differently: Aron (1981, pp. 89-134) calls them 'the crisis of democracy', 'dogmatic liberalism' and 'democratic dogmatism', Dahrendorf (2002, pp. 92-93) labels them 'democracies without democrats', 'the crisis of democracy', 'democracy without freedom', 'new democracies' and 'post-democracy', Zakaria (1997, pp. 22-43) 'illiberal democracy', Held (1987, p. 5) 'radical developmental democracy', Schmitter (1994, pp. 160-171) 'post-liberal democracy', Cohen and Rogers (1994, pp. 149-150) 'associative democracy', Merkel (1999, pp. 361-381) 'defect of democracies' and Dubiel (1994, pp. 67-118, 151-152) 'metamorphoses of civil society'. If we consider Schumpeter's (1950, p. 269) definition of 'democratic method', as well as the possible and impossible types of democracy visible in contemporary political reality and political science literature, it is difficult to conceive of democracy as a 'synonym for a good society'.

The processes resulting from the new democratic realities confirm the Dahrendorfian statement that 'democracy as the all-equality is nothing of the kind, than political democracy' (Dahrendorf, 1992, p. 326).

The first crisis of legitimacy of political democracy after independence, 'The legitimacy deficit of new political institutes' (Lemke, 1997, p. 51) and the 'metamorphoses of civil society' appeared before and after the 1996 presidential elections. There were new mass civil disobediences demanding the resignation of the President. The *Civiliarchic legitimacy* deficit has partially been overcome by the presidential elections that took place in 1998, resulting in the formation of a multi-party cabinet, the establishment of a political council and a human rights council under the auspices of the President of Armenia and the legitimate re-emergence of the Armenian Revolutionary Federation party.

Overcoming the crisis of legitimacy, active civil participation and increased public trust are evident in the parliamentary elections that took place in 1999, which resulted in the creation of the first parliament. The

'Unity' ('*Miasnutyun*',) union, formed by the Armenian Republican Party and the Armenian Peoples Party, won these elections. These elections demonstrated that the party-system of Armenia has been conditioned by leaders, the absence of an established electorate of parties and '*bewegungskultur*', (Lemke, 1999, p. 450) as well as the difficulties associated with new social transformations.

The political disagreements and rearrangements in the 'Unity' alliance after the murder of the leaders of the alliance in the terrorist act of 27 October 1999 illustrate the important role of leaders in the Armenian system. Further, when the comparatively established and 'traditional' parties, such as: the National Democratic Union, *Orinats Erkir*, the Armenian Revolutionary Federation, lost the elections and when the National Self-Determination Union, *Ramkavar* Liberal Party of Armenia, Armenian Democratic Party, Armenian National Movement failed to overcome the 5 per cent barrier, the lack of established parties was confirmed.

As a result of membership of the Council of Europe, the adoption of improved or new laws, such as: Law on trade-unions (2000), Law on non-governmental organizations (2001), Civil Service Law (2001), Law on Parties (2002), Referendum Law (2001) and Electoral Codex (1999), have been of paramount importance in developing political parties, NGOs and the electoral system.

The Constitution and the legislative base are not able to adequately or completely formalize dynamic political life. Thus civil society's construction is not solely based on the content of law in the political science sense. Indeed, it must forge contacts with both the legislative base and the unestablished political system. There is activity of unestablished opposition parties in Armenia, a good example can be seen in the adoption of the Law on television and radio (2000). The opposition parties actively took part in the discussion and adoption of this law. However, after its adoption and in accordance with the established legal procedure, the TV-company, A1-plus, which enjoyed wide popularity, lost its frequency, as a result of increased competition.

There remains nonetheless a *civiliarchic deficit* in civil society institutions but with a twist. That is a surplus of liberalism but a lack of civil participation and limited implementation of liberties and rights; few mass NGOs and limited dynamic political socialization yet secondary schools teach 'civic education' and 'bases of human rights' courses in line with the 'State Program of Development of Education for 2001-2005'. Indeed, it is the paradoxical and insufficient participation of NGOs in influencing policy-makers decisions and creating a less state-centred political process that the deficit is much apparent. Evidently, society cannot always be in an active state, thus transformations in the latent, passive and active realities of social life are unavoidable. However, established NGOs have a role to play in forming its social basis.

From this point of view, the public discussions on the 'Strategic Program of Poverty Reduction in Armenia', organized by the Institute of Human Rights and Democracy are very important and various NGOs and state bodies took part in these discussions. Similarly, the active participation of the Network of Armenian Youth Organizations, 'Pan-Armenian Youth International Centre' Foundation, All-Armenian Youth Foundation and university student clubs in discussions for the draft of 'Law on State Youth Policy' can be considered as an important development. The activities of organizations, such as: the Union of Businessmen and Producers of Armenia, the Armenian Helsinki Association, the 'New Armenia' Humanitarian Support Centre, the National Press Club, the Union of Armenian Lawyers, the Union of Armenian Journalists, the Armenian Association of Political Science, the Association of Private Universities, 'Aravot' (Morning) newspaper, 'Shant' TV company etc. demonstrate increased NGO activity. There are more than a thousand NGOs, a hundred political parties, numerous TV-companies and other mass media organizations as well as religious organizations in civil-Armenia.

The advancement of the legal system from the present political reality is an obligating guarantee and precondition for the adoption of civiliarchic minimums of a democratic nature in Armenian society.

References

Almond, G. A. & Verba, S. (1963). *The civic culture: Political attitudes and democracy in five nations.* New Jersey: Princeton Uni. Press.

Bulletin of National Assembly of RA. (1995). [In Armenian], vol. 1-2.

Alexanyan, A. (1999). The epoch of civiliarchy [In Armenian]. *Bulletin of the Yerevan University,* 2.

Alexanyan, A. (2001). *Post-Soviet area: Globalization and civiliarchy, in: Eurasia – future of Russia: dialog of cultures and civilizations* [In Russian]. Moscow.

Alexanyan, A. (2002). To the question of relation between civiliarchy and globalization [In Russian]. *Bulletin of the Yerevan University,* 2.

Aron, R. (1981). *Über die Freiheiten: Essay* [On the freedom]. Stuttgart: Klett-Cotta.

Aron, R. (1970a). *Demokratie und totalitarismus* [Democracy and totalitarianism]. Hamburg: Christian Wegner Verlag.

Aron, R. (1970b). *Fortschritt ohne ende?* [Progress without an End?], Beselmann Sachbuchverlag Reinhard Mohn.

Cohen, J.L. (1982). *Class and civil society: The limits of Marxian critical theory.* Amherst: Massachusetts University Press.

Cohen, J. L. & Arato, A. (1992). *Civil society and political theory.* Cambridge: MIT Press.

Cohen, J. & Rogers, J. (1994). Solidarity, democracy, association. *Politische Vierteljahresschrift.* Sonderheft (25), 136-159.

Collection of Acting Laws of RA (1990-95) [in Armenian]. Yerevan, 1995.

Dahrendorf, R. (2002). *Die krisen der demokratie: Ein gespräch mit Antonio Polito* [Crisis of democracy: Talk with Antonio Polito]. München: Beck.

Dahrendorf, R. (1992). *Der moderne soziale konflikt* [The modern social conflict]. Stuttgart: Deutsche Verlags-Ansalt.

Dahrendorf, R. (1961). *Gesellschaft und freiheit.* [Society and freedom]. München: R. Piper & Co. Verlag.

Diamond, L. (1994). Toward democratic consolidation. *Journal of Democracy*, 5 (3/July), 4-17.

Dubiel, H. (1994). *Ungewißheit und politik* [Unawareness and policy]. Frankfurt am Main: Suhrkamp.

Gellner, E. (1995). *Bedingungen der freiheit* [Condition of freedom]. Stuttgart: Klett-Cotta.

Gevorgyan, H. (1997). *Nation, national state, national culture* [in Armenian]. Yerevan.

Habermas, J. (1992*). Faktizität und geltung* [Factuality and significance]. Frankfurt am Main: Suhrkamp.

Habermas, J. (1962). *Strukturwandel der öffentlichkeit* [Structural changes of society]. Neuwied und Berlin: Hermann Luchterhand.

Held, D. (1987). *Models of democracy.* California: Stanford University Press.

Kleger, H. (1994). Ziviler ungehorsam, zivilitätsdefizite und zivilitätspotentiale oder: Was heißt 'zivilgesellschaft' [Civil disobedience, civilitet deficit and civilitet potential or: What is 'civil society']. *Forschungsjournal*, NSB 1, 60-69.

Lehmbruch, G. (1967). *Proporzdemokratie: Politisches system und politische kultur in der Schweiz und in Österreich* [Proportional democracy: Political system and political culture in Switzerland and Austria]. Tübingen: J.C.B. Mohr (Poul Siebeck).

Lemke, C. (1999). Neue soziale Bewegungen [New Social Movements]. *Politische Vierteljahresschrift.* Sonderheft (30), 440-453.

Lemke, C. (1997). Protestverhalten in transformationsgesellschaften [Protestant behaviour in transformative society]. *Politische Vierteljahresschrift*, 38.Jg. H.1, 50-78.

Lummis, C. D. (1996). *Radical democracy.* Ithaca: Cornell University Press.

Merkel, W. (1999). Defekte demokratien [Defects of democracies]. In W. Merkel & A. Busch (Ed.), *Demokratie in Ost und West* [Democracy in East and West] (pp. 361-381). Frankfurt am Main.

Pelinka, A. (1974). *Dynamische demokratie.* [Dynamic democracy]. Stuttgart/ Berlin/ Köln/ Mainz: W. Kohlhammer.

Pelinka, A. (1976). *Politik und moderne demokratie* [Policy and modern democracy]. Kroberg/Ts: Scripter Verlag.

Przeworski, A. (1985). *Capitalism and social democracy (Studies in Marxism and social theory).* New York: Cambridge University Press.

Samuelyan, K. (1939). *The history of old Armenian Law Vol. 1* [in Armenian]. Yerevan.

Sartori, G. (1997). *Demokratitheorie* [Theory of democracy]. Darmstadt: Primus Verlag.

Schmitter, P. C. (1994). Interests, associations and intermediation in a reformed post-liberal democracy. *Politische Vierteljahresschrift.* Sonderheft (25), 160-171.

Schumpeter, J. A. (1950). *Kapitalismus, socialismus und demoktatie* [Capitalism, socialism and democracy]. Bern.

Shatski, E. (1997). Protoliberalism: Autonomy of personality and civil society. *POLIS,* No. 6, 15-33.

Talmon, J. L. (1963). *Politischer messianismus.* [Political Messianism]. Köln/Opladen: Westdeutscher Verlag.

Talmon, J. L. (1961). *Die ursprünge der totalitären demokratie* [The Origins of Totalitarian Democracy]. Köln/Opladen: Westdeutscher Verlag.

Walzer, M. (1998). The concept of civil society. In M. Walzer. (Ed.), *Toward a global civil society* (pp. 7-27). Providence: Berghahn Books.

Wesolowski, W. (1995). The nature of social ties and the future of postcommunist society: Poland after solidarity. In Hall, J. A. (Ed.), *Civil society: Theory, history, comparison* (pp. 110-135). Polity Press.

Zakaria, F. (1997). The rise of illiberal democracy. *Foreign Affairs,* 76(6), 22-43.

THE CONSTITUTION OF THE CIVIL SECTOR IN BULGARIA AFTER 1989:

BETWEEN BUSINESS ENTERPRISE AND CIVIC PARTICIPATION

Petya KABAKCHIEVA

This paper[27] analyzes the difficult emergence of Bulgarian civil society and the civil sector after the political change of 1989 and its specific characteristics *vis-à-vis* the institutional culture that it expresses and creates. The main thesis defended is that the contemporary civil sector in Bulgaria is primarily a Western product as a result of the international donors' programs. This factor has both positive and negative consequences. On the one hand, NGOs are acting as subjects of a global institutional culture and they serve as mediators between this culture and the paternalistically-oriented etatist Bulgarian political culture, reforming the latter in the direction of the former. On the other hand, NGOs comprise highly educated professionals as well as **intellectual** and political elites. They are elitist and more money-oriented and they act more as business consultancy firms rather than as civil agents, defending specific interests and rights as well as enhancing civil participation.

Theoretical Framework

Below, I describe the methodological approach and the main concepts used. The specificity and origins of the civic sector are identified in relation to the development of the modern public sphere. The creation of the public sphere was possible because of the emergence of commerce in the late Middle Ages, which led to the differentiation of the private sphere from the public as a sphere of personal and economic autonomy – this was the sphere of private manufacturers who were participants in the market. At the same time, this private sphere gradually acquired public relevance. The public relevance of the private sphere and the consequences of this process for the emergence of civil society are analysed by the erudite scholars Hannah Arendt (1993) as well as Jurgen Habermas (or 1995; in his seminal book *The Structural Transformations of the Public Sphere*).

In short, the contemporary concept of civil society refers to the sphere of public mediation and the defence of the private interests and fundamental rights of individuals. Since Thomas H. Marshall (1996), the commonly accepted term for fundamental human rights – another product of West European Modernity – has been 'citizenship'. Many different forms of association designed to defend the publicly relevant private interests including civic action that varies by degree of structural organization and institutionalization.

The degree to which the main citizen rights are safeguarded, as well as the existence of various forms of civic action, is a sign of the development and sustainability of modern democracies. This is related to an increasingly popular concept of politics based on 'the idea of institutional and ideological pluralism, which prevents the establishment of monopoly of power and truth' (Gellner, 1996, p. 9).

This brief introduction helps identify several preconditions that are imperative for the existence of a civil society or a civic sector. First, the emergence of a civil society presupposes private interests that are of public relevance. In other words, in societies in which property is conceived as belonging to the 'people', there can neither be a civil society nor a civic sector, although there might be some kind of NGO. For example, under communism there were organizations that identified themselves as nongovernmental, but there was no civic sector. Second, the existence of civil society presupposes a certain level of economic development in social relations, the public defence of private interests is formally rational – it is not an act of warm kinship solidarity, which does not distinguish between private and public. Third, civil society presupposes the emergence of autonomous individuals, but also requires self-reflection on their private interests. Civil society does not automatically ensue from social differentiation, i.e., the emergence of different social groups, but results from the self-consciousness of a group identity declaring or asserting itself publicly. Hence, the existence of processes of group formation or group consolidation is fundamentally important for the emergence of civil society. There is no civil society where there are atomized individuals or amorphous social groups that are confined to their privateness, precisely because there is no public mediation for that privateness. Similarly, there is no civil society if the recognized group interests or aspirations cannot be declared publicly, i.e. where there is authoritarian regime.

The role of political parties as a method of representing private interests in government is fundamental to the modern concept of representative democracy. Elitist critiques of representative democracy, however, offer convincing arguments supporting the idea that the practice of representative democracy is illusory. Indeed, if we bear this in mind, Robert Michels' (1959) classical study describing the oligarchic tendencies of political parties has similarly not lost any relevance.

The vulnerability of the political-party-based concept of representative democracy is one of the reasons behind the heightened interest in civic action as a meaningful expression of the degree of a country's real democratization: civic action is the most effective counterbalance to both the tyranny of the majority and the abstract (but sometimes personalised) power of the state. Civic action varies by degree of organization: from spontaneous, ad hoc civic protests regarding a concrete problem; to the structured quest for a solution to a certain problem in the civil movement; to individual and lawful protests against a concrete decision, i.e., civic disobedience; to the formally institutionalized civic associations and foundations registered under law. This paper considers civil organizations, frequently called nongovernmental, nonprofit and nonprofit distributing, which are the most popular method for expressing civic action.

It is widely accepted that the above-mentioned organizations constitute the so-called 'third sector', and a significant amount of the relevant literature attempts to offer a universal definition of that sector, primarily to enable cross-national comparisons. This sector is 'third' insofar as it covers an intermediate zone between the state and private business, and should therefore be both nongovernmental and nonprofit. The 'third sector' claims to include organizations that contribute with their activities to the attainment of some publicly beneficial goal and are nonprofit-distributing as well as not serving political purposes. According to Salamon and Anheir's (1994) much quoted definition, the activities of these organizations are the fruit of the autonomous initiative of groups of citizens who express their will freely and pursue, by all means within the law, some priority objective that they have set which does not contravene the public interest. Defining public interest, however, is a problem, with different definitions appearing in the normative systems of different countries.

The aforementioned definition of the 'third sector' seems reasonable. Yet, if we examine the name, statutory framework and reflections on that sector in different countries, we see that Salamon and Anheir's (1994) formal definition, developed in a multinational comparative nonprofit sector project, does not take into account the numerous national and cultural specificities. Indeed, this definition, as well as other related research, is unconditionally necessary in order to understand the functioning of this sector as a social economy, i.e., as a segment of society that engages a certain number of people for the purpose of performing particular socially beneficial activities. However, I believe that understanding the specificity of civil society, objectified in third sector organizations, requires considering the national and socio-cultural specificities of each country. What is termed the 'third sector' is an ideal model, whereas the significance of its different components varies in different societies depending on the development of civil society in the broadest sense, and its influence on government, its historically established traditions, its culture and concrete social problems.

The different ways of conceptualizing civil society are also discussed by Michael W. Foley and Bob Edwards (1996). They make a rough distinction between two broad versions of the 'civil society argument'. The first version, in their opinion, is crystallized in Alexis de Tocqueville's (1997) *Democracy in America*, with important antecedents in the work of the eighteenth-century 'Scottish moralists' (including Adam Smith, Adam Ferguson and Francis Hutcheson). This approach puts special emphasis on the ability of associational life in general and the habits of association in particular to foster patterns of civility in the actions of citizens in a democratic polity. The second version, which the two authors define as 'dissident', for them is articulated most forcefully by Jacek Kuron, Adam Michnik and their associates when formulating a strategy for resistance to Poland's communist regime in the 1980s. It places special emphasis on civil society as a sphere of action that is independent of the state and that is capable – precisely for this reason – of energizing resistance to a tyrannical regime. Indeed, at least two main views on the specificity and function of the civic sector can be identified: the first view puts emphasis on broader political participation, and is certainly not typical of Poland or the other former members of the Eastern bloc; the second regards the sector as a specific form of expression of social solidarity.

The first understanding of civil society focuses on its political function. This has been expounded most comprehensively by the authors Barber (1996), Bachrach and Botwinick (1992). They uphold the thesis that participatory democracy is the truest form of democracy. They argue for a stronger public presence for civic organizations and citizenship in the life of the community. Further, 'public' is a key word for them, but, following John Dewey, 'public' is conceived identical to the degree of the impact of a given decision on society as a whole or on a particular community and to the extent to which the voices of different people become public (publicly significant), heard by the rest of the people and taken into consideration by the power-holders. Another key word here is 'empowerment' of citizens. This empowerment must be visible in the local communities in which people live and in the nation-state. Certain authors are now considering opportunities for the empowerment of 'normal' people in the context of globalization. 'Civil society grounds democracy as a form of government in which not politicians and bureaucrats but an empowered people use legitimate force to put flesh on the bones of their liberties… Civil society offers us a single civic identity that […] allows us to take control of our governments and our markets' (Barber, 1996, p. 285). According to Barber, different institutions are important in different countries, but the point is to have institutions which give citizens real power over the decision-making that affects their life. In general, however, the main institutions that give such power are local and international civic associations and movements.

The other understanding of civil society as a network of nongovernmental organizations (NGOs) places special emphasis not on civil society's political role but on social connectedness, on association itself – on 'associational life' as a specific form of social solidarity. This understanding is representative of the American tradition. The idea of 'associational life' is currently expanding and developing towards conceptualizing of the civic sector in terms of the development of social capital – a term used by authors such as Robert Putnam (1995) and Francis Fukuyama (1997).

In his much quoted article 'Bowling Alone', published in 1995, the prominent American political scientist Robert Putnam formulates his typology of what we have called the 'third sector' on the degree of social connectedness and civic engagement in society. Putnam argues that civic engagement, or "the networks of organized reciprocity and civic solidarity", i.e., social capital, is an important precondition for stable socioeconomic modernization and democracy.

I have introduced these distinctions to demonstrate that the specific social situation determines the interpretation of the functions of civic associations and lays special emphasis on one of their main 'publicly beneficial' goals. For the ultra-individualized, alienated and socially disengaged American society it is understandable that the main problem will be the degree of 'secondary' and 'tertiary' social connectedness, i.e., association. For civil society in Poland in the 1980s, which strove to defend its independence and autonomy from the all-encompassing communist state, it was natural to have 'political participation' as a leading category. For leftist intellectuals, empowerment of ordinary citizens is of paramount importance and therefore the civic sector is conceptualized in the context of this empowerment. By contrast, conservative thinkers will concentrate on existing forms of social solidarity and voluntary support, through which people find solutions to their daily concerns and problems. In the conditions of non-decreasing poverty and high unemployment levels, economists and politicians consider the civic sector primarily in the categories of social economy, i.e., thinking of the civic sector in terms of the employment and social services that it provides. Depending on the social situation, many other modifications of the civic sector's role are also possible.

It is for this reason that any study of the third sector in any given country should single out its specific characteristics while simultaneously taking into account the universal framework that identifies it precisely as a civic sector as opposed to anything else. However, the ideal model of civil society and the third sector is an expression of the process of Western European Modernity, raising yet another question that is crucial for understanding the third sector: how the specific characteristics of the sector in a given country correlate with that ideal model, i.e., the extent to which the actual sector fits into the ideal model. This, in turn, raises another issue: the discrepancy between the normative concept of the sector and its actual functioning. When discussing this sector some researchers are similarly caught in the trap of normative discourse, describing the sector in its own terms and from the perspective of normative documents or the ideal-typical model. The process of ideological normative construction of the civic sector merits special investigation. The term 'civic sector' is misleading when applied to the Bulgarian case. NGOs in Bulgaria are not operating as civic organizations, necessitating that the boundaries between the political, private and civic sectors be clearly defined.

By uniting the different concepts of civil society and the third sector, we can assume that the sphere of citizenship includes all forms of public representation of private interest, as well as all actions in defence of fundamental individual and group rights and in different structures of mutual association in which people share their various needs and joys as everyday people. This sector comprises all formally registered institutionalized associations as well as spontaneous individual and collective action or informal social associations who are engaged in the aforementioned activities.

What, then, are the boundaries between the 'civic' and the 'political', and the 'civic' and the 'private'? Civic organizations are political insofar as they demand public recognition and aim to safeguard their interests, rights, needs and desires. In this sense, they are a component of what can be defined in modern terms as a democratic polity, where numerous social groups interact with the aim of finding a commonly acceptable solution. Civic organizations are not political with reference to another classical concept of politics, namely state government. They are an expression of the political public sphere, but they are not part of the public power of the state. That is why this type of organization excludes political parties, since the latter's purpose is to acquire state power. The definition 'nongovernmental' is accurate, but does not mean non-political.

With regards to the definition of civic organizations as 'private', they represent the public significance of certain kinds of 'privateness'. In this sense, what is entirely private cannot claim to be part of this sector. The personal aspiration towards profit is entirely private. However, the desire of a group of private employers to achieve a particular profit rate by extending the working hours or restricting leave and workers' resistance to this act can be conceptualized as the public significance of 'privateness'.

In the remaining part of this text I suggest that NGOs in Bulgaria tend to function as a specific type of private enterprise and thus do not fit into the definition expounded above. Yet, they are arguably a prerequisite for the development of civic culture precisely because they tend to function as private enterprises.

The Specificity of the Civic Sector in Bulgaria

There is no regular statistical information regarding the structure of NGOs in Bulgaria. On the basis of their registration, the current number of NGOs in the country is around 9,000. Many of those NGOs however are inactive even though they are registered. This is probably due to the fact that the Persons and Family Act, under which NGOs were registered until recently, barred NGOs from undertaking economic activities, resulting in many organizations being severely under-funded. This has prompted more active NGOs to write project proposals and apply for grants from donor programs. The third sector in Bulgaria is de facto largely the result of Western funding, the major donors being the Phare Programme, Democracy Network, Open Society, the UNDP, the British Know How Fund and several others. In this sense, local NGOs are structured on the model of their Western counterparts and follow the latter's priorities. This has a twofold effect. On the one hand, NGOs are mediators in the 'translation' of Western political and business culture; they import a Western type of behaviour, which is presently necessary given that Bulgarian society is opening up to Europe and the rest of the world. On the other hand, NGO activists tend to set their sights beyond the specific problems of the people. The necessity of winning grants for projects has led to NGOs becoming private consulting agencies rather than forums for the public defence of interests, rights and political participation. The NGO sector is to large extent a social economy. While this is not negative, the sector must ensure that it does not function only as an economy, turning its back on citizens. This preoccupation with projects makes many people sceptical about the NGO sector. Below are the results of a representative poll conducted in 1998:

Table 3.1 What is your opinion about the majority of NGOs in this country?
(per cent, incl. non-respondents)

NGOs defend the interests of citizens	21.0
Tend to work for their personal gain	37.0
The majority serve as a cover for political interests	18.0
The majority serve economic interests	8.0
The majority serve foreign states	2.3
No answer	13.7

From the data, it becomes clear that people perceive NGOs as not serving common public interests, but as a means of acquiring personal gain. They then are not conceived of as a 'third sector' but as a cover for political and private interests. That is why the majority of respondents claimed that in a difficult situation they would turn to family and friends, rather than to the respective authorized organizations, or cope alone.

To identify the concrete specificity of NGOs and their ambivalence, I will trace their origin and role in a case study of a small town, Smolyan (Rhodopi Mountains, South Central Bulgaria), compiled in 2000. The study focused on the local NGO elites. The term 'local elites' is used in the sense of the functional definition of "elite" in political science (without any meritocratic connotations). The method applied was qualitative, namely in-depth interviews.

Nearly all of the existing and active NPOs (that is, non-profit organizations, according to their own definition/labelling) in the town have emerged and survived as a result of European and American funding. Indeed, there is no contradiction between the objectives pursued by American and European program, namely establishing an effective business environment and institutional support for civil society. The NPOs are employed in attaining those objectives and, remarkably, have no 'turf battles'. For example, the promotion of entrepreneurship is 'the turf' of the Regional Development Agency (RDA), the local branches of the Chamber of Commerce and Industry, and the Association of Private Hoteliers and Restaurateurs, while promoting civil society is the 'remit' of the Association of Rhodopi Municipalities, which is mainly concerned with local self-government, and the Centre for Sustainable Development of the Mountain, which focuses on local community issues. The names and missions of the NPOs are indicative of their Western (European and American) priorities, since most of those NPOs are the product of Western funding and are supported by European and American programs. The citation below illustrates that NPOs activists do not see any difference between European and American programs, instead conceiving them as complementary.

Here is the story of one of the most influential NPOs in Smolyan as told by a member:

'The organization opened officially on 27 April 1993, with the ribbon cut by the President of the European Union in Bulgaria [sic., meaning the Head of the Delegation of the European Commission to Bulgaria] *at the time. And the idea was to set up a regional fund with PHARE money, which would help grant small loans to people going into business – small or medium-sized businesses. Unfortunately, however, this was not done in full as planned, i.e., such a forum was not established. And the reason, at least as far as I know, is the Government - it was hard for it to swallow the fact that some regions somewhere would have their own funds. Yet even though what I believe is a very good idea has not come true, in all these years the agency has remained true to its objectives - we have focused on the establishment of small private family hotels, and thanks to the contacts of the agency's director, who has headed the organization for six years now, with the organization of the lending institutions, I'm referring to the Bulgarian-American Investment Fund, the credit line for small and medium-sized enterprises under PHARE, we helped them get funding from those funds and go into business'* (personal interview, 2000, N 4).

As this statement confirms, the efforts were cumulative and the NPO community emerged as a result of successful projects - as in the case of the Association of Rhodopi Hoteliers and Restaurateurs - as well as of the new European priorities: the Eco-World Rhodopi Association; the Stefan Stambolov Bulgarian Youth Legion, whose projects are not associated with Bulgarian history and national issues as it was intended, but with 'The European Union: Our Home and My Civil Rights', funded by Phare Democracy; 'Civil Society Against Corruption', funded by the USAID; Lady Diana: A World Without Tears, a foundation protecting the rights of children and high-risk and marginal youth groups, etc.

The image then of the proper activity of NPOs, as given by 'Europe', is thus objectified as 'private entrepreneurship', 'sustainable development' and 'civil society' understood as 'local self-government', 'civil rights' (see the projects above). Simultaneously, the image of 'Europe' and the 'West' is that of donor, a donor who pays for particular things and expects a particular style of behaviour from the recipients. Thus, the main questions for NPO elite become: how can we secure European money in particular and, more generally, how is money made 'in the world', Europe included?

This prompted a series of training programs. As a case study, I will concentrate on the largest project, which includes a series of training seminars: the CNPO's 'Let Us Prepare for Worthy Dialogue with the World', which had 'the ambition for versatile training of personnel'.

This suggests that for Bulgarians to join 'the West' they must learn planning and management, which subsequently structure all training seminars. The first module is devoted to management and the second to planning. Both management and planning appear to be manifold subjects. Regarding management, NPO activists are informed of the nature of the governing body and trained in day-to-day management, management of different levels and projects, personnel management, resource management, PR and resource management, management of information, monitoring and control (*Informatsionen Byuletin*, 1999, No.1).

With regards to planning, activists are instructed in strategic long-term planning as well as tactical, cyclic, project, day-to-day, contingency and crisis planning (*Informatsionen Byuletin*, 1999, No.1).

These efforts are necessary for 'institution building' in the Third Sector and for training the activists in writing and, even more importantly, winning grants. That is why the training programs and newsletters describe what a project is, how to write a winning project proposal, what the responsibilities of the project coordinator are, how to fill in an application form and how to win a grant. The definitions of 'project' vary and the training emphasizes the need to state the project's uniqueness and to use the donor's language. Projects are described as limited in time but crucial to strategic planning, and that they should generate changes but also be a 'Chicken McNugget', i.e., small enough to swallow but large enough to avoid choking the reader (I guess that means that the bite should be quite small either way), and so on and so forth (*Informatsionen Byuletin*, 1999, pp. 12-14, ff).

Thus, the instrumental, utilitarian image of West and Western type NGOs popularized by non-profit organizations is the image of a successful, well-run commercial enterprise that presumes a particular business and organizational culture - this is not a civic political image, but neither is it related to a specific political culture.[28] Perhaps the promotion of this image is understandable given that the economy, commercial enterprise, etc., are at the centre of the expansion of Western culture. The problem, however, is that there is an attempt to cultivate a new type of formal rationality, a new type of an organized perception of time, alongside the existence of mythical sponsors that these NGOs need at any cost. Applied literally in the existing cultural environment, this model might crack, with formal rationality easily yielding to uncritical compliance with the sponsor. Nevertheless, as long as the sponsors (the European programs) construct themselves and operate as formally rational and transparent, there is perhaps a chance that they will have a positive impact on Bulgarian institutional culture.

This 'business' image of NPOs has already proved to have two important and positive effects. First, the idea surrounding what constitutes a successful style of management has changed. The interviewed NPO leaders spoke Western languages, appointed project coordinators through competition and indeed looked like people with a new organizational culture. Here is how one 'subordinate' described her boss:

'He's exactly what I've always thought a European-type executive should be like. This means he should be very understanding, should be fluent in German, English, Russian - I won't go on with the list - should be able to put a few sentences together in more or less any language. To be a communicator, sort of. With a very clearly formulated goal for the organization itself; he should be clear about what he wants and how to get it. He also succeeds in finding contacts, establishing partnership not only in the country but also abroad. He's creating a very good image' (personal interview, 2000, N 7).

Secondly, it cultivates a real desire to adopt a new type of corporate culture - especially in the business community, which is trying hard to win new niches in the West and to attract Western tourists to Bulgaria.

Perhaps it is not accidental that the Regional Development Agency (RDA) is one of the most successful NPOs, having implemented many projects and encouraged the establishment of new NPOs. The RDA has set out to promote small business and its activities have resulted in the establishment of the Association of Private Hoteliers and Restaurateurs and of small private hotels co-financed by the British Know How Fund and the Bulgarian-American Enterprise Fund. These types of organizations have become effective mediators between Western and Bulgarian business, publishing catalogues of Western companies employed in tourism and in other spheres, forwarding business offers to Bulgarian companies, taking part in investment forums and developing a model for micro-crediting of small and medium-sized enterprises, which resulted in the establishment of the Micro-Fund Smolyan Foundation, financed by the Soros Economic Development Fund in New York and the Open Society Foundation in Sofia. In other words, they have been branching out and *turning into a real and desired information mediator.*

The Association of Private Hoteliers and Restaurateurs admit that grants from the Phare Programme and the Democracy Network have been invaluable, particularly in stimulating the tourism industry rather than on the Association's non-profit activity. Even though they were established with foreign funding, the organizations that promote private enterprise are now becoming pro-active, looking for contacts themselves. For example, the RDA has joined the European Association of Regional Development Agencies on its own (rather than on outside) initiative, hoping to gain gaining admission to the annual business meetings that bring companies from all over Europe together and offering an opportunity to establish direct business contacts that may eventually evolve into contracts.

In addition, the hotels in the Association of Private Hoteliers and Restaurateurs increasingly resemble European hotels: furnished like Western hotels, offering a wider range of services and adopting the ethos of the consumer always being right. This particularly applies to the hotels in Pamporovo (a winter resort near Smolyan), where all signs are also in English and information about services can be found in the main European languages.

For the Smolyan business community, Europe takes the form of concrete business contacts, as well as a culture of information, advertising, actively searching for new partners and the 'import' of European places. For many manufacturers, membership of the Smolyan Chamber of Commerce and Industry is a must if they hope to acquire a European certificate of quality as a guarantee of successful business operation and competitiveness.

In parenthesis, let me note a factor that I believe is of critical importance to the subject of this study. A non-representative survey of professional and business associations in Bulgaria suggested that the overwhelming majority regard membership in a related European association as invaluable, guaranteeing their professionalism and the quality of their goods and services. That is why they themselves are actively trying to establish contacts with European associations. Indeed, many organizations have joined European structures without any mediation by other organizations or public institutions. For example, the Association of Serigraphers in Bulgaria, based in a small town in Northeastern Bulgaria, Popovo, is a member of the European and the World Association of Serigraphers; the Association of Business Evaluators is a member of the European Association of Evaluator

Associations; the Club of Young Entrepreneurs is in the European Club of Young Entrepreneurs. These organizations are not the exception. In other words, these contacts with Europe are the result of a genuine need to adopt European standards, promoting and presenting members of those associations as professional and reliable partners. They are not then simply a source of profit or mimetic emulation.

This suggests that non-profit organizations, which are employed mainly in European and American programs, and their leaders are carriers of a new type of institutional culture - since this is required by their foreign partners - and mediators in the translation/transmission of Western values in the Bulgarian cultural environment, with the aim of forming a new type of corporate culture based on information, advertising and compliance with customer requirements. I interviewed around 15 NPO activists: the oldest one was in his 40s, the vast majority in their late 20s or early 30s. The 'bosses' are popular figures in the region and have self-confidence. I found that they selected their project coordinators through competition and that fluency in a Western language was one of the major requirements - almost all interviewed NPO activists spoke at least one, many two. All have a strong project-oriented mentality, including pragmatism, time planning and actively searching for partners, contacts and projects. Since they earn their living from projects, they are not preoccupied with short-term survival, but give priority to a longer-term strategy. That is why information is one of their prime resources, surfing the Net is a need rather than a duty. Predictably, they were better informed about European programs than the civil servants. Notably, NPOs in Smolyan have divided the spheres of project activity among themselves in an entirely rational and pragmatic way, pooling efforts and winning as many grants as possible for the region, which are subsequently 'assigned' to different NPOs depending on their 'mission', a development out of sync with Bulgarian institutional culture and mentality. They reportedly had to do this in order to avoid NPO internal feuding and mutual damage (regional solidarity proves effective in this case).[29] The interviewees invariably stressed that the most important requirements for an NPO activist were team work, good communication skills and tolerance. Many of them travelled constantly (both in Bulgaria and abroad), had the distinct self-confidence of a local intellectual elite from which the political and economic elites borrowed ideas, and did not have a parochial inferiority complex but, rather, regional self-awareness. The EU emblem appears on the logos of the RDA and the CNPO; the Rotary Club President speaks in terms of 'us members of Rotary International' irrespective of whether 'we' refers to someone in Smolyan, Vienna or New York.

In Bulgaria, we see a very specific model of the civil sector, in which the public goods are used for private interests. NGOs are more money oriented and they act mostly as business consultant firms as opposed to civil agents, defending specific interests, rights and enhancing civil participation. There are numerous reasons for this situation, the analysis of which lay outside the scope of this paper. The big question remains unanswered, however: can we call this a civic sector, or is it just an imitation, or it is a protoform, a precondition for developing of greater citizenship-oriented participation? I am inclined to agree with the latter. While acting as private firms, they are consolidating private interests, showing their public relevance. By gaining money and self-confidence they could develop in the direction of public mediation and in defence of the private interests, which may also include human rights. Further, NGOs are acting as subjects of a global institutional culture and as such they serve as mediators between this culture and the still paternalistically-oriented etatist Bulgarian political culture, changing the latter in the direction of the former.

References

Arendt, H. (1993). *Totalitarizmt* [Totalitarianism]. Sofia: Panorama.

Aristotel (1995). *Politika* [Politics]. Sofia: Open Society.

Bachrach, P. & Botwinick, A. (1992). *Power and empowerment. A radical theory of participatory democracy*. Philadelphia: Temple University Press.

Barber, B. (1996). *Jihad vs McWorld*. New York: Ballantine Books.

Dahl, R. (1971). *Polyarchy: Participation and opposition*. New Haven: Yale Univ. Press.

Dahl, R. (1990). *After the revolution. Authority in a good society* (Rev. Ed.). New Haven: Yale Univ. Press.

Dimitrov, R. (Ed.). (1998). *Grajdanskite organizazii – difiniziya I klasifikaziya* [The civic organizations – Definition and classification]. Sofia: FRGO.

Foley, M. & Edwards, B. (1996). The paradox of civil society. *Journal of Democracy,* 7 (3), 38-52.

Fotev, G. (1992). *Grajdanskoto obstestvo* [The civil society]. Sofia: BAN.

Fukuyama, F. (1997). *Doverieto* [Trust]. Sofia: Obsidian.

Gavrilova, R. & Elenkov, I. (1998). *Kam istoriyata na grajdanskiya sector v Bulgaria* [Towards civil sector's history in Bulgaria]. Sofia: FRGO

Gellner, E. (1996). *Usloviyata na svobodata* [Conditions of liberty: Civil society and its rivals]. Sofia: Obsidian.

Giddens, A. (1999). *Tretiyat pat* [The third way]. Sofia: Prozorez.

Habermas, J. (1995). *Structirni izmeneniya na publichnostta* [The structural transformations of the public sphere]. Sofia: Universitetsko Izdatelstvo "Sv. Kl. Ohridski".

Informatsionen Byuletin [Information Bulletin], 1999, No 1, Smolyan, the CNPO.

Kabakchieva, P. (Ed.). (1998). *Obrazite na grajdanskiya sector. Refleksii varhu isledovatelskata praktika* [The images of the civil sector. Reflection upon research practices]. Sofia: FRGO.

Marshall, T. H. and Bottomore, T. (1996). *Citizenship and social class*. Chicago: Pluto Press.

Michels, R. (1959). *Political parties: A sociological study of the oligarchical tendencies of modern democracy*. New York: Dover.

Minev, D. & Kabakchieva P. (1996). *Prehodat:eliti I strategii* [The transition: Elites and strategies]. Sofia: Universitetsko Izdatelstvo "Sv. Kl. Ohridski".

Salamon, L. & Alheir, H. (1994). Nestopanskiyat sector, nova glabalna sila [The non profit sector – a new global power]. *Soziologicheski pregled*, 1 (2), 2-16.

Sartori, J. (1992). *Teoriya na demokraziyata,* dva toma [Theory of democracy]. Sofia: CID

Putnam, R. (1995). Bowling alone: America's declining social capital. *Journal of Democracy,* 6 (January), 65-78.

Turner, B. (Ed.). (1994). *Citizenship and social theory.* London: Sage Publications.

PART IV

POWER RELATIONS

THE PREDICAMENT OF CIVIL SOCIETY IN POST-SOVIET RUSSIA:
Dynamics of Media Politics

Oktay F. TANRISEVER

Throughout the history of the Black Sea, the developments in Russian politics and society have had considerable impacts on the nature of socio-political transformations in this region as a whole. The fall of the Soviet Union and the rise of the Russian Federation in 1991 resulted in far-reaching changes not only in Moscow's relations with its neighbours in the Black Sea region, but also in Russia's state-society relations. Despite these changes, however, it is difficult to say that there are no problems in the development of civil society in both post-Soviet Russia and the other parts of the Black Sea region.

The collapse of the Soviet Union has been largely considered as a sign of the triumph of civil society and democratic political culture in Russia. In fact, the Soviet Union was ruled by a totalitarian ideology, leaving no significant autonomous role for the development of a civil society independent from state control. However, the post-Soviet optimism regarding the prospects for the development of civil society in Russia was based on a naïve idea that a new political culture could emerge as a mechanical outcome of the neo-liberal process of economic transition. The emerging market economy was expected to transform political culture in a more democratic direction via the leadership of newly formed civil society organizations, including the mass media.

However, the type of political and economic system that has emerged in post-Soviet Russia hardly resembles Western-style democracies where participating individuals face no direct interference from state structures in their civil society activities. Unlike such Western societies, post-Soviet

Russian society has remained largely vulnerable to direct interferences from the state and powerful economic interest groups. The pathological relationship between Russia's civil society and powerful economic and political groups can best be seen in the increase in state pressure on the independent media. This relationship also reflects the problems of Russia's civil society in promoting a democratic political culture in post-Soviet Russia.

This chapter examines the problems of developing civil society in post-Soviet Russia through the prism of the relations between the state and the media. The main argument of this paper suggests that the increasing state pressure on the independent media in Russia marks an authoritarian turn in Russian politics, which could have negative implications for the development of civil society.

It should be stated from the outset that, despite its weak nature, the independent media has played an important role in the post-Soviet process of democratization and in developing civil society in Russia. The survival of some media institutions that have received no direct state funding demonstrates a radical change in Russia where the state maintained complete control over the flow of information during the Soviet period. Following the removal of the state monopoly over the media in the post-Soviet era, Russia's civil society organizations began disseminating their own socio-political views, which would not have been previously tolerated by the Soviet State, through media institutions. Nonetheless, the independent media in Russia has lacked its own sources of funding that could enable it to survive in deteriorating economic and political conditions, especially after the financial crisis of 1998. The situation became even worse for Russian civil society organizations and the independent media following Vladimir Putin's rise to the Russian presidency in 2000.

This chapter discusses the relationship between the mass media and civil society in the context of post-Soviet Russia. It examines the evolution of the independent media in post-Soviet Russia by focusing on a triangular relationship between the state, the business elite and the media during Boris Yeltsin's period in power. I also discuss Putin's policy of pressuring the independent media into submission to the Kremlin with the objective of curtailing the powers of some members of the business elite. Finally, I conclude by exploring whether civil society in Russia is strong enough to protect the independent media and freedom of speech from Putin's authoritarian policies.

The Role of the Media in Developing Civil Society and Democratic Political Culture

The relationship between the development of civil society and democratic political culture has been a very complicated one in the post-Soviet context. It is widely argued that the popularity of political opinions supportive of democracy is evidence of the existence of a democratic political culture in the country. This does not, however, explain how democratic political cultures emerge in countries with an authoritarian background. In this chapter, the development of civil society is understood as a process in which individuals learn how to behave democratically. It is also assumed that this learning process can only take place in the context of a democratic civic culture. Besides, the development of such a civil society is assumed to strengthen the state's role in keeping peace and stability without atomizing society (Putnam, 1993, p. 180).

In order to explore the relevance of the state-media relationship for the development of civil society in Russia, it is essential to clarify the concepts of civil society and independent media. In this paper, civil society (*grazhdanskoe obshchestvo*) is conceived as a self-organizing society. In this sense, this concept presupposes that both state and society accept non-governmental organizations (NGO) as legitimate institutions in their own right. Nevertheless, the notion that there should be intermediaries between the state and society, be they political parties or non-governmental organizations, is still relatively new in Russia (Golenkova, 1999, pp. 4-18).

Among these intermediaries between the state and society, mass media occupies a very special place. This stems from the functions that mass media plays in modern societies. According to Harold Lasswell, mass communication plays three main functions in all modern societies. For Lasswell (1971, p. 85); first, mass media performs the surveillance of the social environment; secondly, it coordinates the responses of different parts of society to the environment: and finally, it serves to transmit the social heritage from the present generation to the future generations.

In this context, independent media is another concept that needs further clarification since the development of civil society in post-Soviet Russia is heavily influenced by the problems associated with developing an independent media (Jensen, 1993, pp. 97-126). The term 'independent media' emphasizes the need to maintain an essential autonomy and freedom of action so that the credibility and integrity of the media can be sustained. From this point of view, some problems with reconciling the mass media's role as an independent social agent with that of an instrument of the authorities become apparent.

However, it is quite clear that independence can never be absolute. Since the media mediates the realms of the state (politics) and economy, some limitations are also necessary to prevent the state or economic actors from abusing this mediating role for their own advantage. The realisation of this condition is very essential for post-Communist states, such as the Russian Federation, that have been trying to overcome the legacy of authoritarian rule because the post-Communist economic elites in these states have exploited the emerging power vacuum since the collapse of the Socialist system (Rogerson, 1997, pp. 329-354).

It is widely shared in Western democracies that the media's relations with the state should be based on laws and principles that do not influence the structure and content of the media. In principle, the media should be objective. In other words, the media should present information impartially without taking sides. However, this does not mean that the press should be above politics. In fact, as Hedwig de Smaele (1999, pp. 174–175) argues, the extent to which the press endorses the idea that it is above politics serves the needs of those in power. The media should also be financially independent, since political freedom is positively correlated with economic independence.

It is in this sense that the existence of independent media institutions plays a crucial role in the development of civil society and democratic political culture. As Jurgen Habermas (1996, p. 367) argues, there are communicative connections between civil society, the public sphere and the state. It is through these media institutions that the interests of civil society organizations are represented. If these media institutions act independently from the state, non-state public interests could be represented in the framework of organized public spheres even if these interests are not the interests of the government in power.

It could be argued that the consolidation of civil society depends largely on the existence of a political culture in which people actively participate in public debates. The fostering of communicative structures within public spheres, such as an independent media, then could potentially strengthen civil society. Accordingly, increasing the independence of media institutions could also increase citizens' access to information. From this point of view, independent media institutions clarify public issues for the public and the free flow of information could improve the public's ability to make sense of policy options as well as provide the policy community with much better access to information.

It is in this context that the independent media's contribution to strengthening nongovernmental organizations and civil society groups may result in an increase in civil society's ability to monitor government accountability, transparency and respect for the rule of law. It is then useful and relevant to explore whether an independent media exists in post-Soviet Russia.

Independent Media in Post-Soviet Russia: Fact or Fiction?

The emergence of an independent media in post-Soviet Russia has been far from complicated. The first major event in the history of post-Soviet Russian media occurred almost immediately after the demise of the USSR when President Boris Yeltsin signed the post-Soviet media law on December 27, 1991. In general, the law established a fairly democratic framework for the development of independent media in post-Soviet Russia (Benn, 1996, pp. 471-480).

Following the end of the strict state control of mass media with the collapse of the Soviet Union in 1991, almost all Russian media institutions started to face new problems stemming from the sharp increases in production and distribution costs in the first years of the post-Soviet era. Consequently, given the financial weakness of the Russian media, several businessmen sought to gain economic and political benefits by controlling the media at very low prices. In 1993, Most Bank founder Vladimir Gusinskii and Boris Berezovskii, the Head of the LogoVAZ holding, started to develop their media institutions (Belin, 1995, p. 88).

In 1996, Russia's main media owners and the vast majority of journalists formed a united front in support of President Boris Yeltsin's re-election bid and against what was perceived as the 'threat of a communist comeback'. Although Russia's presidential system and its oligopolistic economy, dominated by Yeltsin's cronies, played an important role in Yeltsin's success, it was the media's role that shifted the attention of the public opinion from the problematic political situation to the 'successes' of the Yeltsin era. During the 1996 presidential campaign, the privately-owned media joined the state-controlled outlets in supporting the re-election of President Yeltsin. This played a very important role in mobilizing the political support for Yeltsin (Belin, 2001, pp. 324-325).

Given this historical background, it is easy to discern the influences of the Russian state and of big business over Russia's media in the post-Soviet era (Tucker, 1996, pp. 422-438). Even before Vladimir Putin's rise to Presidency in 2000, the Russian State had been still controlling the largest share of the Russian mass media. The state has been completely controlling the TV channels RTR and *Kultura*. Additionally, the State controls the ORT TV channel, which broadcasts throughout the Commonwealth of Independent States (CIS). Moreover, the state owns two radio stations, namely: *Rossiia, Maiak* and *Radio 1*. The official newspaper of the state is *Rossiiskaia gazeta*. Furthermore, the Russian parliament has been publishing *Parlamentskaia gazeta* as its official newspaper since May 1998. The *Rossiia* journal and the *Itar-Tass* news agency are also under state control.

Alongside the federal government, Russia's regional governments have considerable influence over the regional media as well. For example, Moscow, which is also the capital of the federal government, owns *TV Tsentr, Metropolis* publishing house and the following newspapers: *Literaturnaia gazeta, Moskovskaia pravda, Obshchaia gazeta* and *Moskovskii komsomolets*. In addition to the federal and regional governments, the state-controlled oil and gas companies, such as LUKoil and Gazprom, have their own media organs. LUKoil controls *Izvestiia* newspaper, while Gazprom controls the *Rabochaia tribuna* and *Trud* newspapers, *Profile, Kompania* and *Vek* journals and Open radio (Fossato & Kachkaeva, 1999).

Until Vladimir Putin's rise to Russian Presidency in 2000, the 'oligarchs' were the most prominent group among the main non-state owners of the media. Most Bank founder Vladimir Gusinskii controlled a media group that included the newspaper *Segodnia*, the television network *NTV*, the radio station *Ekho Moskvy* and the news magazine *Itogi*. Boris Berezovskii, who was the head of *LogoVAZ Holding*, controlled the second largest media group. Berezovskii also owned the television channel *TV 6* and 8 percent of the ORT television company. In addition, Berezovskii controlled *Nezavisimaia gazeta* and *Novye Izvestiia* as well as the weekly magazine *Ogonek*. Another Holding group Oneximbank-Rosbank-Interros, controlled *Izvestiia* and *Komsomolskaia pravda* newspapers, and the weekly magazine *Ekspert* (Fossato & Kachkaeva, 1999).

The so-called 'independent media' involves media that is owned by neither the state nor the 'oligarchs'. This media is generally owned by Western investors. Therefore, one could question the level of independence that they enjoy too. The following newspapers can be considered as belonging to this category: *Moscow Times* and *Vedemosti*. The *Kommersant, Argumenty i fakty* and *Ekonomicheskaia gazeta* publishing houses could also be considered 'independent media'. *INTERFAX News Agency* is another 'independent media' organization (Fossato and Kachkaeva, 1999). This suggests that most Russian media institutions are either owned by the state or by big holdings or by the foreigners. Consequently, the 'independent media' institutions in Russia have to struggle for their survival in the current economic climate and amid increasing state control (Fadin, 1997, pp. 90-92).

The economic crisis of August 1998 considerably shook the Russian economy, state and society. Evidently, media institutions were not immune from the negative impacts of this financial crisis. As a result, in 1998, the tax exemptions granted to media organizations in 1995 were eliminated. This weakened the independent media's financial basis. Furthermore, the flight of foreign capital resulted in a sharp decline in the advertisement revenues of the independent media. The increases in production costs and the difficulties in distribution weakened this media further (Belin, 2001, pp. 327-328).

The Kremlin has exploited the weakness of Russian media in depressing socio-economic circumstances in order to bring the Russian media under strict state control. For example, the Kremlin created the VGTRK holding company on 8 May 1998, which succeeded in uniting 68 television and 100 radio stations throughout the Russian Federation. On 6 July 1999, Yeltsin has signed a decree for the creation of a Ministry for Press, Television-Radio Broadcasting and Mass Communications. While this move illustrated the determination of the Kremlin to put all independent media under state control, the Kremlin stated that it simply wanted to put an end to the chaotic situation in the media sector. To this purpose, Mikhail Lesin, who was Vice-President of Russian State Television (RTR), was appointed as the Media Minister (Belin, 2001, p. 327).

In general, it could be stated that the Media Ministry succeeded in bringing the federal and regional media under its own control. In this way, the Kremlin became able to suppress any form of political opposition and to shape public opinion in line with its own wishes. Therefore, at that time, the formation of this Ministry was criticized by various politicians from Vladimir Ryzhkov, the head of the centrist Our Home is Russia (NDR) bloc, to Gennadii Ziuganov, the leader of the Communist Party of the Russian Federation (CPRF).

In the face of these criticisms, Lesin felt it necessary to clarify the objectives of the Ministry. According to Lesin, the Ministry was to help the media sector overcome its technological and organizational problems. The Ministry would also supervise electoral campaigns, ensuring that they conform with election legislation. Finally, the Ministry was to develop common norms in the media sector. For Lesin, all these measures were taken in order to increase the credibility of the media institutions in the eyes of the Russian people (Belin, 2001, p. 327).

While the state was trying to gain full control of the media sector, the owners of media institutions entered into a period of infighting after the summer of 1999. These media owners lost their relative power *vis-à-vis* the Kremlin as a result of their economically-motivated conflict of interests. The conflict of interests deepened when Boris Berezovskii and Vladimir Gusinskii differed on their choice of political regime to follow Yeltsin's presidential term.

In the summer of 1999, two influential politicians - Moscow Mayor Iurii Luzhkov and former Prime Minister Evgenii Primakov - formed an alliance, which was backed by Gusinskii but opposed by Berezovskii, who was very close to the Yeltsin family. Reflecting the hostile relations between Berezovskii and Gusinskii, Berezovskii's ORT television channel and Gusinskii's NTV channel declared a media war on each other. The deeply fragmented nature of the media sector enabled the Kremlin to bring the media under its control gradually. Consequently, the media, except Gusinskii's NTV channel, became largely submissive to the wishes of the Kremlin during the State Duma elections of 19 December 1999 (Belin, 2001, pp. 330-331).

The Rise of Vladimir Putin and His Policy towards the Independent Media

In the summer of 1999, the 'new face' of Russian politics appeared when Yeltsin named Vladimir Putin, a former officer in the Federal Security Service (FSB), the agency that succeeded the KGB, as his Prime Minister. In line with the expectations of the Russian masses, bored with the chaotic 'transition' period under Boris Yeltsin, Putin, a rather unknown security officer, was presented as a strong political leader, seemingly ready to drastically improve Russia's state power both internally and externally. In this atmosphere, Russians, including many journalists, supported Putin and his calls for a 'strong Russian state'. Not surprisingly, Vladimir Putin was successfully elected as Russian President on 26 March 2000 (Belin, 2001, pp. 332-333).

As Berezovskii's and Gusinskii's political fortunes worsened substantially in the aftermath of the 2000 presidential election, VGTRK sought to seize the opportunity against the important media outlets owned by Russia's influential business elites. Since ORT and NTV were perceived to be vehicles for Berezovskii's and Gusinskii's political ambitions, the strategy of strengthening VGTRK was clearly profitable politically for the Kremlin. Besides, VGTRK had a powerful and skilful friend in government, Media Minister Mikhail Lesin, who masterminded the creation of VGTRK before becoming deputy chairman of this state holding (Belin, 2001, p. 327). In theory, this could help the Putin leadership re-assume control of the independent mass media smoothly.

In line with Putin's policy of bringing the independent media under state control, Russia's information security doctrine (*Doktrina informatsionnoi bezopasnosti Rossiiskoi Federatsii*) was signed on 12 September 2000. This doctrine aimed to realise the following objectives: (1) the constitutional rights of citizens to procure and use information; (2) the necessity to provide reliable coverage of state policy; (3) the development of new technologies in media-related areas; and (4) the need to safeguard sources of information against illicit access.

Although this doctrine had no legal force, its underlying mentality was similar to the Soviet-era attempts to control information and block foreign broadcasts. In fact, implementing such a doctrine had been considered also during the Yeltsin era in order to protect the state from the media critics of the Chechen war. However, it was not approved at that time. Given that political opposition to the Kremlin weakened after Putin's election, Putin succeeded in getting the doctrine approved.

The first state practices in line with this information security doctrine came in 2001 when Gazprom-Media took control of the NTV channel from Vladimir Gusinskii and the Russian state began bankruptcy proceedings against Boris Berezovskii's TV6. When TV6 was closed by the Russian authorities, Grigorii Yavlinsky, Chairman of the *Iabloko* bloc, stated:

> The closure of TV-6 by the Kremlin shows that the 'dictatorship of law' that the Russian president speaks about so often now appears to be more about arbitrary political preferences than establishing a modern society that plays by the rules. Closing TV-6 in many ways reflects what has gone wrong in Russia since 1991. Many people share the blame for the failures that have occurred since communism's collapse. Indeed, the types of characters involved in TV-6's closure have been with us since then. ... Some in government think that a 'free media' should only champion and praise the ruling elite (Yavlinsky, 2002, p. 9).

These events have shown that state officials have become less tolerant towards the so-called opposition media outlets and started to adopt a more interventionist approach. The cases of NTV and TV6 clearly illustrate the risks to media institutions when becoming involved in economic business. In such an atmosphere, the strengthening role of the state in the media industry minimized the autonomy of independent media and hindered the development of civil society outside the patronage of Vladimir Putin (Aslamazian, 2001).

In fact, the Committee to Protect Journalists (CPJ), the United States-based organization defending freedom of the press globally, named Vladimir Putin, as one of the 'Ten Worst Enemies of the Press' on 3 May 2001. According to Ann K. Cooper, the Executive Director of CPJ, the Russian President was an enemy of the free press for attempting to impose centralized control over mass media, suppress criticism and eliminate the independent press. The CPJ statement declared that:

> Since taking office last year, Vladimir Putin has presided over an alarming assault on press freedom in Russia. The Kremlin imposed censorship in Chechnia, orchestrated legal harassment against private media outlets, and granted sweeping powers of surveillance to the security services. Despite Putin's professed goal of imposing the rule of law, numerous violent attacks on journalists have been carried out with impunity across Russia. In an ominous and dramatic move this April, the Kremlin-controlled Gazprom corporation took over NTV, the country's only independent national television network. Within days, the Gazprom coup had shut down a prominent Moscow daily and ousted the journalists in charge of the country's most prestigious newsweekly. Despite Gazprom's insistence that the changes were strictly business, the main beneficiary was Putin himself, whose primary critics have now been silenced (Nesterova and Vronskaya, 2001).

Vladimir Putin has subsequently revised his policy towards media institutions in 2002, seeking to improve his image as a staunch supporter of media freedom. He ceased supporting further restrictions on the flow of information. For example, he vetoed amendments to Russian media law regarding the coverage of antiterrorist operations in November 2002, stating that the proposed amendments would 'create preconditions for imposing unjustified restrictions on citizens' rights to information.' He also endorsed a law to extend a discount on the value-added tax rate for the media institutions until 2005 (Belin, 2003).

These examples show that Vladimir Putin preferred not to take a hawkish stance towards the media. Instead, he opted for weakening the link between strong economic interest groups and the independent media. This became evident when Putin congratulated the Russian journalists on the Russian Press Day in 2003 as follows:

> I congratulate you on the Russian Press Day. [...] Not a single state can exist without publicity and openness, which are ensured above all by the mass media, following the strict norms of professional ethics. They maintain a constructive dialogue with the authorities and in many respects exert a decisive influence on public opinion. [...] Our common task today is to create the really independent mass media which would rest on a firm economic basis and would be capable to correctly and objectively reflect the complicated processes in our country and abroad (*RIA Novosti*, 13 January, 2003).

Putin's attempts at promoting his image as a supporter of the independent media, however, is not likely to hide his support for increasing state pressure on independent media in Russia. Oleg Panfilov, Chairman of the Center for Journalism in Extreme Situations, contradicts Putin and cites the number of legal cases opened against journalists since Vladimir Putin's rise to the Russian presidency. Panfilov stated: '[T]here have been more legal cases opened against journalists in the two and half years of Mr Putin's rule than throughout the 1990s under Boris Yeltsin' (Jack, 2003). In this way, Putin implied that in order for the state to operate effectively, everyone needed to line up and carry out orders coming from the top. In other words, the Kremlin sought to establish control over the press by intimidating opposition media with politically-motivated measures.

The Prospects for Cooperation between the State and Civil Society in Russia

The increasing state pressure on Russia's independent media highlights the difficulties of developing civil society in post-Soviet Russia. Russia's civil society was not strong enough to exist independently from the state and powerful economic forces when the Russian Federation emerged out of the Soviet Union in 1991. However, a more serious problem concerned the adaptation of political structures to the changing political conditions of the post-Soviet era. According to Timothy Colton and Michael McFaul (2001, pp. 21-22), post-Soviet Russian society has transformed itself more effectively than the political structures governing it. Accordingly, the failure of political structures to adopt a more democratic approach towards the development of an independent media gives us some clue regarding the prospects for state-civil society relations in the near future.

Vladimir Putin's policy toward media institutions reflects his understanding of 'civil society'. According to Putin, the development of a civil society independent of state control was not desirable. As Putin's congratulatory message on Russian Press Day shows, for Putin, the dependence of civil society organizations on foreign grants and on Russia's powerful economic interest groups, as opposed to the Russian state, undermined their independence (*RIA Novosti*, 13 January 2003). Putin saw this as a problem only when civil society organizations act independently from the state. According to Putin's line of thinking, the state should be strengthened in order to provide support and defend the rights and liberty of its citizens. However, this discourse of creating an 'independent' civil society appears as an ideological justification for the emerging authoritarian trends in Russian politics.

In order to bring the newly emerging civil society institutions of post-Soviet Russia under the control of the Russian state, Putin has praised the merits of civil society and called for 'suitable' civil society organizations and figures to participate in a dialogue between the Kremlin and Russian civil society. Although it is understandable that society should engage in a dialogue with the authorities, it has not been clear from Putin's actions whether the Kremlin is genuinely willing to cooperate with the Russian civil society aside from the level of public declarations.

Boris Pustintsev (2001, p. 10), chairman of the St. Petersburg based human rights organization Citizens' Watch, criticized Putin's attempt to create a 'civil society' under his own patronage:

The authorities have, from time to time, attempted to set up their own tame Government Organized Non-Governmental Organizations, or GONGOs, although this has not presented a serious threat to NGO sector development. Actions orchestrated against civil society have never been of a systemic nature. 1998 was probably the most dangerous year when, with the support of the Moscow City Hall legal department, a number of regional elites attempted to launch an attack on citizens' constitutional rights. This was most clearly manifested in the refusals to register or re-register a number of NGOs. This primarily affected human rights and ecological organizations, i.e., the most ardent critics of the federal and regional authorities.

Pustintsev concluded his analysis by stating that 'the main danger currently facing civil society is different. It is the instinct of the new administration - possibly influenced by an influx of former KGB officers to positions in many state institutions - to control everything that moves. Furthermore, the drive to strengthen the state's vertical chain of command is being followed by a drive to increase control over society'. Although Putin's strategy of co-opting civil society institutions hoped to achieve political consolidation in post-Communist Russia, it could be seen as an attempt to manipulate civil society organizations in order to strengthen Putin's position in Russian politics.

The relationship between Putin's media policies and his policies towards civil society could be seen more clearly when one examines Putin's refusal to cooperate on providing the independent media with free access to many sorts of 'open' information that directly affect the vital interests of society. In fact, as Dmitry Pinsker argues, Putin's support for the doctrine on 'information security' clearly runs against the free development of civil society (Pinsker, 2001). This doctrine seems to serve the purpose of making state actions in Russia largely non-transparent. In fact, it is not an exaggeration to state that, without a functioning public oversight of the authorities' actions, there cannot be a fully-fledged civil society in Russia.

Besides, one could also state that potentially, there is no guarantee in Russia's post-Soviet political system preventing Putin from seeking to implement his dream of a submissive 'civil society'. Consequently, the independent media is officially tolerated, as opposed to developing into a strong social force based on the strength of media enterprises. Ignoring the fact that it is impossible to 'build civil society from above' in consolidated democracies, Putin created an image that he has succeeded in controlling the independent media and civil society 'democratically' (Pinsker, 2001). The co-existence of strict state control over the independent media and support of civil society seems to constitute a mutually exclusive contradiction in terms.

Conclusion

This chapter sought to explore the relationship between the dynamics of media politics and the development of civil society in post-Soviet Russia. It could be concluded that although the post-Soviet era has witnessed the emergence of some relatively more 'independent' media institutions in Russia, their dependence on powerful business groups and some state institutions has limited their autonomy considerably. The Russian state has reasserted its control over the independent media by weakening powerful economic interest groups. Having lost their newly-found support from big business groups, the so-called independent media institutions fell under state pressure. Their inability in creating the necessary economic and political conditions for the emergence of a self-reliant independent media resulted in an increase in state pressure on the independent media in post-Soviet Russia.

It is difficult to label the Russian media as 'fully-independent'. The media's failure in carrying out its main objective of enlightening the masses is a welcome development for Russia's post-Soviet elites. Under the difficult socio-economic and political conditions of the post-Soviet transition, the Russian masses are not interested in promoting the independence of the media. It seems that there is no strong demand in Russian society for impartial and objective information from the media. However, it would also be inaccurate to describe Russian society as a malleable mass that can always be molded with limited resistance by Putin's desires.

This analysis suggests that Russia's post-Soviet transition displays many similarities with other post-Soviet states in the Black sea region. What is missing from Vladimir Putin's line of thinking regarding an independent media and civil society is that the autonomy of independent media and the growth of civil society in Russia could aid in dealing with Russia's chronic political instability. The Kremlin could address the xenophobic trends in post-Soviet Russia by promoting civil society networks.

Putin's policies of pressurizing the independent media into submission have undermined the already weak basis for developing civil society in the Russian Federation. The adverse developments in the field of media freedom reflect the problems in Russia's problematic 'transition' process. Although the process of post-Soviet 'transition' aimed to abolish the state's monopoly over the media, the media that is not directly controlled by the state is controlled through indirect economic and political measures. This has provided Vladimir Putin's leadership with a golden opportunity to justify its drive to increase the state pressure on the independent media and civil society in Russia.

References

Aslamazian, M. (21 December, 2001). A year of hard lessons for the media, *Moscow Times*.

Belin, L. (1995). Wrestling political and financial repression. *Transition*, 1 (18), 59-63, 88.

Belin, L. (2001). Political bias and self-censorship in the Russian media. In A. Brown. (Ed.), *Contemporary Russian politics* (pp. 323-342). Oxford: Oxford University Press.

Belin, L. (2003). 2002: A quietly bad year for the Russian media, *RFE/RL Russian Political Weekly*, 3 (2).

Benn, D. W. (1996). The Russian media in Post-Soviet conditions. *Europe-Asia Studies*, 48 (3), 471-480.

Colton, T. J. & McFaul, M. (2001). *Are Russians undemocratic?: Carnegie Endowment for International Peace Working Paper, 20*. Washington: Carnegie Endowment for International Peace.

de Smaele, H. (1999). The applicability of Western media models on the Russian media system. *European Journal of Communication*, 14 (2), 173–189.

Doktrina informatsionnoi bezopasnosti Rossiiskoi Federatsii [Information security doctrine of the Russian Federation]. Retrieved 2000, from http://www.scrf.gov.ru/Documents/Decree /2000/09-09.html

Fadin, A. (1997). In Russia, private doesn't mean independent. *Transitions*, 4 (5), 90-92.

Fossato, F. & Kachkaeva, A. Russian media empires. Retrieved 2000, from http://www.rferl.org/nca/special.

Golenkova, Z. T. (1999). Civil society in Russia. *Russian Social Science Review*, 40 (1), 4-18.

Habermas, J. (1996). *Between fact and norms: Contribution to a discourse theory of law and democracy.* Cambridge, Mass.: MIT Press.

Jack, A. (3 January, 2003). Fear and Kremlin hints turn reporters into Putin's poodles: The Russian media are crippled by self-censorship, *Financial Times.*

Jensen, L. (1993). The press and power in the Russian Federation. *Journal of International Affairs*, 47 (1), 97-126.

Lasswell, H. (1971). The structure and function of communication in society. In W. Schramm, & F. R. Donald. (Eds.), *The process and effects of communication* (pp.84-99). Urbana, IL: University of Illinois Press.

Nesterova, S. & Vronskaya, L. (3 May, 2001). US Press Freedom Group names Putin as enemy of press for 2001, *gazeta.ru.*

Pinsker, D. (16-22 November, 2001). Kremlin tames civil society, *The Russia Journal.*

Pustintsev, B. (22 October, 2001). The Kremlin and civil society, *Moscow Times,* p. 10.

Putnam, R. (1993). *Making democracy work: Civic traditions in modern Italy.* Princeton: Princeton University Press.

Rogerson, K. (1997). The role of the media in transitions from authoritarian political systems: Russia and Poland. *East European Quarterly*, 31 (3), 329-354.

RIA Novosti, 13 January, 2003.

Tucker, E. (1996). The Russian media's time of troubles. *Demokratizatsiya*, 3, 422-438.

Yavlinsky, G. (9 February, 2002). Putin's media war damages Russia's move to normalcy, *The Taipei Times,* p. 9.

SOCIAL POWER
AND POST-SOVIET
ECONOMIC TRANSFORMATION

Neil ROBINSON

It has become apparent over the last few years that political factors are a key variable explaining different outcomes in post-communist economic transition. Extensive economic reform and post-communist economic development in states such as Poland, Hungary, and Czechia, have been locked in place by democratic development supporting economic reform through the creation of a virtuous circle in which the emergence of new economic actors and relative economic success encourage the continuation of reform and support democratic governance. At the opposite end of the reform spectrum, states where there has been little or no economic and political reform – most notably Belarus and Uzbekistan – remain largely unchanged as dictatorships with politically controlled economies. These states have not experienced economic growth, but neither have they experienced large-scale contraction of industrial production. The worst economic performers are those states that have reformed both their political and economic systems half-heartedly. These partial reform states – most notably Russia and Ukraine – enjoy neither the benefits of reform nor the certainties of continuity. They suffer the economic cost associated with embarking on reform without experiencing the benefits of reform that help to lock it in place and create a virtuous reform circle. Instead, the inequalities produced by partial reform create a sub-optimal reform outcome in which actors who gain from reform's partiality – reform winners – oppose measures that would complete the movement to full reform and subvert moves to democratic government. As a result, states that only manage partial reform exist in a situation of equilibrium, unable to move forward to greater change and prosperity (Hellman, 1998).

Equilibrium creates a particular form of political economy that is inimical to democratization. Partial reform facilitates a raw form of 'social power', the ability to employ 'resources in order to protect [one's] self and take advantage of others'. The source of this social power is the 'assets and resources acquired under the old regime ... [and] easily converted into individually useful resources, thus generating positions of power and advantage unregulated by legal rules' (Elster et al., 1998, p. 25). Connected to this development of social power the failure of marketization creates 'virtual economy' (Gaddy & Ickes, 1998, 1999). 'Virtual economy' is characterized by the transfer of value from households and wealth producing sectors of the economy to loss-making industries. Virtual economy permits many of those who seized control of economic resources at the collapse of communism to derive economic benefit from those resources and hence consolidate their power. Virtual economy is based on particularistic, rather than market, exchange, on barter, corruption and access to resources due to the political influence, rather than purchasing power in an open market. Particularistic exchange acts as a barrier to the acquisition of power by those outside of networks leftover from the communist system and devalues resources held by actors other than social power holders. Having no access to resources, the bulk of the population depends on local elites for the satisfaction of their basic economic needs. Consequently, society at large is placed in a position where it cannot act autonomously of elites and in its own interest. In this way, Zon (2000, pp. 151-160, 172-177) has argued, virtual economy perpetuates a culture rooted in a 'psychological syndrome' of anomic, asocial behaviour, dependency, avoidance of responsibility. This syndrome creates a 'comprehensive mechanism' that hinders economic change. Being based in psychology and providing some degree of continuity in the chaos of post-Soviet political life, virtual economy and partial reform, are not actively struggled against, but are 'robust, deep-rooted and broadly popular' (Gaddy & Ickes, 1998, p. 54). The belief system that underpins them is 'shared by both the majority of the ruling elite and the larger part of the population' (Zon, 2000, p. 175).

The new consensus about the comparative political economy of reform has much to commend it. However, it is incorrect in several important dimensions. I contend that partial reform, virtual economy and social power are not as stable or in equilibrium, as proponents of these ideas argue. Although strong social power holders may desire its stabilization, partial reform is not necessarily created or held in place by these actors. Partial reform can be a response to, and subsequently a cause of, the post-communist fiscal crisis. This crisis prevents social power holders from stabilizing control over the political process and stops partial reform from becoming an equilibrium position. To make this argument, I will concentrate on the case of Russia. Both the idea of partial reform and virtual economy have been used to describe other post-communist and post-Soviet states (Zon, 2000; Ganev, 2001), but Russia is often said to be the exemplar of both. I will argue that in fact partial reform in Russia has not been in equilibrium, but has seen constant upheaval in state-economy relations;

there is partial reform and virtual economy are not products of psychology or inherited political culture. People may still be in a position of dependency because there has only been partial economic reform; there are limits to the extent that this paper is a corrigent to partial reform and virtual economy. But this position of dependency and weakness are not cultural givens that are destined to be reproduced *ad infinitum*. Finally, I will consider the possibility that Russia is unique. Just as we should not infer that Russia is in partial reform equilibrium from aggregate analysis of all cases of post-communist economic change, so too we should not assume that other cases of partial post-Soviet economic change display the same characteristics as Russia. Consequently, I shall consider what might make partial reform stable. I will argue that if there is stability in virtual economy it is because of material factors. There is some basic evidence for this and I will draw some tentative conclusions from this evidence, most notably that although there are factors that may stabilize partial reform in some post-Soviet states excluding Russia, these factors are themselves highly unstable. Even where it looks stable, therefore, partial reform is very likely to undergo change in the near future.

The Theory of Partial Reform Equilibrium and a Test for its Validity

The argument that some post-communist states have reached a position of partial reform equilibrium is based on the observation that economic reform has been most successful where there has been a dispersal of political power. This is contrary to ideas on reform that were common as communism collapsed. Then, it was assumed that consumption would fall at the start of economic transition. This fall would be caused by the constriction of welfare regimes as political priorities changed, as well as by the economic disruption caused by the introduction of market exchange and price liberalization. Certain political assumptions followed from these expectations. Few people would have any particular interest in exerting themselves in the cause of reform, but actors threatened by a decline in their fortunes because of reform would press for policy to accommodate their particular interests. In short, reform would create a collective action problem; there would be little widespread action in support of reform, but plenty of protest against it from a population suffering falling living standards under the tutelage of vested interests. Assuming this to be the case, it was thought best to reduce the time of transition by choosing a radical reform strategy. Although this would raise incentives to protest reform because radical reform would initially cause a very steep fall in living standards, this would be compensated for by the shortening of the time that collective action problems were a threat to reform and by the more rapid construction of constituencies who benefited from reform (Sachs, 1993a). However, this raised the question of how to maintain the momentum for reform during the initial period of transition when the population would not, in the main, be experiencing its benefits, the collective action problem of reform would be at its most critical and incentives to lobby for policy to accommodate particular interests at their height. It was assumed that the best way to resist these efforts would be to use a honeymoon period at the moment of regime change and construct a centralized executive with sufficient power to operate economic policy free of social pressure in the short-run and until market mechanisms had introduced economic rationality sufficient to enable the population to make sensible choices about reform (Haggard & Kaufman, 1995, pp. 163-165; Sachs, 1993b).

Initial expectations of reform were thus that reform would progress most rapidly where power was centralized because economic policy would be implemented and not subverted by social interests and by extant economic cultures. This expectation was not validated by the experience of reform. Centralization of power was most marked in states with presidential systems, but these did not perform as well in fostering reform and recovering from the initial shocks it provokes as states with parliamentary systems and high rates of governmental turnover. In the latter – Hungary, Poland and the Czech Republic – reform became entrenched and comprehensive, and there was a recovery in GDP to a point higher than at the end of the communist period within four years of starting transition (Hellman, 1998; EBRD, 1999, pp. 102-114). In contrast, Russia, despite having a presidential regime with a high concentration of executive power, did not develop reform as far and soon began to stagnate; per capita GDP recovered somewhat after an initial slump, but did not reach a level comparable to that enjoyed at the end of the communist period and the start of economic transition. The reasons for this lie in how partial and comprehensive reform and different institutional arrangements provide public goods as a part of economic reform, and the patterns of resource distribution that the two modes of reform create, and which are perpetuated by their institutional structures. Economic reform should deliver certain public goods – such as secure property rights, a relatively stable currency that is a universal medium of exchange, or the enforcement of economic contracts between entrepreneurs, business and labour etc – that are crucial to market consolidation. Political openness created by parliamentarism aids in the provision of these public goods because competition between political factions and the checks on government by parliamentary bodies prevent authorities from accumulating the power to either obstruct their development, or trade them off to lobbies and social power holders for political support. Parliamentarism thus creates conditions that sustain market reform by ending and controlling the 'needless uncertainty' prevalent in Soviet-type economies due to the arbitrary use of political power and the need to secure political protection for economic activity (Olson, 1992, p. 68; Clague, Keefer, Knack & Olson, 1997). Indeed, the fact that parliamentarism and reform can deliver public goods before economic benefit helps to create consensus for reform. The opposite is true of states where partial reform is the norm. In these states, with their presidential regimes, the isolation of policy making from parliamentary scrutiny and unstructured political competition enable politicians to use their power to satisfy social power holders that lobby for their interests to predominate over the common good without censure. Consequently, political consensus does not develop behind reform and neither do the prerequisites for market economy (such as secure private property rights), or for economic growth (such as the confidence that investment will be protected through contract enforcement). This means that first, reform stalls, and second that those with social power become very wealthy at the expense of society at large. This wealth can then be used to further extend lobby interests so that the influence of social power holders and Soviet-style practices and dependencies are perpetuated. Where this occurs, differences in wealth become extreme as lobbies transfer the wealth of society to themselves and pass any costs of change to the wider society instead of bearing their share of them. Partial reform thus creates much more distinct winner and loser groups than comprehensive reform. The ability of losers to do anything about their disproportionate shouldering of the reform burden is low since they do not have resources to support political organization, or overcome the collective action problem of organizing to achieve redistribution. Winners, on the other hand, have the power and the incentive to block reforms that might create equitable distribution and the provision of public goods by the state to society as opposed to the private goods that they enjoy.

The idea that partial reform thus reaches equilibrium is thus premised on the belief that winner groups come to have the power to block reform. Again, there is some empirical evidence to back these claims. The idea that winner groups have the power to block reform fits with the idea that Russia developed a form of 'oligarchic capitalism' in the 1990s. Survey evidence also distinguishes between the extent to which political processes are captured by social power holders in partial and comprehensive reform states (Hellman, Jones & Kaufman, 2000). However, although we can see a rough fit between particular cases with the patterns of reform identified through comparison of all of the cases of post-communist reform, we should not automatically make explanatory inferences about actual behaviour and developmental trajectory in any individual case from the comparative conclusions. Making any inference about any individual case from conclusions reached through aggregate level analysis runs the risk of committing an ecological fallacy (W. S. Robinson, 1950). For aggregate level analysis to explain individual cases requires the confirmation of its results through theory-confirming or infirming case study. Furthermore, drawing a conclusion about Russia from the observation that state policy in partial reform states seems to favour winner groups because of the latter's power runs into a classic problem in the study of states that are democratic (even if they are only weakly so). This is the problem of assuming that state autonomy – the 'institutional differentiation of formal collective decision making from the overall system of inequality' (Rueschemeyer, Huber & Stephans, 1992, p. 63) – has been compromised if state policy favours a powerful group. This assumption turns the issue of state autonomy into a zero-sum game for analytical purposes; we can only see the state as being autonomous when it is seen to be taking action against the rich, and conversely view its autonomy as compromised where it takes action that favours them. The assumption that the autonomy of the Russian state has been compromised is quite a common one and is central to the view that the rough correspondence of Russia to the partial reform norm constitutes explanation (see McFaul, 1998, for example). However, as Nordlinger (1981) has pointed out, state actions that serve the interests of the powerful and appear to be the result of a compromise of autonomy, may in fact be motivated by officials' desire to achieve some goal of their own, or to secure some desired end for the state; serving the interests of the rich may be incidental, and even if it is an intentional end of policy, it is not necessarily proof of compromised autonomy.

Assuming that policy which creates partial reform is a result of social power holders' ability to affect state capture in any particular case is thus to make two leaps in explanatory logic by inferring motive across different levels of data, and by assuming motivation and power relations from the outcomes of policy in only one dimension, that of elite interests. We have to consider whether partial reform is caused by something other than social power and that the state may not be helpless before that power even if it does satisfy elite interests. If it turns out that state officials' actions were inspired by some motive other than to please the rich, then it is not sensible to predict either that partial reform endures as a result of winner power, or that partial reform equilibrium is inescapable. In other words, if we see that state officials were motivated by something other than pleasing the rich we will have grounds to suspect that there is no embedded consensus over virtual economy or partial reform.

This begs the question of what other motives state officials might have. Such motives are likely to be multiple according to office held and personal inclination. However, whilst this observation recognizes that the state is not a unitary actor, it is still possible to argue that state officials have a common interest in securing conditions in which the state can replicate itself as an institutional ensemble and continue in existence as a vehicle that can be used for individual ambition. Practically, and with regard to partial reform, this means, first, that we have to consider whether state officials' actions that compromise reform and perhaps autonomy are in fact trade-offs that enable the survival of the state as much as they are actions that satisfy some powerful social interest. Second, it implies that compromises on autonomy will not endure if a point is reached where partial reform comes to threaten the state's future. Winner groups/social power holders, although they may shift much of the burden of economic reform on to losers and collude with the state to do this, have to be able or prepared to countenance the transfer of resources from themselves to the state sufficient for it to replicate itself if they are to hold partial reform in equilibrium. If they either cannot or will not do this, they run the risk of the state taking action against them. We can therefore test the strength of virtual economy and partial reform equilibrium quite simply: is it produced by winner/social power, or by state officials concerned as much with state continuity as with satisfying elite interests? If the latter, there is no reason to assume equilibrium rather than mutual convenience in the first instance. However, it may also be equilibrium emerges over time, that convenience evolves into equilibrium and stable virtual economy. We therefore also have to see if partial reform lasts due to the force of winner power, or through the mutual adaptability of state and social power holders. The former suggests that state capture is a more powerful block on reform than the latter, and that equilibrium will be harder to escape. The rest of the paper examines these questions in light of the Russian experience of economic reform.

Testing Partial Reform Equilibrium in Russia

The crucial aspect of economic reform for the replication of the state is its ability to avoid fiscal crisis. A fiscal crisis is not simply the incidence of budgetary deficit, but the point where a budget deficit threatens the state's ability to replicate itself and fulfil its functions. How states are affected by fiscal crisis varies according to the demands made of them. In capitalist states, fiscal crisis is the product of expenditures exceeding revenue due to increased demands being made of the state; in post-communist states, fiscal crisis is caused by revenues declining faster than expenditure (Campbell, 1995). The fiscal crisis of a post-communist state is a result of two things: the continued demand for state subsidy from industry and welfare recipients and the transition from a system of taxation based on being a 'property state' to a 'tax state' (Hausner, 1993, p. 192). The latter is responsible for the crisis of revenue collection. As a 'property' state, the USSR raised taxation from the property it owned and maintained a high level of tax returns through its control of wages and prices (Olson, 2000). Tax payments were thus made between branches of the state and the fiscal survival of the state did not depend on the state's capacity to appropriate surplus through taxes on the private sector. This form of taxation generated a large amount of revenue and investment for a time, but at the cost of low factor productivity. This low factor productivity, and the other problems associated with planning, meant that overtime the economy stagnated so that the state's ability to generate large amounts of revenue declined. This tendency of revenue to fall overtime was compounded by collusion between bureaucrats and the existence of soft-budget constraints; revenue had to be diverted to combat the misappropriation of state resources and could not be maximized through the promotion of efficiency (Urban, 1985; Kornai, 1986). Finally, the ability of political authorities to take tax was undermined by political reform during which the state's ability to claim possession of its property was questioned and its resources stolen from it by being put beyond its use (Solnick, 1997). As a result, the budgetary legacy of the Soviet system was a poor one and there were few administrative mechanisms available to resolve it through the easy creation of a new tax system.

The problem of budget deficits was widely recognized by future reform leaders such as Gaidar before the collapse of the USSR, and was one of the key tasks that reform strategy was designed to deal with in its first stages (Birman, 1990, p. 25). If the Gaidar reforms had worked as planned, the budget deficit should have been tackled by a mixture of expenditure cuts and the creation of a tax system. The former would have been achieved by price liberalization and the commercialisation of economic policy, which would, it was hoped, have eased the state's budgetary problems by cutting subsidies to both consumers and customers. The latter would have been achieved via the monetization of economic exchange that price liberalization and the commercialisation of economic activity were to create. As money regained its functions of representing the value of goods as set by the neutral market (as opposed to being determined by planners) and became a universal medium of exchange, it would become possible to replace the negotiation of tax rates and exemptions between authorities and enterprises with a transparent, universal system of taxation paid in a single medium, money. The monetization of economic exchange would thus create the basis for a new tax system. In this way, economic reform was also to help create state capacity and overcome the weaknesses of post-Soviet administration. Being transparent and universal, the new tax system would require less administrative capacity to operate.

With these changes in mind, Yeltsin announced at the start of reform that the 'budget deficit for 1992 should be almost non-existent or minimal' (*Sovetskaya Rossiya*, October 29, 1991). This expectation was, of course, far from realized, despite the Gaidar administration's efforts at cost cutting. Expenditure doubled in every quarter of 1992; a budget surplus as a percentage of GDP of 1.4 per cent in the first quarter of the 1992 turned into a deficit of 10.1 per cent in the second quarter, and ended as a deficit of 3.4 per cent for the year as a whole (Obzor, 1994, p. 81). At the same time, privatization meant that the government's ability to take tax from economic activity as a property owner ended as it transferred its property rights to enterprises without affecting wide scale turnover in management. In short, the Russian government managed to create the worst of both worlds. It destroyed the basis of tax collection through ownership, but did not create either a form of economic exchange that supported a transparent system of tax payments in money, or insure that property had devolved to entrepreneurs who might have expected to pay taxes in money and regularly. Instead, property was now largely owned by – or at least remained under the control of – to social power holders who were used to making payments to the state in kind and/or at rates that were negotiated to perpetuate soft budget constraints. The revenue position of the Russian state was thus fundamentally compromised in 1992 the same time that it failed to control expenditure or demand for subsidy. The budget crisis that ensued peaked in 1994 as revenue collection fell to new lows. The shortfall in tax collection in 1993 had been 30 per cent (*Rossiiskie vesti*, 5 March, 1994). By the autumn of 1994, the shortfall in collection was just under 50 per cent (*Segodnya*, September 27, 1994). The collapse of revenue gathering caused a huge expansion in the deficit in 1994, as it more than doubled as a percentage of GDP (Tikhomirov, 2000, pp. 50-52). This ballooning deficit created intense pressure on the rouble and it collapsed against the US dollar in October 1994. The October 1994 rouble crisis brought home the depth of reform's failures in the area of budget financing in the previous three years. It showed that the state could not rely on the productive economy inherited from the USSR to finance it; by and large this had not responded to the new tax system and was able to lobby for relief from taxation at too many points in the political system to be quickly brought under the fiscal control of the state.

Mass expenditure cuts were introduced in 1995 and 1996 to try to control the budget deficit, but this did not resolve the revenue. The state therefore tried a new tack. In the absence of improved tax collection, it tried to cover the shortfall in its finances by turning to the one set of actors in Russia with some liquidity, the commercial banks. In turning to the banks, the Russian government was turning to a classic winner group that had grown through taking advantage of the state's inability to force reform through to an end. The government tapped into this pool of liquidity through bond issues (primarily of short-term GKOs) and the 'shares for loans' programme. Commercial bank investments in government securities rose eightfold between the rouble crisis and mid-1996 and were equal to 7.1 per cent of GDP in 1996, rising to 12 per cent by May 1997 (Treisman, 1998, p. 255; EBRD, 1997, p. 197). 'Shares for loans' was a less effective means of transferring funds from the banks to the state, but the programme meant that the revenue raised from the sale of smaller number of enterprises in the period of 1995-1997 was roughly equal to that earned during the period 1993-1994 when the bulk of Russian privatizations took place.

It is this turn to the banks, and these policies that are generally regarded as marking the point at which the autonomy of the Russian state was fatally compromised and the economic power of winner groups becomes fungible as political influence. In the words of one Russian newspaper at the time, events in the months after the October 1994 rouble crash moved state and banks 'from shapeless co-operation without fixed rules to highly formalized co-operation' (*Kommersant*, 31 March, 1995). However, the first point to note is that both deficit financing through the sale of government debt and the 'shares for loans' programme had reformist intentions. Deficit financing by GKO sales was justifiable in reformist eyes in that it was not inflationary and could therefore aid currency stabilization. There were hopes, therefore, that like shock therapy' before it, the expansion of the government debt market might increase the rouble's attractiveness as a means of exchange. This in turn would have had a positive affect on the ability of the government to raise tax revenue in forms other than in kind. 'Shares for loans', on the other hand, had attractions for reformists in that it appeared to link industries to sources of investment finance, could be justified as a means of changing corporate governance in major strategic industries, and was supposed to create two waves of revenue for the state (Kokh, 1999). The first wave of revenue was to come through the initial loan from bank to state that would secure stock for the bank to hold in trust and manage, the second from the eventual sale of stock held in trust by the banks for the state, stock which would, it was hoped, have increased in value under bank management. Not only did the policies compromising state autonomy have reformist intentions, there were also few other options for a weak state to take to raise revenues, but to finance itself through schemes that created incentives for those economic agents with money to pay it over to the state. The state was not strong enough to appropriate this revenue through confiscatory schemes, and could not force substantial taxation revenue out of the rest of the economy since it was increasingly demonetised, reduced to paying tax in kind, and able to collude with regional authorities to deliver less than was due to the central state. Although the schemes that were introduced were to make the commercial banks very rich and heralded the emergence of 'financial-industrial groups' (FIGs), there were thus few other sources of revenue available that could be tapped. Moreover, both schemes were cheap to run for the state – fewer personnel are needed to issue bonds than to collect taxes – so that they generated revenue at little economic cost to the government.

There are thus good grounds for stating that the policies of deficit financing through the GKO market and 'shares for loans' were designed at least as much to maintain revenue flows to the state so that it could avoid a total collapse of its finances, as they were intended to satisfy the interests of a powerful group. Partial reform was thus not the invention of social power holders, as much as recognition that to restore some level of state finances, reform had to be supported by an alliance with one sector of the economy and tailored accordingly. The banks gained from government policy in the absence of any other group that the state could turn to for financing, not because of some inherent characteristic, or power that they possessed over the government. The apparent compromise of state autonomy that emerged through the alignment of state and private interests after 1994 thus does not create any grounds for assuming that partial reform lifted the power of a particular group above the power of the state, at least at its moment of creation. It is still possible to argue, however, that the subsequent expansion of the GKO market and the 'shares for loans' programme expanded the wealth of the commercial banks and their 'oligarchic' heads and raised them to a point where they had the means to block policies that would endanger partial reform. Making this argument stick, however, depends on whether or not the state was constrained by the interests created by partial reform to maintain virtual economy. Arguably, it was not, or at least was not for long; the close relationship between bank-led FIGs and the state only lasted for two years – 1995 and 1996 – before the threat of fiscal crisis pushed the state into taking action against the banks.

The move to deficit financing through bond sales helped to ease some of the strain on the state budget. After the peak deficit year of 1994, the deficit dropped from 9.4 per cent of GDP to 3.2 per cent in 1995. This seemingly favourable turn of events was, however, not sustainable. GKO sales could not substitute for failure to collect taxes over the longer term. Revenue continued to drop in 1996 and the deficit began to grow again. Moreover, by the autumn of 1996, Russian commercial banks no longer had the liquidity to fund the continued expansion of the government debt market (EBRD, 1998, p. 13). The cost of borrowing from a small range of institutions also began to outweigh the benefit it brought to the state. Interest rates on government stock rose to over 100 per cent in 1996 and the state's domestic debt tripled (*Izvestiya*, October 15, 1997). Lowering the cost of borrowing and expanding the debt market were thus necessary for the government if it was to control the growth of its deficit and be able to fund it. The only way to do this was to seek out external sources of deficit financing so as roll over debt repayments in to fresh bond issues and expand the debt market at a lower cost. The GKO market was opened up to foreigners in 1996, with a major influx of foreign money in 1997. The strategy worked. The value of foreign holdings of short-term government debt rose threefold in 1997 and interest rates on government debt fell to 9-10 per cent in the summer of 1997 from the high of over 100 per cent in 1996 (RET, 1998a, p. 58; *Izvestiya*, October 15, 1997).

The expansion of the market in treasury bills did not mark a breakdown in relations with the banks. The size of the profits that they could take from the GKO market fell as the cost of government borrowing was reduced, but they were compensated by the fact that they acted as agents for foreign money wishing to purchase Russian treasury bills. However, there was a corollary to the opening up of the market in government debt that did affect the banks. To create investor confidence the Russian government had to be able to show that it had a revenue base sufficient to service its debt obligations: it had to collect its taxes. This ability was in serious doubt since the demonetization of the economy though the creation of virtual economy had reached endemic proportions by the end of 1996 and non-payment of taxes grew massively. In 1996, non-payments were 18.94 per cent of planned tax revenues and equal to 4.9 per cent of GDP (Tikhomirov, 2000, p. 66). Further losses were sustained as the government compensated energy firms with for making deliveries to cashless firms that could not pay for them with tax and export concessions equivalent to 7.2 per cent of GDP by the end of 1996 (Treisman, 1998, pp. 260-264; EBRD, 1997, p. 121).

These concessions had to be curtailed and the overall level of tax collection had to be improved if the government was to maintain its external sources of debt financing. The problem facing the Russian state was how to create a mechanism that could force the payment of taxes in cash, rather than in kind given the demonetized nature of much economic activity. Subsidy cuts were of dubious usefulness; government spending had already been cut, had not produced a commercial response and had contributed to the demonetization of the economy. A revised tax code was necessary to help to simplify the assessment of tax liability and collection, but was not in itself a means of forcing payment in cash. The only solution was to deal with the biggest and most obvious tax defaulters and to try to force regional governments to collect taxes in cash rather than kind. The state did not have the capacity to collect it from defaulters in the economy as a whole; it only had the capacity to target a few major enterprises and try to squeeze more tax from them. This was bound to bring the government and the banks into conflict. Many of the biggest tax defaulters were industries in the energy and petrochemical sectors controlled by FIGs (RET, 1998b, p. 36). Against this, there was a hoped for side-benefit that when squeezed by tax authorities, the FIGs might insist on payment in cash from their debtors so that barter and tax in kind payments would decline throughout the economy. In short, by forcing energy firms to pay tax the state hoped to make them work against virtual economy; they would work to monetize the economy as a whole, something that the state had the aspiration, but not the capacity, to do.

An attack on the privileges of the bank-led FIGs was thus a natural step for the government when they could no longer finance the state budget and when the government had to seek out new revenue sources in a situation of virtual economy. Reform of tax collection began in late 1996 and was stepped up after a government reshuffle in March 1997. State policy was therefore detrimental to social power holders' interests in 1997. If equilibrium was to be restored, as the idea of partial reform suggests, this threat to status and income should have provoked winner groups into action. Action took place, but it did not develop to protect their income sources and status. Winners tried to secure their income by fighting both the government and each other, rather than working against policy. This infighting took the form of competition for the blocks of shares to be allocated under the 'shares for loans' scheme and in the 1997 and 1998 privatization rounds. Control of these shares would have created new income streams; the shares on offer were in firms where there was potential for income generation through export earnings (Norilsk Nickel, the Rosneft oil group), or linkage with foreign investors (the Svyazinvest telecom network). Competition to control these enterprises intensified over the summer of 1997 and soon became political as access to politicians was seen as a key ingredient to a successful bid. These 'bank wars' had an effect on government, in that the state personnel caught up in them were exposed to allegations of corruption and government responsibilities were reshuffled as a result, but they did not lead to a change in policy. If anything, the affect of intra-winner group competition was to make the government more reformist. Yeltsin restored his control over government not by conceding to the wishes of bankers or energy lobbies, but by removing Chernomyrdin in March 1998 and replacing him with a new prime minister, Sergei Kiriyenko, who was committed to continuing efforts to restore the state's financial health.

However, whilst effective action against policy did not emerge from winner groups, the government's efforts at improving its financial position still failed. This failure was because of the intractability of the Russian economy as a whole and global economic change, rather than because of social power holders. The intractability of the Russian economy was shown by the general response to the state's efforts at tax collection in 1997. The government managed to force up collection of tax payments in cash for a short time, but it could not increase its revenues in general. Tax collection at the end of 1997 was about 15 per cent higher in cash terms than at the same time in 1996, but the overall level of enterprise tax indebtedness rose over the course of 1997 by 50 per cent (BOFIT, 1997, 1998, p. 2). The impact of global economic change on Russian economic policy built up from late 1997 onwards as investor confidence in emerging markets began to fall and Russia's trade performance declined (N. Robinson, 1999). On its own, the decline in trade performance would not have been a problem. The Russian current account was still positive. However, it magnified the effect of declining investor confidence caused by the crisis in Asian markets in late 1997. Most of the foreign money that had entered the government debt market in late 1996 and 1997 was in short-term debt that matured in under a year. Maintaining investor confidence was therefore very important because as debt matured the government sought to roll it over in new GKO issues. When this confidence began to decline as a result of the Asian crisis, money began to leave the government debt market. The outflow of foreign money was impossible to halt over the course of 1998, putting pressure on the rouble to a point in August 1998 where the government was left with no choice but to devalue and declare a debt repayment moratorium.

Conclusion

Fiscal crisis was a constant threat to the Russian state after 1992. After radical reform failed to create a new taxation system, the weakness of the state meant that it had little choice but to seek resources from the one sector of the economy that had them, the commercial banks. These resources had been accumulated through the opportunities for speculation and arbitrage created by the uneven development of the market in Russia. The state's relationship with this winner group was not a sign that it had lost the ability to take autonomous action even though the policies it pursued enriched the banks. It was a necessary response to avert further fiscal collapse after October 1994 given the state's limited capacity to direct change in the economy as a whole. At most, the relationship was a search for mutual advantage with the banks, rather than a surrender of sovereignty. Indeed, the state's autonomy was reasserted after 1996 as fiscal crisis loomed again. This reassertion of sovereignty was aimed at breaking down partial reform by attacking one of its main supports – the demonetisations of Russia's virtual economy – using the most prominent of social power holders, the bank-led FIGs. There was thus little deep-rooted accord over the economy between state and social power holders based on psychology, or shared cultural traits; virtual economy had been created as a result of state-business compromise and its survival as a partial reform equilibrium position lasted only as long as that compromise was beneficial to the state. When the benefits declined, so to did the shared understandings about how the economy should be run and to who's advantage, and the government acted to try to force industry to be micro-economically efficient through ending barter and virtual economy practices. The economic chaos that the August 1998 crisis caused brought the push to reform state finances to a halt and changed the composition of the government. However, the fact that efforts to pressure resources out of winner groups was halted in August 1998 does not mean that an equilibrium was restored through their efforts. Policy change came from outside and because of the depths of Russia's problems rather than because of a shared understanding about how the economy should work between government and social power holders.

The Russian example thus shows that partial reform and virtual economy need not be stable due to any immanent properties that these forms of political economy might possess such as affinities to past practices and cultural forms. Such affinities may exist, but they may not have a determining effect on economic policy as some proponents of virtual economy and partial reform imply. Is what I have argued for the Russian case true for other post-Soviet cases and what does this mean for thinking more generally about the relationship of political to economic reform?

No other state in the area has had as volatile a history of economic reform as Russia and social power therefore seems to be more stable in the wider post-Soviet world than it is in Russia. However, this stability may not be durable over time. There are two main reasons for this.

First, where social power is at its most stable, a crisis ridden future is likely because the problems of post-Soviet modernization have yet to be confronted. We can see this if we distinguish between Russia, and other partial reform cases in the area, and those states where social power has seized control of the economy most fully, and been challenged least. Examples of where this has happened are Belarus, Turkmenistan and Uzbekistan. In these states, elites have been able to transfer value from society as a whole to enterprises that they control much more effectively than elsewhere. In these societies, the flow of resources from society to elites has been maintained through high state spending (N. Robinson, 2004). This has taken place at great economic or political cost. Social power holders in Uzbekistan have maintained their grip on the economy and the transfer of resources to the enterprises that they own at the cost of a large build-up of debt (general government debt rose from 27 to and estimated 49 per cent of GDP between 1994 and 1998) and the population has suffered falling living standards as evinced by cuts in services and declining consumer good possession. Belarus has avoided debt build-up, but at the price – paid willingly – of dependency on Russia, from which it has received cheap energy and maintained trade; Belarus trades with other CIS states far more than any other CIS state – 60 per cent of exports and 70 per cent of imports were sourced to the CIS in 2000 – and most of this is with Russia (nearly 90 per cent of Belarus's CIS trade was with Russia in 1999) (Statkomitet SNG, 2000, pp. 70-71). Stable social power thus equates with mass impoverishment and avoidance of economic restructuring and that problems of economic transition are being stored up, not dealt with. The greater the stability of social power, that is the more politically controlled by its successor elites a post-Soviet state is, the more this is the case. This makes the continuance of social power dependent, first, on other states needing the markets and goods from unreformed economies, something that cannot be relied on in perpetuity as other states slowly reform and seek to deal with the effects of competition in their more open economies, and, second, on the ability to keep transferring wealth from society to the elite, a practice that elsewhere in the world has ultimately led to state breakdown (the Congo under Mobutu is a classic example of this pattern of development, see Wrong, 2001). Belarus and Uzbekistan may be the most extreme cases of stable social power, but what is true for them is true for other states where there has been low to partial reform like Azerbaijan and Kazakhstan.

Second, some other states that have partially reformed have not had as tempestuous a ride as Russia because of two things: size and resources. Although Russia is the most materially rich of all of the post-Soviet states, it has not been able to enjoy the benefits of its natural assets in the same way that other states have and has not been able to use wealth generated, or attracted, by its natural resources to offset its budgetary problems. Although Russia has attracted the largest total amount of inward investment of all of the post-Soviet states, this has not had the same impact on Russia as it has elsewhere. In Russia, this money has just disappeared into the vastness of the Russian economy and has had no positive general effects; in smaller states, it has helped to lessen the severity of investment crises. Azerbaijan and Kazakhstan, for example, have received about seven times as much foreign direct investment per capita as Russia (calculated from EBRD, 2000, p. 74). Smaller states, with less fractious elites and lacking Russia's federal system, which has historically dissipated control over revenue collection, have also been able to tax natural resource wealth more effectively or maintain some greater degree of control over natural resource production. As a result, possession of natural resources has ameliorated fiscal crisis to some extent in the CIS. Size and resources matter in one other way: they give international commitments. Russia has, for geo-strategic reasons, maintained material assistance to some post-Soviet states. This has not always been a smooth process since Russia has used this assistance for political leverage. However, the amounts of money involved are substantial and have eased some economic problems for the states concerned, and allowed them to generate revenue for themselves. A good example of this energy exports to states like Ukraine. By February 2000, Ukraine owed Russia some $3.5 billion in trade debt, with most of this outstanding amount being owed for gas imports. This unpaid fuel bill is a major factor that enables Ukraine to continue trading with the rest of the world: if fuel costs were paid, many Ukrainian exports would become uneconomic and unsaleable (Zon, 2000, pp. 113, 117). Although the Ukrainian state is not efficient at taxing trade, it does raise revenue from exports, particularly through licences and the arms trade. To an extent then, its ability to maintain a form of virtual economy is built upon the internationalization of that economy and its support from Russia.

Exogenous factors, and geographical chance may thus have been important stabilising factors outside of Russia in the first decade of transition. Unfortunately, as Russia's experience in 1998 shows, they may not always be beneficial. Resource prices and geo-strategic interests can change and become liabilities. Moreover, relying on beneficial exogenous circumstances means that reform choices, in particular the build up of state capacity to manage change and future exogenous shocks, are not made. That crisis and change has not been more widespread is thus not necessarily because of stable elite and mass beliefs, then, but because material factors have enabled hard decisions to be delayed and facilitated continuity. These factors cannot be relied upon to give elites and their subject peoples the space to avoid change over the long term. Change may not, of course, be in the direction of greater market democracy. Markets are not likely to be any more attractive to many future post-Soviet leaders than they have been in the past. In common with many other late developing states, post-Soviet states do not have the capacity to manage markets effectively and with confidence (Chaudry, 1993). The most likely pattern of development, therefore, is that states will alternate between reform to build up their economies and create mechanisms for dealing with the crises that partial reform may cause them, and backsliding as their inability to manage markets is exposed. As for economics, so for structures of power more generally: concentrations of economic wealth may not be stable as governments move to control crisis, but they will be recreated at cost to wider post-Soviet societies and their ability to accumulate the wealth necessary to support political pluralism. The mutual, reinforcing development of markets and democratic governance that we can see in some parts of Eastern Europe will thus not develop quickly, if at all in the near future.

References

Birman, I. (1990). The budget gap, excess money and reform. *Communist Economics*, 2, 25-45

BOFIT. (1997). Russian and Baltic economics - the week in review 51/52. Newsletter posted to BOFIT electronic mailing list, archived at http://www.bof.fi/bofit/

BOFIT. (1998). Russian economy. *The month in review*, 2.

Campbell, J. (1995). Reflections on the fiscal crisis of post-communist states. In J. Hausner, B. Jessop & K. Nielsen. (Eds.), *Strategic choice and path-dependency in post-socialism* (pp. 84-112). Aldershot: Edward Elgar.

Chaudry, K.A. (1993). The myths of the market and the common history of late developers. *Politics and Society*, 21, 245-274.

Clague, C., Keefer, S. Knack, S. & Olson, M. (1997). Democracy, autocracy, and the institutions supportive of economic growth. In C. Clague (Ed.),

Institutions and economic development (146-175). Baltimore: Johns Hopkins University Press.

EBRD. (1997). *Transition report 1997: Enterprise performance and growth.* London: European Bank for Reconstruction and Development.

EBRD. (1998). *Transition report 1998: Financial sector in transition.* London: European Bank for Reconstruction and Development.

EBRD. (1999). *Transition report 1999: Ten years of transition.* London: European Bank for Reconstruction and Development.

EBRD. (2000). *Transition report 2000: Employment, skills and transition.* London: European Bank for Reconstruction and Development.

Elster, J., Offe, C., Preuss, U., Boenker, F., Gottling U. & Rueb, F. (1998). *Institutional design in post-communist societies.* Cambridge: Cambridge University Press.

Gaddy, C. and Ickes, B. (1998). Russia's virtual economy. *Foreign Affairs*, 77, 53-67.

Gaddy, C. and Ickes, B. (1999). Stability and disorder: an evolutionary analysis of Russia's virtual economy. *William Davidson Institute Working Paper,* No 276.

Ganev, V. (2001). The Dorian Grey effect: winners as state breakers in postcommunism. *Communist and Post-Communist Studies*, 34, 1-25.

Haggard, S. & Kaufman, R.R. (1995). *The political economy of democratic transitions.* Princeton: Princeton University Press.

Hausner, J. (1993). Financial crisis of the state: appearances and causes. In J. Hausner & G. Mosur. (Eds.), *Transformation processes in Eastern Europe* (pp. 185-195). Warsaw: Institute for Political Studies.

Hellman, J. (1998). Winners take all: the politics of partial transition. *World Politics*, 50, 203-234.

Hellman, J., Jones, G. & Kaufmann, D. (2000). "Seize the state, seize the day": State capture, corruption and influence in transition. *World Bank Policy Research Working Paper,* No: 2444.

Izvestiya, October 15, 1997.

Johnson, J. (1998). Russia's emerging financial groups. *Post-Soviet Affairs*, 13, 335-365.

Kokh, A. (1999). Gosudarstvo-prodavets [The state as salesman]. In A. Chubais (Ed.), *Privatizatsiya po-rossiiskii* [Privatization Russian style] (pp. 247-269). Moscow: Vagrius

Kommersant, March 31, 1995.

Kornai, J. (1986). The soft budget constraint. *Kyklos*, 39, 3-30.

McFaul, M. (1998). Russia's "privatized" state as an impediment to democratic consolidation part I. *Security Dialogue*, 29, 191-199.

Nordlinger, E. (1981). *On the autonomy of the democratic state.* Cambridge, MA: Harvard University Press.

Obzor (1994). *Obzor ekonomiki Rossii 1993 II* [Review of the Russian economy 1993 II]. Moscow: Izdatelskaya gruppa "Progress".

Olson, M. (1992). The hidden path to a successful economy. In C. Clague & G. Rausser. (Eds.), *The emergence of market economies in Eastern Europe* (pp. 92-128). Oxford: Blackwell.

Olson, M. (2000). *Power and prosperity. Outgrowing communist and capitalist dictatorships*. New York: Basic Books.

Przeworski, A. (1991). *Democracy and the market. Political and economic reforms in Eastern Europe and Latin America*. Cambridge: Cambridge University Press.

RET. (1998a). *Russian Economic Trends*, 7 (1).

RET (1998b). *Russian Economic Trends*, 7 (3).

Robinson, N. (1999). The global economy, reform and crisis in Russia. *Review of International Political Economy*, 6, 531-564.

Robinson, N. (2004). The post-Soviet space. In A. Payne (Ed.), *The new regional politics of development* (pp. 169-192). Basingstoke: Palgrave.

Robinson, W.S. (1950). Ecological correlations and the behaviour of individuals. *American Sociological Review*, 15, 351-357.

Rossiiskie vesti, 5 March, 1994.

Rueschemeyer, D., Huber, E. & Stephens, J. (1992). *Capitalist development and democracy*. Cambridge: Polity.

Sachs, J. (1993a). *Poland's jump to the market*. Cambridge, MA: The MIT Press.

Sachs, J. (1993b). Western financial assistance and Russia's reforms. In S. Islam and M. Mandelbaum (Eds.), *Making markets* (pp.143-175). New York: Council for Foreign Relations.

Segodnya, September 27, 1994.

Solnick, S. (1997). *Stealing the state. Control and collapse in Soviet institutions*. Cambridge, MA: Harvard University Press.

Sovetskaya Rossiya, October 29, 1991.

Statkomitet SNG. (2000). *Sodruzhestvo Nezavisimykh Gosudarstv v 1999 godu. Statisticheskii ezhegodnik* [Commonwealth of Independent States in 1999. Statistical yearbook]. Moscow: Statkomitet SNG.

Tikhomirov, V. (2000). *The political economy of post-soviet Russia*. Basingstoke: Macmillan.

Treisman, D. (1998). Fighting inflation in a transitional regime. Russia's anomalous stabilization. *World Politics*, 50, 235-265.

UN (2000). *Statistical yearbook. Forty-fourth issue*. New York: United Nations.

Urban, M. (1985). Conceptualizing political power in the USSR: patterns of binding and bonding. *Studies in Comparative Communism*, 18, 207-226.

Woodruff, D. (1999). *Money unmade. Barter and the fate of Russian capitalism*. Ithaca: Cornell University Press.

Wrong, M. (2001). *In the footsteps of Mr Kurtz. Living on the brink of disaster in the Congo*. London: Fourth Estate.

Zon, H. Van. (2000). *The political economy of independent Ukraine*. Basingstoke: Macmillan.

STATE FORMATION, CIVIL SOCIETY AND DEMOCRATIZATION:

COMPARING THE TURKISH EXPERIENCE WITH MEDITERRANEAN AND EAST EUROPEAN CASES[i]

Fethi AÇIKEL

Since the early 19th century, the process of transition from one socio-political system to another has been a central focus of social scientific inquiry. Theorising the historical process of transition, making 'macrosociological predictions', in terms of 'state breakdowns and revolutions' (Collins, 1995, p. 1552), and understanding the dynamics of democratization (Moore, 1991) have pre-occupied historical sociologists and political scientists. Over the last two decades and numerous examples of authoritarian regimes (e.g., the Mediterranean military-fascist regimes, the East European bureaucratic-communist systems), we have noted the various patterns of democratization that have taken place. Economic and political developments in these regions and/or zones have typically been categorised in terms of successive waves, e.g., the third/fourth waves of democratization. Irrespective of whether they are economic-institutional or political-ideological in nature, such systemic changes deserve examination, primarily to aid in forming trans-cultural comparisons and generating some theoretical guidelines for possible transitions of the future (Offe, 2001; Collins, 1995; Burawoy, 2000b; Schopflin, 1991; Szelenyi & Kostello, 1996; Bernhard, 1993; McFaul, 2002; Fligstein, 1996).

By considering the dominant characteristics of transition in the Mediterranean, East European and Black Sea cases, I will identify striking parallels and differences with the Turkish case. The main thematic axis of comparison is the processes of state formation, democratization and nationalization. An analysis of this kind is far from exhaustive thematically and geographically, yet even such a preliminary examination provides some comparative insights. This study then should be considered as a modest attempt to sketch out the dominant trends and constraints in these societies.

Preliminary Observations on Transitional Formations

Almost fifteen years of radical transformation in the post-Communist societies of Central Europe and the Black Sea region has provided historical sociologists and scholars of comparative politics with yet another field area for study. Referring to Karl Polanyi's notion of the great transformation, Burawoy (2000a, pp. 693-695) considers these processes of transformation in the post-Communist world as 'the second great transformation' (p. 5). In fact, in terms of the patterns and deadlocks of transition – from state paternalism to democracy, from state-led command economies to market liberalization, and from centralised bureaucratic traditions to bourgeoning civil societies – these societies have experienced remarkable change. Perhaps more strikingly, these transformations were accelerated by the external dynamic of potential EU membership. Claus Offe (2001, pp. 167-168) considered the post-Communist experience of transition as *the fourth wave*. According to this account, the post-Communist experience of transition has qualitative parallels with the experience of the 'Latin group of Mediterranean Europe', or, in other words, with the Third Wave of democratization. Macrosociological transformation of this kind deserves to be studied closely for many reasons. In particular, we must consider it from the viewpoints of i) state-building, ii) economic reform and iii) democratization (Collins, 1995, pp. 1552-1593; Shevtsona, 2001, p. 66). Indeed, the histories of authoritarian political regimes, their weak democratic traditions as well as almost non-existing civil societies suggests that the post-Communist experiences can be conceived – without underestimating major socio-political differences – as following similar patterns to the Mediterranean post-military regimes.

From this perspective, developments in the Mediterranean societies of the 1970s and in East European societies of the 1980s evoke interesting axes of comparison. The 1980s symbolise the ascendancy of neo-liberal economics and the New Right ideology in the West. Similarly, the 1990s are representative of significant political change in post-Communist societies (Gill, 2002). By the 1980s, the post-war formula of the Welfare state was gradually replaced by rising neo-liberalism in Western Europe, while the institutional heritage of the Communist regimes in the East of Europe was challenged by new politics. These two remarkable changes – irrespective of whether they are considered positive or negative developments – in the Western and the Eastern frontiers of Europe encouraged optimists to envisage the possible collapse of the Communist systems. It was hoped that this would further contribute to the harmonization of economic and political systems in the broader European context. Despite remarkable differences in the patterns of transition to multi-party politics, the rule of law, political accountability and democratization of state-society relations, East European societies emerged as fertile case studies of transition by which scholars could test the validity of this analysis. Both the post-authoritarian period and the prospect of EU membership further contributed to the newly emerging dynamics informing democratization and civil society's reconstruction. These processes had a differing effect in the Mediterranean and the East European cases. We can argue that the collapse of the military-dictatorial regimes in Spain, Portugal and Greece and the collapse of the Communist Party regimes in East Europe are representative of different patterns of democratization, civil society formation and economic reconstruction. Contrary to the expectations of smooth and radical changes, these societies displayed different performances in economic and political terms. Their experiences also varied at the regional and intra-regional levels.

In the aftermath of the regime changes, Shevtsona (2001, pp. 65-70) regrouped East European societies with regard to their new political trajectories. This account categorises these societies under three sub-leagues of political formations: i) the Baltic states, which are in the process of becoming a part of the broader Western liberal-democratic societies, despite the vulnerability of their political liberalization and their limited consolidation of civil society; ii) the league of patrimonial states, which exhibit varying degrees of authoritarianism, such as the Central Asian republics, Azerbaijan and Belarus; and iii) Russia, Ukraine, Armenia, Georgia and Moldova, which still experience the negative effects of Soviet bureaucracy, a low level of institutionalized democracy and personalistic governments. Despite striking differences between these societies (in terms of democratic institutions and the consolidation of civil societies), some parallels between the Mediterranean and the Black Sea societies do become apparent, particularly for post-authoritarian regimes. The decline of military dictatorships and oligarchic politics in Spain, Greece and Portugal in the 1970s (Pollack & Taylor, 1983; Danopoulos, 1983) is in stark contrast to that of the collapse of communist rule. Nevertheless, both the post-junta and post-communist societies displayed a similar condition: semi-peripheral development (Mouzelis, 1986).

Equally, the cases of transition in Turkey, the Mediterranean, the East of Europe and the Black Sea region can comparatively contribute to our repertoire of macro-processes, particularly *vis-à-vis* societies on/in the periphery of Europe (Offe, 2001; Burawoy, 2000a; Laitin, 2000, pp. 117-148; McDonough, 1995). While such a comparative analysis is beyond the scope of this article, the reader should note that the Turkish experience is an interesting example by which to elaborate comparatively. Indeed, Turkey is located at the intersecting point where the Mediterranean post-military regimes and the post-Communist societies converge. Turkey continues to display similarities with both these semi-peripheral zones without losing its relatively peculiar characteristics. The Turkish experience of democratization resembles that seen in the post-authoritarian cases of Spain, Portugal and

Greece, yet the problems of transition from a state-led economy to a market-oriented one reminds us of the East European experience. One could argue that the Turkish case stands at the juncture where the particularities of the post-military regimes and the post-etatist bureaucratic states intersect. At first glance the placement of the Turkish experience at the centre of the axis of comparison looks arbitrary; a closer look reveals quite a different story. Both the Mediterranean societies' experiences of shaky democratization, authoritarian elite formation and nation building and the Communist societies' bureaucratically centralised systems, state-led economies and new oligarchic class formations demonstrate the validity of doing so.

Before expanding on the Turkish experience *vis-à-vis* that of the post-junta and post-communist societies, I should point out the problems of democratization and civil society in Turkey. The first appears in military-bureaucratic managerialism, which decisively affected the political process and the political culture, including elite formation and the nation state-building processes. The second relates to the neo-liberal economic restructuring, which undermined the economic foundations and emergence of a pluralistic civil society. By focusing on these processes, I draw attention to two significant phenomena that hinder the consolidation of democracy and civil society in Turkey, namely: patrimonial modernization in the shadow of military-bureaucratic managerialism and the patrimonial expansion of capitalism in the shadow of post-etatist neo-liberal economic transition.

Further, I will identify two significant theoretical approaches that undermine comparative macro-sociological analyses of democratization and civil society: *market universalism* and *cultural essentialism*. While the former is optimistically inclusive and universalistic in its claim that consolidating civil society and democratization are products of economic liberalization, the latter is particularistic and confrontational in its claim that civil society and democratization are culture-bound and peculiar to Western societies. I maintain that the dynamics informing democratization and civil society cannot be reduced to the dynamics of the market or privatization. The economic dimension certainly plays an important role; yet market universalism underrates the social networks and structures that may hinder the operation of the capitalist market and question the irreducibility of civil society in forming the market (Fukuyama, 1992). Cultural essentialism adopts a rather relativistic stance and regards non-Western societies as inherently incompatible with plural democracy and civil society. According to this account, neither the East European societies, which are predominantly Orthodox Christian (e.g., Russia), nor Turkey, a Muslim society, are capable of complying with the Western values of democracy and civil society (Huntington, 1996). Both approaches then have limitations in explaining the dynamics of transitions both in the Turkish case and in post-Communist societies.

These approaches tend to reduce a multi-dimensional phenomenon to either economic or cultural determinants, thus neglecting the interwoven relations between political culture, legal framework, political institutions and economic dimensions. These accounts overlook the constitutive elements of plural democratic societies and the dynamics of democratization, overstating market capacities or cultural differences. In fact, recent developments in post-Communist societies and Turkey indicate that the outcomes of transition from a command to a market economy are not necessarily in congruence with the initial expectations of smooth and transparent reforms (Szelenyi & Kostello, 1996, pp. 1082-1096; L. P. King, 2001, pp. 493-538; Evans & Mills, 1999, 23-46; Brada, 1996, pp. 67-86; Murrell, 1996, pp. 25-44). Similarly, the transitions from authoritarian politics in the Mediterranean were not a natural outcome of cultural essentialism. The *nomenklatura* type of privatization, collapsing public services in health, higher education and housing, etc., suggest that these economies are susceptible to regressive political and economic moves (Schopflin, 1991, pp. 245-250). The liberalization of the market appears to be driven by the newly born technocratic and/or oligarchic economic powers. In many cases, the strategies of economic transition from state socialism to market liberalism failed to produce the expected socio-economic outcomes. Instead, a rather mixed system has developed where neither the new nor the old socio-economic forms are strong enough to dominate, resulting in a hybrid process of transformation.

The logic of economic liberalization in these societies has not automatically led to political liberalization and the democratic reconstitution of society. Autocratic politicians and technocrats drive the policies of neo-liberalization. Under these conditions, the liberalization of markets that have no prior check and balance mechanisms in place does not create synchronic democratization. Instead, amorphous forms of capital accumulation patterns and oligopolies appear. It would not then be incorrect to argue that post-communist economies (with their giant state enterprises, factories, vast natural reserves and state-owned distribution networks) were articulated in the bureaucratic-political remnants of the Communist regimes (L. P. King, 2001, pp. 519-529) or in the new economic and political elites in Turkey. (This is indeed contrary to the flawless transitionalist expectations of neo-liberal grand theories and market universalism.) Although the degree of articulation between the old political-managerial elites and the new ones varies from society to society, the symbiosis between the two continues to be a significant factor. Thus, new patterns of class inequality, poverty and mass deprivation follow the process of transition in these societies. In the Turkish case, as I will demonstrate, the malformation of market dynamics have similarly had negative consequences for the foundations of civil society and the development of a plural economic system.

The story is no different if we consider the process of democratization. The transition to multi-party politics did not automatically lead to democratization in the political sphere nor did the breakdown of party-state apparatuses result in the emergence of an organised civil society and non-oligarchic and inclusive elite formation. Apart from a few exceptional cases (e.g., the Solidarity Movement in Poland, which created an autonomous political space distinct from the socialist party-state), most East European societies proved incapable of organising opposition and creating an independent civil society (Bernhard, 1993, pp. 307-326). The Polish Worker's Movement of the 1970s and 1980s created a fracture between civil society and the party-state, and thus led to the birth of a new non-bureaucratic political elite (Gill, 2002, pp. 24-27). The presence of dissenting intelligentsia, apart from in a few cases (such as the Czech Republic), did not radically challenge the monolithic political structures that hindered the growth of a plural democratic society. In many cases, their contribution to broadening civil society and consolidating democracy remained limited, in part because those elites were recruited from the ranks of the previous ruling parties or from the opposition benches within the party. As Gill (2002, pp. 32-4, 66-67) indicates, the old communist elite managed to stay in power after the collapse of communism instead of giving birth to new genres of political elite/networks in civil society. Bulgaria and Romania are the two most prominent examples of this trend.

In the cases of the former republics of the USSR, the former communist elite grasped the initiative by raising the flag of nationalism and independence-seeking politics, consequently establishing a plebiscitary democracy in Georgia (Gill, 2002, pp. 49-51). In Russia and Ukraine, 'an amalgam of the oppositionist and old regime forces' claimed power and almost in a stalemate fashion ruled the country. In these cases, both communists and nationalists seem to merge, with the nomenklatura regime gradually being replaced with presidential systems where the populism of charismatic leaders overshadowed parliamentarians (Gill, 2002, p. 61). In the Turkish case, however, a dual structure has emerged in the ruling elite, an elite informed by two distinctly different traditions: the state's elitist republican tradition and the populist tradition. From 1997 onwards, this bifurcation became increasingly visible at the political-ideological level and influenced, unsurprisingly, the dynamics of civil society (associations, parties, intellectuals, etc.). Civil society was divided along this line of confrontation, a confrontation in which the former proved strong enough to counterbalance the latter. This suggests that the structure of civil society is subjected to competition, primarily between the fractions of the ruling elites. Inner divisions within civil society were superimposed via the reshuffling of political elites. Indeed, the numerous political positions also index the fractures in political society. This dual structure appears to be representative of democratization in Turkey.

In East European societies, socio-economic patterns of transition indicate how certain segments of the old nomenklatura and new oligarchs succeeded in uniting their interests. Lawrence King (2001, pp. 493-507) suggests that strategies of close interaction between the new economic elite and the old political elite were characteristic of clientelistic post-Communist market formation. However, many of the unequal and clientelist distribution patterns prevailed even during the communist period (Tarkowski, 1981). As Lawrance King emphasises the 'presupposition of neo-classical theory of transition, [...] the introduction of markets and private property do not create efficient organizational outcomes', nor do new oligarchic elites lay the foundation for capitalist market mechanisms (2001, pp. 526). To illustrate the complexity of transition, Tomusk examines the process of new and old forms of elite formation, aided by Pierre Bourdieu's (1998b) notion of *state nobility* (Tomusk, 2000, pp. 269-282). The new patterns of elite formation and capital accumulation appear to be oligarchic and clientelist in nature, and clearly contradicts the logic of plural and open civil society. Indeed, in many cases, the new networks of political power and economic distribution exclude large sections of the working classes and are controlled by small circles of corrupt politicians, senior bureaucrats and businessmen. In these societies, including Turkey, we do not see the creation of an open public sphere and competitive market relations for various sections of society, instead we see an oligarchic economic transition from state-led economies. Non-transparent market liberalization has not encouraged the participatory dynamics of civil society and aided the formation of oligarchic elite.

An important factor that shapes the future of democratic transition in these societies is the formation of new nation states with no substantial experience of self-governance. In some of these cases, in part related to the Soviet heritage, the state's institutional capacities and civil society's autonomous formation did not occur. Some of the Central European and the Black Sea societies have been dramatically challenged by the revival of ethnic-regional identities (Peteri, 2000, pp. 367-384; Offe, 2001, pp. 178-182; McIntosh et al., 1995, pp. 939-968; Derluguian, 1999, pp. 3-27). In some cases, the re-generation of separatist or autonomy seeking sub-national identities vertically divided state-elites, and even some networks of organizations and civil society (Cornell, 2002). The weakening of the state apparatus created a crossroad that could either lead to further democratization and the restructuring of political liberties or to chaotic civil wars and the violation of rights (as in Romania, Georgia, Yugoslavia and Albania). Given the fact that democratization is also directly linked to governmental capacities (Tilly, 2002, pp. 6-9), the collapse of state capacities led to severe crises and intra-societal conflicts, even before civil society was reconstructed in a plural way. Therefore, various particularistic tendencies in society – organised along ethnic, religious, regional, political etc. cleavages – may also undermine the sustainability of a plural and democratic society, unless these cleavages are checked and balanced by democratic principles and mechanisms. Coming to terms with multi-ethnic and multi-religious society has dominated the political agenda in Turkey, as well as constituted one of the main problems with regards to democratization.

Where the centralist capacities of governments are overwhelming, both democracy and freedoms are threatened by the state. In these societies, the state appears either unaccountable or non-transparent in its dealings with civil society. These extremes illustrate that democracy emerges as a middle-point between blatant authoritarianism and rampant chaos. Therefore, it is important to comprehend how the state and civil society have historically been posited against each other. When the state/government lacks those centralising capabilities, society experiences different forms of decentralisation, organised violence and/or civil wars. When neither the legal-institutional framework nor the political culture is able to balance excesses of this kind, arbitrary violation of human rights and the destruction of liberties is the likely outcome. If we consider Tilly's argument further, what makes a society or a political system work democratically is not civil society as such, that is, as a transcendentally democratic entity, but rather a democratically organised civil society, which balances the state's authoritarian tendencies. While such a dichotomy appears to suggest that the state and civil society are the two dominant constituent parts for democracy in most cases, democracy can only be sustainable if civil society is also democratically structured. Therefore, it is a common mistake to presume that the equation is necessarily a zero-sum equation. Democratic mechanisms are not necessarily immanent in civil society but need to be incorporated into traditions and institutions. This suggests that both the state tradition and civil society must evolve along pluralistic democratic principles and culture. In some cases, the overt militant pursuit of particular interests at the expense of others or uneven institutionalisation of power in society (either between interest groups or political, ethnic, regional and/or religious minorities) undermines the very foundations of democracy. Such particularistic groups and political cleavages may constitute the individual parts of civil societies, yet, if they cease to function democratically, they jeopardise both civil society and democracy. The presence of a political authority that maintains the rule of law is similarly a precondition of plural civil society. Without this, the power vacuum is filled by illegal armed gangs, regional warlords and the mafia, resulting in the criminalisation of large sections of economic and social life (Barany, 2002, p. 150; Nodia, 1995, pp. 104-116).

The unchecked intervention of a strong state authority in ethnic and religious issues represents the other extreme. This certainly appears to be the case for most Black Sea region societies, societies that have a relatively non-homogenous ethnic background (C. King, 2001, pp. 529-552). In Russia (a multi-ethnic and multi-religious society), the political agenda appears to be eclipsed by the issue of coping with autonomy-seeking regions and republics (Duncan, 1999, pp. 63-83; Rowley, 2000, pp. 23-42). Excessive and disproportionate use of force in Chechnya and other similar (potentially forthcoming) problems with other regions indicate that under the influence of rising Russian nationalism Russia could move towards de-liberalization, silencing dissident views and suppressing mass media. Unlawful state intervention was also prevalent in Bulgaria during the 1980s. The Turkish minority's struggle to resist discriminatory policies and to gain cultural rights in the 1980s and the 1990s was similar in nature to the struggle of the Hungarian Catholic population in Romania (Verdery, 1993). Georgia's tension with autonomy/independence seeking Abkhazia and South Ossetia (Cornell, 2002, pp. 245-276) and the conflict between Azerbaijan and Armenia regarding the status of Karabagh, leading to the irredentist occupation of Armenia, are also the result of ethnically diverse societies.

These cases of ethnic decentralisation tend to pose serious challenges to nations-states. When addressed democratically, the demands for ethno-cultural rights strengthen plural civil society. However, when not, they further deteriorate democratization. Such sub-national demands either lead to the restoration of authoritarian centralism or to the vertical fragmentation of the democratic capacities of civil society along ethnic, regional and religious lines. In Bulgaria, the excessive authoritarian capabilities of the Bulgarian state in the mid-1980s systematically discriminated against the ethnic Turkish minority, which constituted approximately 8.5 per cent of the Bulgarian population. Although these policies continued during the early years of the post-communist rule, the process of democratization and closer ties with the EU in the 1990s has almost resolved the situation democratically (Dimitrova & Dragneva, 2001, pp. 89-90). The Movement of Rights and Freedoms (MRF), a predominantly ethnic Turkish party, has been part of post-communist coalition governments, somewhat compensating for Bulgarian state actions in the 1980s. Contrary to the secessionist expectations of the ethnic Turkish minority, MRF became an important component of Bulgarian democratic life, successfully allied with both the Bulgarian Socialist Party and the NDSV of Simeon II (Barany, 2002, p. 147). Irrespective of these positive developments, the Roma minority in Bulgaria has not experienced similar benefits nor been included into Bulgarian democratic composition. Discrimination against the Roma population in Bulgaria, which is as large as the Turkish community, has not been totally eradicated (McIntosh et al., 1995). However, despite these difficulties, Barany (2002) argues that the development of civil society and the consolidation of democracy in Bulgaria have progressed far beyond the Balkan standards.

One of the most pertinent examples in terms of acute inter-ethnic tensions and weak government is Georgia. As Ghia Nodia (1995, pp. 104-116) claims, Georgia has been through various stages of paramilitary fights, civil wars and coup attempts. The rise of the populist nationalist leader, Zviad Gamsakhurdia, to the office of president of Georgia in 1991 was accompanied by another period of turbulent politics. The authoritarian populism of Gamsakhurdia created conflicts among the Georgian elite and stirred ethnic tensions with South Ossetia and Abkhazia. Despite being removed from power, inter-ethnic conflicts dominated Shevardnadze's presidency. The ethnic composition of Georgian society in the post-communist period has undermined nation-state formation and democratization. The ongoing tension with Abkhazia and Ossetia hindered the capacities of central government and made the political impasse durable (C. King, 2001, pp. 533-535). Politically and economically, Georgia appears in constant search of foreign aid and international support. Indeed, the weakness of the state appears to be the main obstacle for further democratization and economic recovery as well as for re-structuring Georgian civil society. All the aforementioned cases indicate that the components of civil society are strongly affected by the dynamics of nation building. The political problems of these societies are directly linked to the questions of how to balance overly strong authoritarian state traditions, which monopolistically control the public sphere and hinder the flourishing of civil society and certain rights, and/or how a weak decentralised state is incapable of providing the basic conditions for democracy to function effectively, such as: a working judiciary, minimum security and the rule of law, without resulting in bloody civil wars or mafia-led systems.

Attila Agh (1999, pp. 263-279) indicates that both democratization and civil society in post-Communist societies are connected to the manner in which state sovereignty is perceived. Furthermore, their political evolution during the period of nation-state formation similarly impacts on democratization. The relevance of nation building for democracy and civil society may appear insignificant at first glance, however ethnic and regional issues procure central positions in the political agendas of many, if not all, Black Sea societies. The solution of ethno-regional tensions via nation-state building is then significant for democratization and the development of plural civil society. The problems surrounding democratization in Black Sea societies are linked to the granting of cultural and/or administrative rights to minorities (Grodeland et al., 2000, pp. 43-66). If the demands of ethnic, religious and regional identities are democratically solved, the development of authoritarian state strategies considerably diminishes. In some countries, e.g., the Czech Republic, Slovakia, Yugoslavia, Bulgaria, Georgia and Russia, the fate of civil society and plural democracy is linked to the democratic solution of ethnic-regional questions. The Turkish case displays similar characteristics. Democratization in Turkey throughout the 20th century can be viewed through the process of nation building by the political and military-bureaucratic elite, as well as how this process impacted on the creation of a plural society.

In addition to political processes, socio-economic processes have a decisive effect on the consolidation of an organised civil society. Transition from etatist-command economies to market economies radically changes the patterns of class formation and the role of political elite (Szelenyi & Kostello, 1996; L. P. King, 2001; Evans & Mills, 1999; Brada, 1996; Murrell, 1996). As Brada (1996, pp. 70-76) indicates the process of privatization in post-Communist societies follows different patterns from simple market liberalization. The former East Germany, currently incorporated into the body of strong German economy, has experienced a different transition. While privatization in Hungary was primarily based on foreign investors, problems still exist. The voucher privatization programmes in Poland and the Czech Republic are designed to balance large participation and concentrate ownership, yet the success of these programmes remains questionable. Apart from the privatization programmes, start-up firms and small enterprises have impacted economically. Brada suggests that entrepreneurs of start-ups firms 'tend to come from well-educated backgrounds and from the managerial ranks of state-owned enterprises, from research institutions/centres or from the state bureaucracy'.

The privatization policies of the 1980s and the mushrooming of private companies and conglomerates in Turkey suggest that in transition economies one method of securing capital accumulation requires establishing strong links with government officials and the bureaucracy (Buğra, 1994). The new pattern of accumulation was structured around the symbiotic relationship between corrupt politicians, senior bureaucrats and business. Relationships of a similar nature have been identified and theorised by scholars in post-communist transitions, irrespective of significant variations in the scale and scope of these relationships in the different post-communist societies (Bourdieu, 1998a; Tomusk, 2000). Market liberalization was interpreted as an opportunity to make public resources available to party members and the party elites, as well as one that creates extra economic incentives and loans from public banks. From this perspective, the transition to a market-oriented society has yet to materialise. A high level of corruption, resulting from the shady relationships between the bureaucracy, the political elite and the new generation of business tycoons, is a typical characteristic of these economies. Widespread corruption and clientelist management undermined the economic foundations of plural civil society and, in some cases, led to the creation of authoritarian populist parties.

Democracy, Civil Society and Military-Bureaucratic Managerialism in Turkey

Turkey's pattern of semi-peripheral development began in the 20th century with the disintegration of the agrarian-bureaucratic empire (and its backward rural economy) and the commencement of a questionable democratic tradition under the auspices of a parliamentary monarchy. The first decades of the century were representative of a semi-colonised society unable to control its market and resources (İnsel, 1996). Furthermore, its democracy was not institutionalized and protected from autocratic rulers and the putschist-tendencies of the military and its civil society was not sufficiently structured to counter an autocratic state tradition. As a result of centuries of dependency on capitalist core markets, the Turkish social formation evolved bureaucratically and was centralised politically. However, it continued to be socio-economically backward and the centralisation programme was largely ineffective. The imperial legacy also resulted in significant impacts on the successive processes of contemporary nation building, national elite formation and civil society. The weight of industrial production and the power of working class movements in the Ottoman society were negligible (Quataert, 1994). Indeed, the politically active class was the Ottoman bureaucracy.

In this system, the state elite immediately attempted to undermine the influence of local notables (*Ayan*), who demanded greater autonomy and recognition of their rights through the administrative centralisation. The non-Muslim merchant class was also not exempt from the interventions of the state, albeit for those that were under the protection of foreign powers. As a result of this protection, the non-Muslim bourgeoisie emerged as the dominant opponent of the ruling bureaucratic elite, which had systematically and gradually increased its influence on the economic and cultural life of the empire.

As an Asiatic social formation (İslamoğlu-İnan, 1987; Keyder, 1976), where political power was monopolised by the Sultan and his patrimonial bureaucracy, private ownership of land was considerably limited until the late 1850s and the confiscation of the wealth of state bureaucrats common practice. Religious foundations, which provided certain services, however managed to gain limited autonomy and exemptions. The excessively centralised political-administrative system hindered the development of semi-autonomous local authorities or city-states during the Ottoman period (Mardin, 1969, pp. 265-267); the imperial state apparatus undertook military, bureaucratic and religious functions via a relatively tight monopoly. This perhaps explains why the short-lived tradition of local and/or regional self-rule did not evolve after the 1808 *Sened-i Ittifak*. An asymmetry between political-bureaucratic and socio-economic institutions marked the Ottoman social formation. In contrast to Western development, neither a strong land-owning class nor a politically demanding urban bourgeoisie developed in Turkey. The progress of a relatively autonomous civil society *vis-à-vis* 'the political society' has then not been visible. The decision-making processes were protected with zeal by the military-bureaucratic state apparatus. Ironically, the strategies that hoped to modernise the obsolete institutions of the state further contributed to this process via the centralisation of resources and the means of control. Exposure to European modernity allowed the ruling bureaucratic-military elite to counterbalance the decentralising trends visible in Ottoman society. Modernization in the Ottoman context implied the modernization of state institutions rather than society in general. Administrative and cultural modernization surpassed the modernization in social, technological and economic fields.

Hegel in his *Philosophy of Right* (1953, p. 41) argues that the right of possession and appropriation are necessary conditions of civil society (*Bürgerliche Gessellscahft*), yet they are insufficient unless this right is recognised. In the first quarter of the 19th century this *right* had not been institutionalized, and non-Muslims' and Muslims' rights were limited by the patrimonial state tradition. The recognition of the right of property and the right of life, formulated under *Habeas Corpus* and the tradition of civil society, began to gain weight in Ottoman society after the introduction of reform packages, designed by westernised bureaucrats, for non-Muslim subjects. Similar to Hegel's (1953, p. 39, 121-122) criticism of Roman agrarian laws in creating a clash between public and private ownership of land, Western states criticised the Ottoman legal-political system for arbitrarily making non-Muslim citizens' rights vulnerable. As a reaction to the logic of the patrimonial bureaucratic system that considers the economic, cultural and social levels subordinate, Western influence on the Ottoman Empire hoped to institutionalise and enshrine the cultural and economic rights of subjects. Both the *Tanzimat* (Reorganization) and *Islahat* (Rehabilitation) verdicts hoped to create the foundations for institutionalising those rights, albeit with different concerns (Lewis, 1968).

The reforms hoped to impact on the Ottoman social structure, a structure organised along religious and ethnic lines (*Millet* system) (Ortaylı, 1995; Mardin, 1997). Given this social structuring and the numerous ethno-religious communities that existed in the empire, the networks of solidarity were not structured on general social principles but on cultural-religious distinctions. The formation of civil society in Turkey then appears to display an atypical pattern of post-imperial development characterised by ethno-religious cleavages in civil society rather than economic-legal. The existence of such cleavages compensated for the weakness nature of organizational networks and civil society, even in contemporary Turkey. The extent to which civil society lacked structural and institutional foundations meant that these cleavages tried to fill the gap, serving a similar function to Hegelian *corporations*. Delayed capitalist development, which developed under an agricultural imperial social formation, and the lack of an institutional framework aided the appearance of this phenomenon.

Under such conditions, the formation of the bourgeoisie as a legally recognised class – through the recognition of property rights – was hindered. The lack of an industrial revolution in Ottoman territories similarly limited the formation of a mature working class movement struggling for political and economic rights. The relatively late emergence of the industrial revolution in Ottoman society explains why labour movements and professional organizations were infantile. The existing labour organizations (such as guilds) were either weak, particularly when compared to their western counterparts, or were formed along ethnic and local lines (Quataert, 1994, pp. 19-36). Foreign funded projects, such as the construction and maintenance of railways, tended to employ non-Muslim workers; indeed, non-Muslim workers outnumbered Muslims (Tunçay & Zürcher, 1995, p. 253). Towards the end of the 19th century, some trade unions and socialist ideas were identified by their ethnic-class elements (Adanır, 1995). In such an agro-bureaucratic empire neither the working class nor civil society were shaped along notion of a conflict of interests. While society was vertically divided *vis-à-vis* culture, it was horizontally structured in terms of status (both for the bureaucracy and the peasantry). Ottoman civil society then was susceptible to vertical divisions and clientelistic ethnic-regional ties of solidarity. The process of democratising Ottoman society suggests that the class dimension of civil society was embryonic and fragmented. It also suggests that civil society was incapable of balancing the power of political society.

In the Ottoman-Turkish context, the principal dynamic of change was not social-economic forces but international dynamics and the state's new generation of western-leaning and educated bureaucrats. Modernization thus authorised the monopoly of systemic design to state bureaucrats. As a result of the uneven modernization of institutions, the ruling military-bureaucratic elite was exposed to modernization significantly more than other sections of society. This phenomenon also appears in the development of civil society in modern Turkey. Given that the modernization of the military-bureaucratic elite exceeded that of socio-economic institutions, the process itself can be characterised as happening 'from above', which similarly impacted on the development of civil society. The Ottoman-Turkish modernization granted authority to the bureaucratic elite and thus the political society monopolised the means of decision-making, designing the cultural, social and economic reforms that were to be adopted and the direction that modernization would followed. The managerialism of the bureaucratic elite suggests that it is not incorrect to conceive of the Ottoman elite in Gramscian terms, namely as *the state's organic intellectuals*. Kemal Karpat (1985, pp. 96-97) also employs such phraseology, referring to the bureaucrats as *bureaucratic-intelligentsia*. However, the process of modernization by state bureaucrats (the new intelligentsia) did not automatically imply democratization or the strengthening civil society. On the contrary, it frequently represented the centralisation of political power as well as the means of control and representation. Turkish modernization thus took the form of patrimonial modernization, a modernization that evolved at the expense of the popular masses' discontent and without seeking a broad consensus. The reforms proposed and implemented by the state's organic intellectuals were indicative of *passive revolutions* where mass mobilisation remained low and democratization was perceived to be secondary goal. The 19th and 20th century reforms introduced by enlightened autocratic bureaucrats and the Sultans were Janus-faced, displaying both progressive (liberal) and conservative (authoritarian) features. The Janus-faced nature of modernization is symptomatic of *the dialectic of modernization from above* and reflects the *Weltanschauung* of military-bureaucratic managerial strategies in Turkey. This led to a polarisation between the military-bureaucratic managers' *political capital* and the non-Turkish bourgeoisie's *economic capital*. In this sense, nation-state formation in Turkey evolved as a type of 'military-bureaucratic nation building', similar to that seen in the early stages of Spanish nationalism (Jensen, 2000, pp. 257-274).

The class configurations visible in this case suggest that, even after the non-Muslim bourgeoisie were replaced with their Turkish counterpart, neither the economic nor the institutional-legal frameworks for organised civil society were established. Moreover, between the two world wars, the monopolist tendencies of the state increased both politically and economically. The Turkish business class, closely in agreement with the protectionist policies of the state, failed to develop autonomy from the state; indeed, this dependence remained a dominant characteristic into the 1990s (Buğra, 1994). Patrimonially and clientelistically attached to politics, the

Turkish middle class became conscious of the significance of being on good terms with the political-bureaucratic circles (Güneş-Ayata, 1990). Furthermore, the monopolising tendencies of the state's bureaucrats ensured that the newly formed national bourgeoisie was under the protective-clientelist wings of political capital (Buğra, 1994; İlkin, 1993). Listian protectionism and Durkheimian solidarism, introduced by the state to combat class-warfare, authorised that labour movements and the middle classes did not challenge the unity of national interests. It was not until the mid-1960s that labour movements and the bourgeoisie were freely institutionalized, coinciding with a relative relaxation of the scrutinising of the freedom of association and union organizations. The social progressivism of the Republican People's Party (RPP) further consolidated the monopolistic control of civil society, non-governmental organizations and political culture. Given the elite's tendency to adopt various forms of *authoritarian modernization,* the Turkish revolution moved away from its initial *bourgeois-democratic character* and established itself as a *bourgeois-bureaucratic revolution.* The bourgeois-bureaucratic revolution enabled military-bureaucratic managerialism to create the socio-economic conditions for a series of socio-political reforms. The end result was the creation of a social order in the shadow of the state. Patrimonial modernization from above then created *a shadow civil society* and *a shadow democracy* where their preconditions, framework and content were formed by the modernising state. The state's monopolistic tendency to design a mission for social institutions overshadowed the development of autonomous institutions and, in light of the possible excommunication of social institutions, survived into the recent period. Numerous examples of ostracism are visible, including human rights associations (Çalı, 2003), ethnic-religious organizations and associations (Schüler, 2000, pp. 197-250) and dissident movements.

The managerial logic's eagerness to colonise civil society and incorporate it within the framework of national security and a unitarian division of labour turned civil society into an *object,* rather than an active subject of transformation. Through this process, civil society became the field of experimentation as opposed to the realisation of autonomous institutions and traditions. As a result, unlike the well-organised political core, social networks and organizations are without institutionalized autonomy. For structural historical reasons, *authoritarian progressivism* outbalanced *populist-libertarian politics,* and the gap between the popular domain and the parties of the state elite could not easily be bridged. Thus, the split between the *high culture of the elite* and the *low culture of the masses* remained as relevant for Turkish political culture (Gellner, 1995; Mardin, 1973) as the rift between state elitism and political populism. The paradox of patrimonial modernization begins with the state's perceived role in teaching 'civil society what to do and what not to do' and around which issues to mobilise. Such macro-pedagogical strategies created a replica of political society at the expense of civil society and democratic traditions (Açıkel, 2002, pp. 117-139).

Military-bureaucratic managerialism and *nomenklatura culture* in the Mediterranean and East European societies attempted to monopolise *the political capital* (Bourdieu, 1998a). The birth of 'state nobility' in the Bourdieuan sense (1998b) is not only a symptom of a military-bureaucratic managerial culture but also a sign of semi-peripheral state formation, if not malformation. This malformation indicates the dialectic of modernization from above. Historically, managerialism of this kind dates back to the pre-Republican periods and was shaped by the Asiatic military-political system of Ottoman society. However, the nationalization of the monopoly of power strengthened its capabilities in the more recent period. The principal ideological priorities of this managerial logic in Turkey are threefold, namely to develop: a staunchly defined Turkish nationalism that rejects centrifugal sub-national cultural identities; a strictly defined notion of secularism/laicism that resists various forms of religious populism in politics; and a corporatist notion of class formation that limits class-based understandings of politics (Ahmad, 1995). These three objectives, which aimed to establish a unitarian social fabric, hinder the formation of civil society along ethnic-regional, religious-sectarian and class lines. Indeed, the contours of civil society were drawn with these criteria in mind.

Undoubtedly, these objectives had severe repercussions on the nature of civil society in Turkey. The clientelist dependency of the Turkish bourgeoisie and the visible weakness of labour movements allowed the military-bureaucratic managers to appear as the most effectively organised force in Turkish society. Given that the vast majority of population was rural and illiterate, it seems inevitable that a patrimonial managerialism of a bureaucratic kind would evolve. Patrimonialism as a Janus-faced tradition has had both protective and restrictive effects on civil society (İnsel, 1996; Mardin, 1980; İlkin, 1993) and on the bourgeoisie. Although reformist in its intentions, the strategies of modernization from above (Trimberger, 1978) reproduced the imperial tradition in modernist disguise, resulting in a constant confrontation between the state elite and the popular masses/elites. Military-bureaucratic managerialism developed against liberal-populist politics as well as the democratic dynamics of civil society.

The military interventions and memorandums in 1960, 1971, 1980 and 1997 introduced new institutions and cadres into the political realm from above and hindered the institutionalisation of social 'check and balance' mechanisms. Thus, the military-bureaucratic logic gained relative autonomy (Karaosmanoğlu, 1993, pp. 19-34) above 'the conflicting and anarchic tendencies of civil society', rather than civil society gaining autonomy from the state. The somewhat patronising idea that the state should regulate society on the grounds that society is immature and prone to self-destruction in Turkey is typically justified in a Hegelian fashion. Authoritarian-military interventions, besides legitimising this view, also influenced the constitutions. Both rightwing and leftwing movements in the 1950s and 1970s, for different reasons, encountered the reservations of the military; successive constitutions created after *coup d'etats* were designed accordingly. The constitutions of 1961 and 1982 and the amendments of 1971 and 1973 were formulated after *coup d'etats* with the help of bureaucratic elites and with limited consideration of the dynamics/demands of large sections of society. Each of the constitutions was created with an idea of the type of society that should be avoided.

These constitutional changes, particularly the 1982 Constitution, displayed an inherent suspicion towards party politics in particular and a distrust of autonomous social dynamics in general. During that period, the State Security Courts – composed of military and civilian judges and designed to deal with what was conceptualised as threats to national security – tried thousands of intellectuals, academics, union leaders, students, journalists, politicians, etc. As a result, *coup d'etats* – contrary to the thesis of modernization from above – had 'a regressive and de-modernising effect on the Turkish society'. The 1961 and 1982 Constitutions and the more recent 1997 Western Study Group (*Batı Çalışma Grubu*) considered how best to administer civil society. The logic of bureaucratic managerialism assumed that civil society is flexible enough to respond to *political engineering* from above.

Despite its democratic outlook, the 1961 Constitution attempted to balance the popular rightwing parties' majoritarian rule with a form of mild state elitism. Undoubtedly, the broadly defined political liberties and rights and the appearance of minority parties in parliament (enshrined in the 1961 Constitution) improved the conditions for creating the foundations of a democratic civil society. However, military-bureaucratic managerialism attempted to limit the possibility of a populist party monopolising the political scene, as was the case with the Democratic Party in the 1950s. To serve this objective, the 1961 Constitution enshrined the protection of democratic rights and laid the legal foundations for a democratic and plural society (Tanör, 2000; Soysal, 1987). Nonetheless, the desire to keep progressive parties in power led to the introduction of a subtle patrimonial-pedagogic approach, perhaps further reflecting the distrust of the state elite of the masses and populist elites. For this reason, the Constitution of 1961 visibly increased the role of the military and high bureaucrats in the political system, granting them lifetime membership of the National Unity Committee in Parliament and authorising the formation of semi-autonomous bureaucratic institutions to check the 'excesses' of political parties.

The 1961 Constitution also granted the military a consulting role in the National Security Council (Tanör, 2000, pp. 388-402). The NSC was initially formed as an advisory body, but after the implementation of the 1982 Constitution it proved itself to rather autonomous, representing the general views of the Turkish military. The 1982 Constitution authorised that members of the High Command were immune from judiciary procedures and were given the unprecedented right to design the 'electoral system, judiciary, the police, martial law, universities, associations, unions and collective bargaining etc.' (Özbudun, 2000, p. 115). Through constitutional regulations and the political culture (shaped after the military interventions) the military's systemic position as 'the custodian of the Republic and the Constitution' was strongly confirmed and reaffirmed. Such a systemic position confirms Heper's (1993, pp. 3-9) belief that Turkish bureaucratic elites are reluctant to consider democracy as the reconciliation of conflicting social interests, rather than the application of purely enlightened models. Metin Heper (1985, p. 94) argues that since the foundation of the new republic the bureaucracy, rather than positioning itself ideologically to the left or the right, developed *Weltanschauung*, and thus perceived of itself as the guardian of the state.

The most regressive development during the 1980 *coup d'etat* was the introduction of a series of anti-democratic laws, which restricted freedom of association and freedom of expression with the rhetoric that conflicts of interests would be avoided as a result. The unions, universities, public sector workers and the mass media, alongside many other sections of society, were closely scrutinised. Thus, the institutional grounds for civil society to regulate itself were paralysed. Instead of encouraging the process of social reconciliation (based on the position that imminent conflicts of interest would be avoided), the military regime opted for limiting or abolishing associational grounds. As a result of a great level of distrust of social mechanisms and non-governmental initiatives, Turkish society became susceptible to chronic atomisation and the interests of large segments of the working masses remained underrepresented.

In the fields of economics, this managerialism created new forms of *technocratic tutelage*, in part indicative of the post-military government's invitation to many technocrats/managers from the US to launch radical economic liberalization programmes. These new elites were given unprecedented authority and were allowed to climb to the highest levels of power. These technocrats were meant to aid the speedy integration of the Turkish economy into global capitalism. Yet such a reshuffling of the elite, at the expense of traditional bureaucrats (Heper, 1989, pp. 460-471), did not simply bring about a radical shift in terms of the process of decision-making but also impacted on state-society relations. It marked a new stage of managerial strategies, which like military-managerialism, similarly disregarded civil society and social dynamics. The stabilisation programmes, which addressed the issues of high inflation and public deficit, in particular neglected social aspects (Boratav, 1992, pp. 63-76). These privatization policies were implemented with the support of the state's economic enterprises (SEEs) (Saraçoğlu, 1994, pp. 63-75; İlkin, 1994, pp. 77-86) and the vast majority of municipal services (Waterbury & Suleiman, 1990). 1980s and 1990s' neo-liberal technocratic strategies of privatization did not create institutions that would aid in the development of civil society, but instead gave birth to new paternalist-clientelist corruptions and widespread partisanship and nepotism. As a result, technocratic managerialism was inefficient management plagued by widespread fraud and clientelism. As this technocratic managerialism could not be checked by an already dis-organised civil society, or by the obsolete legal system and discouraged judiciary, the process of (mal)liberalization was aborted, partly because of a lack of transparency and accountability and partly because of a lack of check and balance mechanisms.

The dramatic decline in the state's capabilities to carry out its judiciary, security and legal functions gave momentum to widespread corruption and facilitated the involvement of Italian-style mafia networks in business and politics. Both the legal infrastructure and the enforcement of law proved inefficient in dealing with such a malformation. The privatization and tendering processes became open to non-market dynamics, i.e., the corrupt networks of bureaucrats, mafia and politicians. This trend continued until the early 2000s when the State Security Courts decided to try organised crime gangs. (Mal)liberalization of this kind, which undermined the market mechanisms and the economic foundations of civil society, led to the birth of new forms of shady favouritism instead of leading to the creation of an open, competitive and efficient economy. As a consequence of a decade of corruption, the process of market (mal)liberalization created a siphoned and mismanaged economy. While not as acute as its counterparts in post-Communist societies, it would not be wrong to argue that – given the weakness of organised civil society and the non-transparent state services – the transition from state-led economies to market-oriented ones were frequently characterised by widespread corruption and oligarchic class formation. Indeed, we could consider this period in Turkey as a period of 'patrimonial capitalism' (L. P. King, 2001, p. 506); patrimonial in the sense that uneven and corrupt distribution of wealth was sheltered or overlooked by the political and bureaucratic elites.

With regards to the crippling effects of (mal)liberalization on Turkish civil society, parallel developments are also observable in post-Communist societies. Crony capitalism, shady tenders and (mal)liberalization allowed a new class of entrepreneurs to flourish, a class whose influence of public opinion and political processes increased over time. As a result of partisan privatization and government's incentive strategies, a new generation of tycoons in Turkey subsequently developed. During the 1980s, aided by low interest rate loans, tax exemptions and shady business relations with governments and bureaucrats, the formation of an oligarchic class gained momentum. As the process of clientelist liberalization benefited a handful of the new generation's holding companies, its impacts on civil society turned to be greater than expected. The increasing number of national and local TV channels allowed the new oligarchs to gradually extend their influence over politics and public opinion. The widespread involvement of the new business circle in the media assured the political and economic ties and maintained their market positions *vis-à-vis* rival tycoons. At this point, another serious threat to democracy and self-reflexive civil society emerged. The clientelisation of the means of mass communication, which were based on shady business affairs, led to feuds between business and journalists.

Under the regime of non-accountable patrimonial capitalism then neither a purely market-oriented civil society nor patrimonial networks in political and bureaucratic channels benefited democratization.

Despite the progress of Turkish mass media to create a multi-vocal society, their lack of institutionalized autonomy *vis-à-vis* those oligarchs remain a pressing problem. The democratic representation of numerous viewpoints and the circulation of less-distorted forms of information, therefore, are also fundamental concerns for the consolidation of democracy and civil society. Indeed, without a multi-vocal and free media, public opinion is vulnerable and subject to manipulations. Accountable mass media is a constitutive element of democracy and civil society (Keane, 1993) and thus the nature of the state authority and the power of economic oligarchs similarly impacts on the uncensored production and dissemination of information. In the Turkish case, the misrepresentation of public opinion has been connected to: the state's and governments' direct/indirect intervention – which took the form of economic incentives/sanctions – in some media institutions (Alpay, 1993, pp. 69-91); destructively distorting competition between various interest groups through mass communication (including political blackmail and vilification); the control of the market by a few giant oligopolies; and the marginalisation – if not disappearance – of other media.

The nationalist-etatist agenda undermined the birth of a plural-democratic society by insisting on an 'official line' for the public; the decreasing state monopoly in mass media regarded by many as a healthy development, proved otherwise. The pluralist representation of views also soon turned out to be a symptom of the conflict of interests between emerging oligarchs. The 1990s witnessed great competition between the newly created holding companies and the bosses/managers – especially in the areas of privatization of state enterprises, huge-budget tenders, government incentives and low interest loans – allowing us to better understand the dynamics behind intra-oligarchic conflicts over mass media. In the context of competing political and economic interests, private TV channels became effective instruments for interest-optimisation and political feuds. It would not be incorrect to argue that both the democratization process and civil society have been substantially hindered by the oligopolistically control and structure of mass media.

The experience of mass society was even bleaker. Despite the level of organization that some segments of civil society reached, the labour movement – primarily for ideological and organizational reasons – plunged into a deep crisis and the Turkish peasantry went through a period of massive *depauperation* (Boratav, 1991). Similarly, civil servants, blue-collar workers, agricultural workers, petty-producers and labour experienced real losses compared to previous decades. The low level of salaries both in the public and private sectors was accompanied by widespread poverty. (Mal)liberalization was followed by radical de-stabilisation of the labour market in general. Apart from a well-organised segment of the labour aristocracy, large sections of the working classes in industry, agriculture and services were forced to live just below the poverty line. Evans and Mills (1999, pp. 42-43) indicate a parallel trend in post-Communist societies where the re-structuration programmes primarily impacted on the traditional working class employed in heavy industry and the service sector. They also argue that – unlike the highly educated and entrepreneurial groups, which were on good terms with the political-bureaucratic elites – large sections of the masses could not benefit from the new economic system. As privatization created immense opportunities for the new generation of entrepreneurs, strategic connections with bureaucratic and political figures were of unprecedented importance.

For many of the newly flourishing, ambitious businessmen personal relations with political leaders were presented as an effective business card, including politicians such as Turgut Özal, Süleyman Demirel, Mesut Yilmaz and Tansu Çiller. Beside the high degree of favouritism at the top level, partisan methods of resource allocation also became quite common at the lower level. The involvement of bureaucrats and politicians in the networks of construction and other tenders indicates, in the Bourdieuan sense, the convertibility of *political-bureaucratic capital* into *economic capital*. Given the fact that the judiciary system and legal regulations systematically lagged behind in the new economic era, deterrent judiciary measures could not be taken to prevent widespread corruption and bribery. Even the highest judges expressed their concerns regarding their position and that of the more general judiciary, i.e., low salaries, politicisation and shady businesses. The transition to a corrupt system of administration through unguided and unbalanced liberalization inevitably left civil society paralysed. As the rule of law and accountability of the institutions failed, kleptocracy and nepotism were rampant. Moreover, various forms of financial and political corruption were sheltered by political-bureaucratic machine. In reaction to clientelist-usurpation networks, from the mid-1990s onwards, the masses (alienated by malliberalization) began to support either religious or nationalist populist parties. Turkish politics became vulnerable to a constant swing between bureaucratic-elitist and populist movements.

Both alternatives suffered from various deficiencies. It could be argued that the axis of democratization was shaped by the tension between technocratic managerialism and economic populism. The appeal of populism proved so effective that the deprived masses and conservative middle classes opted for populist parties. In the case of Turkey, this reaction to neo-liberalism was apparent in Islamic-conservative populism (Birtek & Toprak, 1993; Boratav, 1995). In some post-Communist societies, the reaction to both bureaucratic managerialism and clientelism allowed the masses to express their frustration in populist channels. Evans and Whitefield (1993) suggest that the social bases of party competition in post-Communist societies are based on 'cross cutting patterns of socio-economic, regional, ethnic or populist forms' (pp. 523-524). In some East European societies, these reactions were mobilised by ethnic and religious populist movements (Gregor, 1998, pp. 12-13). Under economic strain, the electorate may become susceptible to various forms of authoritarian-nationalist solutions, which are heavily coloured by the slogans of justice and national pride.

Various forms of populism marked by nationalist or religious rhetoric were also appealing and effective in 1990s Turkey. The oscillation between nationalist leftwing populism and nationalist right-wing populism (of either the ultra-nationalist or Islamic forms) interchangeably dominated the political agenda. Populist politics were founded on the charisma of leaders and their ethical and political promises to address deep-rooted problems. Compared to leftwing and nationalist versions of populism, the Islamic-populist movement relied on different networks and had a tendency of being more communitarian. Although Islamic-populist parties also relied on strong leadership (utilising their organizational ability to mobilise different sectors of society), they display certain distinctive features. Islamic-populist movements in Turkey appear to have taken advantage of both traditional and modern organizational forms (e.g., brotherhoods, foundations, modern political parties) (Ayata, 1993). Ironically, some elements of civil society have been incorporated into these movements. From the late 1980s onwards, many traditionally secular civil society organizations moved away from secular-modernist stances. The Islamic-populist movements – besides owning means of mass communication and securing the support of a number of intellectuals – have also been supported by traditionally leftwing and liberal organizations such as trade unions and business associations. The support of HAK-İŞ and MÜSİAD (the leading conservative trade union confederation and the association of medium-size businessmen) authorised the integration of Islamic populism into the modern institutions of civil society. With the support of several conservative foundations (*Vaqfs*) and brotherhoods (*Tariqats*), Islamic populist movements accessed financial opportunities and developed network capability (Bulut, 1997, pp. 395-425), as well as proved themselves effective in vertically shaping the channels of mobilisation along solidarist-communitarianist lines.

Islamic-populist parties then tried to unite the socio-cultural expectations of the urban poor and conservative rural areas, medium scale entrepreneurs and blue-collar workers, and the culturally alienated masses and the conservative electorate. The rise of Islamic-populist parties in Turkey was a direct outcome of governments' inability to address the socio-economic problems resulting from massive migration and cultural transformation. As leftwing parties dramatically failed to develop any tangible solutions to these problems, preoccupied instead with reshaping institutions that do not necessarily enhance civil society but consolidate official culture in different forms, they gradually lost electoral support in the outskirts of metropolitan cities. Despite the fact that new forms of official non-governmental organizations were launched by neo-Kemalist and centre-left groups (e.g., *Atatürkçü Düşünce Dernekleri* (ADD) (The Associations for Kemalist

Thought), *Çağdaş Yaşamı Destekleme Dernekleri* (ÇYDD) (the Association for the Support of Modern Life) (Erdoğan, 2000, pp. 251-282)), their activities remained limited to metropolitan cities and the educated urban middle-classes and their effect proved far beyond the scope of their network.

The polarisation between secular-republican and religious-Islamic traditions necessitates that we discuss a particular section of civil society: the *Alevi-Bektaşi* movement. Various Alevi Associations expressed their demands for greater recognition and representation in the public sphere, albeit unconnected from the outcome of the National Security Council memorandum of 27 February 1997. Alevi citizens (a persistently neglected and repressed group) in Turkey experienced a radical process of transition, attempting to re-define Alevism from that which dominated in the 1960s and 1970s. Alevi identity incorporates a political (usually centre-left or socialist) dimension and a religious-cultural dimension. The political dimension was naturally incorporated into secular-republican parties, i.e., CHP (Republican People's Party), however the religious dimension was not easily accommodated into the political system. Thus, the political and religious identities and expectations of Alevis differed: the former consolidated the official line and the latter did not. The question of recognition for the Alevis, as for many other ethnic and religious groups, remained one of the most challenging questions that the modern Turkish state has faced, especially given that the republican state formation rejected community-based definitions of citizen rights. The failure to recognise Alevi identity further contributed to the creation of barriers in building plural civil society (Schüler, 2000, pp. 200-211).

In stark contrast to the rise of the neo-Kemalist civil society, which coincided with an official desire to neutralise the anti-systemic effects of religious-conservative associations, the Alevi Association fulfilled a dual role in civil society *vis-à-vis* the official ideology: consolidating secular-republicanism and simultaneously consolidating their cultural-ethnic-religious rights in a plural civil society. While the secular state apparatus failed to control Islamic religious-conservative associations, foundations and networks, the Alevis and secular-republican circles approached each other. As a result of the military-bureaucratic managers' determination to create a shadow/dependent civil society, these secular associations – along with Kemalist NGOs (ADD, ÇYDD) – were encouraged to counterbalance their conservative-Islamic counterparts. In recent times, the relationship between secular-republican circles and the Alevis has changed. The Alevi associations have openly expressed their disappointment with official restrictions on the freedoms of belief and organization. It was not until the later 1990s that Alevi citizens were granted permission to open their prayer and gathering houses (*Cemevi*). Despite improved relations between the state and Alevi associations, there are still problems, primarily resulting from the rejection of recognition and restrictions on free association. Some Alevi organizations vocalised their demands to EU representatives, leading to a certain discomfort in nationalist-republican circles.

The systemic expectations of ADDs and ÇYDDs as NGOs are strikingly similar to the 1960s Associations for the Struggle against Communism. Paradoxically, while the generals after the 1980 *coup d'etat* pragmatically supported Islamic-conservative associations and networks as antidotes to leftwing activists and Communist ideology, in the late 1990s, the westernised, educated urban middle-classes were mobilised against the danger of Islamic fundamentalism. A similar strategy was also pursued in the 1970s when some sections of the ultra-nationalist Grey Wolfs were encouraged to stand against rising leftwing mobilisation. It would then be incorrect to theorise the interventions on civil society as merely repressive; they were in fact meant to engineer civil society in line with the projects of military-bureaucratic managerialism. From the 1997 military memorandum onwards, the axis of the confrontation is primarily ideological, perhaps representing two contradicting ways of life influenced by two antagonistic *Weltanschauungs*. The two sides simultaneously tried to reclaim political and ideological ground in civil society, suggesting that civil society should not simply be reduced to the activities of NGOs (Kaldor, 2003, pp. 5-27). However, the question mark remains over whether these institutions progress beyond monopolistic and semi-authoritarian tendencies and work for and towards a plural democratic civil society. The fact that these organizations (NGOs) are defined as outside of political society does not necessarily imply that their *Modus Operandi* is democratic and their objectives pluralistic and democratic. Indeed, assessing the polarisation between secular-republican and religious-Islamic organizations suggests that both currents lacked certain democratic characteristics in the past. The former tended to adopt a universalist form of authoritarianism, the latter an intolerant communitarian authoritarianism (Keyman & İçduygu, 2003, pp. 229-223).

The tension between secular-republican and conservative-Islamist politics was exacerbated when competition for the control of the state apparatus reached its climax. As the crises of unbalanced liberalization and the fragmentation of the political scene peaked, a new type of elite, originating in the political periphery, appeared, initially in the municipalities and then in parliament, i.e., populist-Islamic politicians. Similar to the centre-left ideology/movement of the 1970s, they gained increased electoral support among socio-economically deprived classes as a result of their populist and solidarist rhetoric. Having successfully won local elections in the big metropolitan cities (e.g., Ankara, İstanbul, Konya etc.), the conservative-Islamic municipalities gained greater opportunity to create their own associations and networks. It was via these new networks that the underrepresented currents of society began to be represented. Although the Islamic-conservative movement mobilised its well-organised communitarian networks in the poor neighbourhoods effectively, we should not assume that they were exclusively comprised of the lower-middle class masses. On the contrary, the interesting feature of the Islamic-conservative movements in Turkey is that they vertically cut civil society in such a way that – from the lower middle class and underpaid urban poor to the Islamic-conservative business circles and intellectuals – they represented a large fragment of society. Unsurprisingly, these networks channelled a substantial amount of material and human resources to the party and brotherhood members. In some respects, religious or semi-religious organizations operated like the Hegelian communitarian corporations, that is, against the egotistical and particularistic tendencies of the market, or, as Hegel termed, *the system of needs* (Hegel, 1953, pp. 152-153). Similar to what Cohen and Arato regarded as the welfarist trend in Hegel's work, which tried to overcome the deficiencies of the system of needs/market, Islamist-conservatives also attempted to compensate for what the system lacked. Like many other networks of solidarity (ethnic, religious-sectarian (*dini-mezhebi*), regional (*hemşehrilik*) or political), they hoped and attempted to transcend the overly individualistic structure of market liberalization. During the 1990s, NGOs as well as national-ethnic and religious movements were the strongest actors in civil societies throughout the world (Kaldor, 2003, pp. 23-24). It is then unsurprising that the rise of various types of communitarianism is interpreted as a response to the failures of neo-liberal states and markets. For this reason, Arato and Cohen (1992, p. 102) emphasise the implicit meaning behind Hegel's critique of the system of needs, i.e., the market. When the state fails to provide such welfare, the opportunity and need for alternative populist movements or clientelist networks to provide it grow. The reactions to such failures have led to a revival and/or reproduction of traditional social institutions in the age of globalisation. Similarly, in the Turkish case, when the modern political and economic institutions fail to address the complicated problems of participation and distribution, traditional networks are regenerated in existing structures.

However, in many cases and in contrast to the universalistic rhetoric of communitarianism, these networks are comprised of complicated clientelist networks, which are not necessarily open to the ordinary public. Irrespective of the religious, sectarian, ethnic, regional, etc., formations of civil society, they all appear to be eclipsed by the particularistic tendencies of identity politics or communitarian corporatism (in the Gramscian sense). At one point or another, all formations of civil society fail to fulfil their egalitarian promises, either by creating employment opportunities only for their members or by allocating resources exclusively to their sympathisers. In the case of Islamic communitarianism in Turkey, many sub-contracting firms (mostly from members of MÜSİAD) took advantage of the large budgetary capacities of the metropolitan municipalities, suggesting that populist strategies are frequently replaced with clientelistic networks created along partisan networks. Therefore, what appears to be a constitutive element of civil society, i.e., economic NGOs, are also components of clientelist networks, which are inclined to privatise the public sphere. The privatization of the public sphere suggests that NGOs and other similar institutions/organizations in Turkey, contrary to common belief, are not de-politicised, but are highly politicised in a partisan manner.

Conclusion: From Stalemate to a Pluralist-Democratic Civil Society

The preliminary analyses discussed above are far from capable of exhausting the theoretical and empirical implications of a broader analysis both in the Mediterranean and in the post-Communist contexts. The questions asked and the temporary answers provided should not be viewed as concrete or final. Our preliminary findings suggest that simplistic theses of market universalism and neo-liberal reconstruction are incapable of providing a satisfactory explanation of the development of civil society in Turkey. Similarly, the classical approach, emphasising NGOs' progressive role, does not fully apply to the Turkish case since these NGOs tend to operate as extensions of political society. Political partisanship and clientelist networks further particularise the objectives and the scope of non-governmental organizations. De-politicised institutions, hyper-politicised partisan institutions and sections of civil society have all failed to fulfil their role in creating a plural and democratic civil society in Turkey.

However, in spite of the impasses of previous *coup d'etats*, the constraining 1982 Constitution, the myth of the patrimonial state and clientelistic political networks, Turkish society represents an interesting example of semi-peripheral development. Despite 'various forms of inefficient oligopoly-like market structures and political networks' (Özbudun, 1981; Güneş-Ayata, 1990), Turkish society has visibly moved forward, questioning the paternalist/patrimonial culture of the state and the malfunctioning and unaccountable technocratic managerialism. In its encounter with legal and institutional restraints, Turkish society appears more mature than the establishment, an establishment where conservative managerial strategies resist change.

Rather than clinging to old clientelistic and patrimonial relations, Turkish society appears to have been more responsive to systemic failures and more willing to express its discontent in different ways. Besides widespread cynicism and civil disobedience, open criticism has become common practice in citizens' lives. While the institutionalisation of discontent at the level of civil society is far from satisfactory (due to a restrictive and illiberal legal framework), the demands for political rights and liberties are on the rise. Despite restrictions and discouragements, new forms of *spontaneous civil protest/disobedience* have recently been influential in expressing disappointment with the current political establishment (e.g., *One-Minute Darkness Campaign for a Clean Society*, civil servants' protests against the ban of unionisation and chronically low wages, headscarf protests by conservative women, cultural-linguistic demands of students).

The demise of the mythological image of the patrimonial-Asiatic state – as in Russia (Urban, 1998; Howard, 2002) – further contributes to the rise of effective social movements. The demystification of high politics should be considered as an important improvement in Turkey. The sharp decline in *the myth of state* is perhaps an unintended consequence of numerous governments' inability to deliver basic public services and to overcome deep legitimation crises. Similarly, the state's transcendental image as the ultimate moderator of corporatist national interest is increasingly challenged as rampant crony capitalism continues to remain unchecked and radical measures to ameliorate the conditions of lower-middle classes are not taken. However, as the state's declining willingness and capacity to redistribute becomes apparent, the more criticism and disillusionment with technocratic-bureaucratic strategies surface. This is especially the case for the lower-middle classes (which are in the worst position in terms of the level of organization compared to business associations), chambers and some trade unions who have become disillusioned. The economically unprotected segments of society (i.e., those portions of labour not belonging to the relatively well-protected labour aristocracy) are more likely to vote for populist parties with the expectation of socio-economic compensation.

The fragmentation of the labour movement – between public and private sectors, civil servants (KESK) and workers, labour aristocracy and large sections of minimum-waged working class, large and politically divided confederations (such as TÜRK-İŞ, DİSK and HAK-İŞ) – counterbalanced and limited the effectiveness of labour movements. Uneven competition in the market regarding the distribution of the wealth resulted in various conflicting interests being represented (medium scale producers—large conglomerates, trade unions—other pressure groups). During the period of the state's declining monopoly, both TÜSİAD (the Association of Turkish Industrialists and Businessmen) and TOBB (the Union of Chambers and Bourses) visibly increased their impacts on political processes through public discussions. This can be seen in different fields, e.g., economic policies, foreign policy, democratization, demands for constitutional reform (Bora, 2000, pp. 99-142). In the 1990s, these organizations also emerged as influential lobbying organizations in the corridors of power (including tax reforms, protectionist measures and incentives), altering and influencing the political scene. The disproportionate representation of interests meant that unorganised yet large segments of society were unable to have their voices heard.

Nonetheless, some of these associations published several reports on the consolidation of democratization and the pluralisation of civil society. Many issues were brought to the public's attention as a result, e.g., EU integration, the Kurdish problem, human rights, legal-administrative reforms, economic policies, privatization, etc. These reports created numerous opportunities for the discussion of these issues in depth and have had a remarkable impact on public opinion, even though their conclusions were not always warmly welcome and (occasionally) the authors were ostracised by jingoist politicians and journalists. This is especially the case on the prolonged and sensitive issues of human rights and the Kurdish question (Kirisçi and Winrow, 1997). The ongoing EU accession partnership appears to have guided some of the much needed discussions and reforms. Of these NGOs, TÜSİAD and TOBB have proved themselves to be particularly capable of creating broader discussions on the necessary reforms.

In conclusion, 21st century Turkey has failed to solve the problems associated with democratization and the creation of a free and pluralistic civil society. This does not necessarily imply that the forces of democratization are in retreat. At the turn of the century, the balance of power reached a stalemate between the forces of democratization – be they political or economic – and the forces of status quo – the representatives of patrimonial modernization and patrimonial capitalism. This stalemate suggests that the forces struggling to bring greater democracy and economic equality are not yet strong enough to change the systemic matrix. Similarly, they are not so weak to let the current situation get worse. At this crucial juncture, the future of civil society and democratization in Turkey is dependent, similar to the past, on an external wave. Whether this will contribute to transforming Turkey or not remains to be seen.

References

Açıkel, F. (2002). Devletin manevi şahsiyeti ve ulusun pedagojisi [State's spiritual personality and the pedagogy of the nation]. In T. Bora, (Ed.), *Milliyetçilik: Modern Türkiye'de siyasi düşünce: Cilt 4* (pp.117-139). [Nationalism: Political thought in modern Turkey] İstanbul: İletişim Yayınları.

Adanır, F. (1995). Osmanli İmparatorluğunda ulusal sorun ile sosyalizmin oluşması ve gelişmesi: Makedonya örneği [National question and the development of socialism in the Ottoman Empire]. In M. Tuncay & E.J. Zürcher (Eds.), *Osmanli İmparatorluğunda sosyalizm ve milliyetçilik* (pp.33-72) [Socialism and nationalism in the Ottoman Empire], *1876-1923*. İstanbul: İletişim Yayınları.

Ag'h, A. (1999). Process of democratization in the East Central European and Balkan States: Sovereignty-related conflicts in the context of Europeanization. *Communist and Post-Communist Studies*, 32, 263-279.

Ag'h, A. (2001). Public sector reforms, institutional design and strategy for food governance in East Central Europe. *Studies in East European Thought*, 53, 233-255.

Ahmad, F. (1995). The development of class-consciousness in Republican Turkey, 1923-45. In D. Quataert & E. J. Zürcher (Eds.), *Workers and the working class in the Ottoman Empire and the Turkish Republic 1939-1950* (pp.133-161). London: I.B. Tauris.

Ahmad, F. (1996). *Demokrasiye geçiş sürecinde Türkiye: 1945-1980* [Turkey in transition to democracy]. İstanbul: Hil Yayınları.

Alpay, S. (1993). Journalists: Cautious democrats. In M. Heper, H. Kramer & A. Öncü (Eds.), *The Turkey and the West: Changing political and cultural identities* (pp. 69-91). London: I.B. Tauris.

Ayata, S. (1993). The rise of Islamic fundamentalism and its institutional framework. In A. Eralp, M. Tünay & B. Yeşilada (Eds.), *The political and socioeconomic transformation of Turkey* (pp.51-68). Westport: Praeger.

Barany, Z. (2002). Bulgaria's royal elections. *Journal of Democracy*, 13(2), 141-155.

Bermeo, N. (1995). Classification and consolidation: Some lessons from the Greek dictatorship. *Political Science Quarterly*, 110 (3), 435-452.

Bernhard, M. (1993). Civil society and democratic transition in East Central Europe. *Political Science Quarterly*, 108(2), 307-326.

Birtek, F. & Toprak, B. (1993). The conflictual agendas of neo-liberal reconstruction & the rise of Islamic politics in Turkey: The hazards of rewriting modernity. *Praxis International*, 13(2), 192-212.

Bora, T. (2000). Professional chambers and non-voluntary organizations: The intersection of public, civil and national. In S. Yerasimos, G. Saufert & K. Vorhoff (Eds.), *Civil society in the grip of nationalism* (pp. 99-142). İstanbul: Orient-Institute

Boratav, K. (1982). *Türkiye'de devletçilik* [Etatism in Turkey]. Ankara: Sosyal Yayınları.

Boratav, K. (1991). *Türkiye'de sosyal sınıflar ve bölüşüm* [Social classes and distribution in Turkey]. İstanbul: Gerçek Yayınevi.

Boratav, K. (1992). Distributional dimensions and macro-economic policy implications of external liberalization under structural adjustment. *Social Scientist*, 20(12), 63-76.

Boratav, K. (1995). *İstanbul'dan sınıf manzaraları* [Class profiles from Turkey]. İstanbul: Tarih Vakfı Yayınları.

Bourdieu, P. (1998a). *Practical reason: On the theory of action*. Cambridge: Polity Press.

Bourdieu, P. (1998b). *The state nobility: Elite schools in the field of power*. (L.C. Clough, Trans.). Oxford: Polity Press.

Brada, J.C. (1996). Privatization is transition or is it?. *The Journal of Economic Perspective*, 10 (2), 67-86.

Brown, M. B. (1995). *Models in political economy* (2nd ed.). London: Penguin Books.

Buğra, A. (1994). *State and business in modern Turkey: A comparative study*. Albany: State University of New York.

Bulut, F. (1997). *Tarikat sermayesinin yükselişi* [The rise of the Islamic capital]. Ankara: Doruk Yayınları.

Burawoy, M. (2000a). A Sociology for the second great transformation. *Annual Review of Sociology*, 26, 693-695.

Burawoy, M. (2000b). Marxism after communism. *Theory and Society*, 29, 151-174.

Collins, R. (1995). Prediction in macrosociology: The case of the Soviet collapse. *American Journal of Sociology*, 100 (6), 1552-1593.

Cohen, J.L. & Arato, A. (1992). *Civil society and political theory*. Cambridge: The MIT Press.

Cornell, S.E. (2002). Autonomy as a source of conflict: Caucasian conflicts in theoretical perspective. *World Politics*, 245-276.

Çalı, B. (2003, March). *Human rights discourse in Turkey: A study of domestic human rights organizations*. Paper presented at the University of Essex, Human Rights Centre, London.

Danopoulos, C. P. (1983). Military professionalism and regime legitimacy in Greece: 1967-1974. *Political Science Quarterly*, 98 (3), 485-506.

Derluguian, G. M. (1999) Che Guevaras in Turbans, *New Left Review*, October-November 237, 3-27.

Dimitrova, A. & Dragneva, R. (2001). Bulgaria's road to the European Union: Progress, problems and perspectives. *Perspectives on European Politics and Society*, 2 (1), 79-104.

Duch, R. M. (1995). Economic chaos and the fragility of democratic in former communist regimes. *The Journal of Politics*, 57 (1), 121-158.

Duncan, P. (1999). Russia: Accommodating ethnic minorities. In D. MacIver. (Ed.), *The politics of multinational states* (pp. 63-83). London: MacMillan.

Ekiert, G. (1991). Democratization process in East Central Europe: A theoretical reconsideration. *British Journal of Political Science*, 21 (3), 285-313.

Eralp, A., Tünay, M. & Yeşilada, B. (1993). *The political and socio-economic transformation of Turkey*. Praager.

Erdoğan, N. (2000). Kemalist non-governmental organizations: Troubled elites in defence of a sacred heritage. S. Yerasimos, G. Saufert & K. Vorhoff (Eds.), *Civil society in the grip of nationalism* (pp. 251-282). İstanbul: Orient-Institute.

Evans, G. & Mills, C. (1999). Are there classes in post-communist societies? A new approach to identifying class structure. *Sociology*, 33 (1), 23-46.

Evans, G. & Whitefield, S. (1993). Identifying the bases of party competition in Eastern Europe. *British Journal of Political Science*, 23, 521-548.

Evans, P. (1982). Reinventing the bourgeoisie: State entrepreneurship and class formation in dependent capitalist development. *American Journal of Sociology*, 88, 210-247.

Fligstein, N. (1996). The economic sociology of the transitions from socialism. *American Journal of Sociology*, 101 (4), 1074-1081.

Fukuyama, F. (1992). *The end of history and the last man*. London: Penguin Books.

Gill, G. (2002). *Democracy and post-communism*. London: Routledge.

Goldstone, J. A. (1998). Initial conditions, general laws, path dependence, and explanation in historical sociology. *American Journal of Sociology*, 104 (3), 829-845.

Gellner, E. (1995). *Muslim Society*. Cambridge: Cambridge University Press.

Göçek, F. M. (1996). *Rise of the bourgeoisie and demise of Empire: Ottoman modernisation and social change*. New York & Oxford: Oxford University Press.

Gramsci, A. (1996). *Selections from prison notebooks*. Q. Hoare & G. N. Smith (Ed. & Trans.). London: Lawrance and Wishart.

Greenfeld, L. (1994). *Nationalism: Five roads to modernity*. Cambridge: Harvard University Press.

Gregor, A. J., (1998). Fascism and the new Russian nationalism. *Communist and Post-Communist Studies*, 31 (1), 1-15.

Grodeland, A., Miller, W.L. & Koshechkina, T.Y. (2000). The ethnic dimension to bureaucratic encounters in postcommunist Europe: Perceptions and experience. *Nations and Nationalism,* 6 (1), 43-66.

Gülalp, H. (1994). Capitalism and the modern nation state: Rethinking the creation of the Turkish Republic. *Journal of Historical Sociology,* 7 (2/June), 155-176.

Güneş-Ayata, A. (1990). Class and clientelism in the Republican People's Party. In A. Finkel & N. Sirman. (Eds.), *Turkish State, Turkish Society* (pp.159-184). London: Routledge

Hale, W. (1994). *Turkish politics and the military.* London: Routledge.

Hegel, G. W. F. (1953). *The philosophy of right.* (T. M. Knox, Trans.). Oxford: Clarendon Press.

Held, D. (1996). *Models of democracy.* (2nd ed.) Cambridge: Polity Press.

Heper, M. (1985). The state and public bureaucracies: A comparative and historical perspective. *Comparative Studies in Society and History,* 27(1).

Heper, M. (1989) The Motherland Party governments and bureaucracy in Turkey: 1983-88. *Governance: An International Journal of Policy and Administration,* (2), 457-468.

Heper, M. (1993). Bureaucrats: Persistent elitists. In M. Heper, H. Kramer & A. Öncü (Eds.), *The Turkey and the West: Changing political and cultural identities* (pp. 35-68). London: I.B.Tauris.

Heper, M. (1997). Islam and democracy in Turkey: Toward a reconciliation? *Middle East Journal,* 51(1), 32-45.

Howard, M. M. (2002). The weakness of postcommunist civil society. *Journal of Democracy,* 13(1), 157-169.

Huntington, S. P. (1996). *The clash of civilisations and the remaking of world order.* New York: Simon & Schuster.

İlkin, S. (1993). Businessmen: Democratic stability. In M. Heper, H. Kramer & A. Öncü (Eds.), *The Turkey and the West: Changing political and cultural identities* (pp. 177-198). London: I.B.Tauris.

İlkin, S. (1994). Privatization of the state economic enterprises. In M. Heper & A. Evin (Eds.), *Politics in the Third Turkish Republic* (pp.77-86). Boulder: Westview Press.

İnsel, A. (1996). *Düzen ve kalkınma kıskacında Türkiye* [Turkey in the trap of order and development]. İstanbul: Ayrıntı Yayınları.

İslamoğlu-İnan, H. (Ed.). (1987). *The Ottoman Empire and the world-economy.* New York: Cambridge University Press

Jensen, G. (2000). Military nationalism and the state: the Case of *fin-de-siecle* Spain. *Nations and Nationalism,* 6 (2), 257-274.

Kaldor, M. (2003). Civil society and accountability. *Journal of Human Development,* 4(1), 5-27.

Karaosmanoğlu, A. L. (1993). Officers: Westernization and democracy. In M. Heper, H. Kramer & A. Öncü (Eds.), *The Turkey and the West: Changing political and cultural identities* (pp. 19-34). London: I.B.Tauris.

Karpat, K. H. (1985). *Ottoman Population: 1830-1914.* The University of Wisconsin Press: Madison.

Keane, J. (1993). Democracy and the media – Without foundations. In D. Held (Ed.), *Prospects for democracy* (pp.235-253). Stanford: Stanford University Press.

Keyder, Ç. (1976). The dissolution of the Asiatic mode of production, *Economy and Society*, 5 (2), 178-196.

Keyder, Ç. (1987) *State and class in Turkey: A study in capitalist development*. London & New York: Verso.

Keyder, Ç. & Öncü, A. (1994). Globalization of a third-world metropolis: İstanbul in the 1980's. *Review*, XVII (3/Summer), 384-421.

Keyman, F. & İçduygu, A. (2003). Globalization, civil society and citizenship in Turkey: Actors, boundaries and discourses. *Citizenship Studies*, 7(2), 219-234.

King, C. (2001). The benefits of ethnic war: Understanding Eurasia's unrecognized states. *World Politics*, 53, 524-552.

King, L. P. (2001). Making markets: A comparative study of postcommunist managerial strategies in Central Europe. *Economy and Society*, 30, 493-538.

Kirişçi, K. & Winrow, G.M. (1997). *Kürt sorunu* [The Kurdish question]. İstanbul: Tarih Vakfı Yurt Yayınları.

Laitin, D. (2000). Post-Soviet politics. *Annual Review of Political Science*, 3, 117-148.

Lewis, B. (1968). *The emergence of modern Turkey*. London: Oxford University Press.

Mardin, S. (1969). Power, civil society and culture in the Ottoman Empire. *Comparative Studies in Society and History*, 11(3), 258-281.

Mardin, S. (1973). Center-periphery relations: A key to Turkish politics?. *Deadalus*, (102), 169-190.

Mardin, S. (1980). Transformation of an economic code. In E. Özbudun & A. Ulusan. (Eds.), *The political economy of income distribution in Turkey* (pp.23-53). New York: Holmes & Meier.

Mardin, S. (1991). *Türk modernlesmesi: Makaleler IV* [Turkish Modernization: Essays IV]. İstanbul: İletişim Yayınları.

Mardin, S. (1997). *The Ottoman Empire*. In. K. Barkey & M. Von Hagen. (Eds.), *After Empire* (pp.115-128). Oxford: Westview Press.

McDonough, P. (1995). Identities, ideologies, and interests: democratization and the culture of mass politics in Spain and Eastern Europe. *The Journal of Politics*, 57 (3), 649-676.

McFaul, M. (2002). The fourth wave of democracy and dictatorship: Noncooperative transitions in the postcommunist world. *World Politics*, 54, 212-244.

McIntosh, M., Mac Iver, M. A., Abele, D. G. & Nolle, D. B. (1995). Minority rights and majority rule: Ethnic tolerance in Romania and Bulgaria. *Social Forces*, 73 (3), 939-968.

Minnasian, G. (1998). The road to economic disaster in Bulgaria. *Europe-Asia Studies*, 50 (2), 331-349.

Miscevic, N. (2001). National identities in transition. *Studies in East European Thought*, 53, 197-219.

Moore, B. (1991). *Social origins of dictatorship and democracy*. London: Penguin Books.

Mouzelis, N. (1976). Greek and Bulgarian peasants: Aspects of their sociopolitical situation during the Interwar period. *Comparative Studies in Society and History*, 18 (1), 85-105.

Mouzelis, N. (1978). *Modern Greece: Facets of underdevelopment*. London: MacMillan Press.

Mouzelis, N. (1986). *Politics in the semi-periphery*. Hong Kong: Macmillan.

Murrell, P. (1996). How far the transition progressed?. *The Journal of Economic Perspective*, 10 (2), 25-44.

Moore, B. (1991). *Social origins of dictatorship and democracy*. London: Penguin Books.

Nodia, G. (1995). Georgia's identity crisis. *Journal of Democracy*, 6(1), 104-116.

Offe, C. (2001). Political liberalism, group rights and the politics of fear and trust. *Studies in East European Thought*, 53, 167-182.

Ortaylı, İ. (1995). *İmparatorluğun en uzun yılı*. İstanbul: Hil Yayınları.

Özbudun, E. (1976). *Social change and political participation in Turkey*. Princeton, New Jersey: Princeton University Press.

Özbudun, E. (1981). Turkey: The politics of political clientelism. In S.N. Eisenstadt & R. Lemnarchand (Eds.), *Political clientelism, patronage and development* (pp. 173-88). London: Sage.

Özbudun, E. (2000). *Contemporary Turkish politics: Challenges to democratic consolidation*. London: Rienner.

Peteri, G. (2000). Between empire and nation-state: Comments on the pathology of state formation in Eastern Europe during the 'Short Twenty Century'. *Contemporary European History*, 9 (3), 367-384.

Pollack B. & Taylor J. (1983). The transition to democracy in Portugal and Spain. *British Journal of Political Science*, 13 (2), 209-242.

Poulantzas, N. (1974). *Fascism and dictatorship: the Third International and the problem of fascism*. (J. White, Trans.). London: New Left Books.

Poulantzas, N. (1978). *State, power, socialism*, (P. Camiller, Trans.). London: NLB.

Quataert, D. (1994). Ottoman workers and the state, 1826-1914. In Z. Locman. (Ed.), *Workers and working classes in the Middle East* (pp. 21-40). New York: State University of New York Press.

Rowley, D. G. (2000). Imperial versus national discourse: The case of Russia. *Nations and Nationalism*, 6 (1), 23-42.

Saraçoğlu, R. (1994). Liberalization of the economy. In M. Heper & A. Evin. (Eds.), *Politics in the Third Turkish Republic* (pp. 63-76). Boulder: Westview Press.

Schopflin, G. (1991). Post-communist: Constructing new democracies in Central Europe. *International Affairs*, 67 (2), 235-250.

Schüler, H. (2000). Secularism and ethnicity: Alevis and social democrats in search of an alliance. In S. Yerasimos, G. Saufert & K. Vorhoff (Eds.), *Civil society in the grip of nationalism* (pp. 197-250). İstanbul: Orient-Institute.

Shevtsona, L. (2001). Russia's hybrid regime. *Journal of Democracy*, 12 (4), 65-70.

Sohrabi, N. (1995). Historicising revolutions: Constitutional revolutions in the Ottoman Empire, Iran and Russia, 1905-1908. *American Journal of Sociology*, 100 (6), 1383-1447.

Soysal, M. (1987). *100 Soruda anayasanın anlamı* [The meaning of constitution in 100 questions]. İstanbul: Gerçek Yayınları.

Spenner, K. I. & Derek, C. J. (1998). Social economic transformation in Bulgaria: An empirical assessment of the merchant capitalism thesis. *Social Forces*, 76 (3), 937-65.

Szelenyi, I & Kostello, E. (1996). The market transition debate: Toward a synthesis?. *American Journal of Sociology*, 101 (4), 1082-1096.

Tanör, B. (2000). *Osmanlı-Türk anayasal gelişmeleri* [The Ottoman-Turkish constitutional developments]. İstanbul: Yapı Kredi Yayınları.

Tarkowski, J. (1981). Poland: Patrons and clients in a planned economy. In. S.N. Eisenstadt & R. Lemnarchand (Eds.), *Political clientelism, patronage and development* (pp. 173-188). London: Sage.

Tilly, C. (2001). Mechanisms in political processes. *Annual Review of Political Science*, 4, 21-41.

Tilly, C. (2002). Processes and mechanisms of democratization. *Sociological Theory*, 18 (1), 1-16.

Tomusk, V. (2000). Reproduction of 'State Nobility' in Eastern Europe: Past patterns and new practices. *British Journal of Sociology of Education*, 21 (2), 269-282.

Trimberger, E.K. (1978). *Revolution from above: Military bureaucrats and development in Japan, Turkey, Egypt and Peru.* New Jersey: Transaction Books.

Tunçay, M. & Zürcher, E. J. (1995). *Osmanlı İmparatorluğunda sosyalizm ve milliyetçilik* [Socialism and nationalism in the Ottoman Empire], *1876-1923.* İstanbul: İletişim Yayınları.

Urban, M. (1998) Remythologising the Russian State, *Europe-Asia Studies,* 50(6), 969-992.

Vaner, S. (1987). The army. In I. C. Schick & E. A. Tonak. (Eds.), *Turkey in transition: New perspectives* (pp.236-267). New York: Oxford University Press

Verdery, K. (1993). Nationalism and national sentiment in post-socialist Romania. *Slavic Review*, 2, 179-203.

Vincent, M. (1999). Nation and state in twentieth-century Spain. *Contemporary European History*, 8 (3), 473-485.

Waterbury, J. & Suleiman, E. N. (Eds.). (1990). *The political economy of public sector reform and privatization.* Boulder: Westview Press.

NOTES

PART I

1 The term 'Post-Westphalian' refers to permeable boundaries and layered and compromised state sovereignty as opposed to the Westphalian understanding of sovereignty as a highly centralized, monolithic, and uncompromising notion.

2 Black Sea regional cooperation is often referred to as a sub-regional framework. Since the collapse of the Cold War several subregional cooperation initiatives emerged from the Northern tier to the Southern tier of Europe. In this sense, the BSEC, like other subregional cooperation frameworks in Europe, can be seen as the integral part of European globalization. The prefix 'sub' could imply to a lesser status, but it can also be interpreted as part of a larger sum, namely the Pan-European political and public space as defined by membership of Pan-European organizations, such as: the Organization for Security and Cooperation in Europe (OSCE), the Council of Europe, etc.

3 At this point, an important conceptual distinction must be made between regionalism and regionalization. Regionalism refers to a project or attitude as an organizing political principle that can be measured by the political willingness or voluntarism of elites and decision makers to promote regional cooperation and political institutions within defined geographical boundaries, or rather around regional economic, ecological and social concerns. Regionalization, on the other hand, is the deepening of the actual and perceived interdependence on salient regional issues and the intensifying of regional flows of energy, population and economic transactions (Aybak, 2001, p. 55). Whereas regionalism is the formal establishment of regions as political units, regionalization refers to the manifestation of the global process of economic integration and the changing structures of production and power (Grugel, 1999, p. 10).

4 Interview, October 13, 2000.

5 These include: Black Sea University, Black Sea University Network (Costantza), Future Foundation (Chisinau), Black Sea Region Association for Shipbuilders and Shiprepairers, Turkish Marine Environment Protection

Group (İstanbul), Black Sea International Shipowners Association (Odessa), Euro-Mediterranean Trade, Distribution and Services, Forum of Architects of the Black Sea Region (Tbilisi), Russian Maritime Register of Shipping (St Petersburg), Russian Foreign Policy Foundation, (Moscow), Regional Energy Working Group (Ankara), and Balkan Centre for Small and Medium Enterprises (Varna).

PART II

1 Research for this chapter was funded by Economic and Social Research Council Grants No. R000222380 and L213252021.

2 The survey referred to in this paragraph was carried out by the Kyïv International Institute of Sociology. Further details are available from the author upon request.

3 The relationship between the findings reported in Table 3 and those reported in Table 4 appear to be rather peculiar: there are more party identifiers on the left of the political spectrum, though fewer leftists support multipartism. This is most likely because for many on the left only their party (for most the Communist party) is legitimate and multiparty competition is not seen as desirable. The reverse is true for many right-wing voters – they support multipartism in principle but do not identify with any particular party.

4 The law governing the elections of 1998 was passed on 24 September 1997, and came into effect when it was published in Holos Ukraïny on October 25, 1997.

5 The electoral law does not require parties to open such accounts, and it does not explicitly prohibit them from using other sources for the purposes of financing their campaigns.

6 Low-cost mobilization of the Russian ethnic vote does not appear to have been possible, however. The parties most clearly allied with ethnic Russian causes -SLOn and the PRVU- ran relatively expensive campaigns (especially the PRVU), but both garnered less than one per cent of the list vote.

7 The authors would like to express their thanks to Alexandru Boer (regional campaign manager for CDR 2000 in Cluj-Napoca, Romania) and Horia Ungur (regional coordinator of the electoral staff of CDR 2000 Bistrita, Romania) for their time and assistance with their research.

8 'Voteaza schimbarea' ('Vote for change') was one of the main themes of the CDR's message.

9 For a sample of the messages used in the 2000 campaign see Isarescu's and Iliescu's official websites (http://www.mugur.isarescu.ro and http://www.iliescu.ro).

10 Interview with Emil Boc, Vice-President of PD (The Democratic Party), August 23, 2001.

11 Interview with Emil Boc, Vice-President of PD (The Democratic Party), August 23, 2001.

12 Interview with Oliviu Gherman, Romanian Ambassador to France, former President of the Romanian Senate and former leader of PDSR (1992-1996), August 10, 2001.

13 The full independence of Ukraine was declared as a goal of Rukh in October 1990·

14 For a more detailed overview of the creation of the party system in Ukraine see Haran', 1991; Haran', 1993; Kuzio & Wilson, 1994.

15 Figure cited in the Central Election Commission's web-site (www.cvk. gov.ua)

16 However, Mykola Azarov had to resign from this post in December 2001, after vigorous discussion regarding the incompatibility of this post with the post of Head of the Tax Administration·

17 I do not claim that the 'party of power' is a uniquely Ukrainian phenomenon. For a discussion on Russia's "party of power" compared to the Ukrainian case see Kuzio (2002a).

18 Indeed, the Ukrainian President expressed his desire to head the bloc once it transformed into a party. However, he later retracted the statement in order to retain his non-party status.

19 The 'Our Ukraine' bloc was dominant in Kyiv, Western Ukraine, some regions in the North, and in the majority of the Central region: The 'ZYU!' bloc primarily drew its votes from the East, the Donetsk region in particular The Communist Party traditionally relied on the electorate in the South, while the Socialist party relied on the electorate in the Centre, especially in the Poltava region·

20 It acquired the popular name after both original Rukhs formed the 'Our Ukraine' bloc.

21 These include: the CPU, the SDPU (united), the Party of Greens of Ukraine, the All-Ukrainian Party of Workers, the SDPU and the Ukrainian National Assembly·

PART III

1 Birlik was the second biggest association after the People's Front of Azerbaijan (PFA). It was mainly formed by Iranian Azerbaijanis and aimed to create a united Azerbaijan. Observers noted that, unlike the PFA, 'it openly expressed its sympathy for pan-Islamic ideas'. See Michaeli, M. & Reese, W. (September 1, 1989) 'The "Birlik" Society in the Azerbaijani Democratic Movement', RFE/RL Report on the USSR, p. 30.

2 Chenlibel was first established as a cultural and historical movement, becoming more politically oriented as time progressed (Michaeli & Reese, 1989, p. 30).

3 Interviews with Meryem Oruclu and Aydin Balayev, July 2000, Baku.

4 The formation of the Organization for Freedom of Karabagh (Garabaga Azadliq Teshkilati) and the National Resistance Movement (Milli

Mukavemet Harekati) are indicative of the centrality of the Karabagh problem in the subsequent years of independence.

5 There is not any official data regarding the number of organizations that applied for registration. Some of the organizations are quite well known by their activities but have not yet been registered. These include: the Institute of Peace and Democracy, Inam Pluralism Centre, Azerbaijan Modernization Centre, Azerbaijan Committee of Democracy and Human Rights, United Azerbaijan Union, the Defence Committee of Journalists' Human Rights. Interviewees from these organizations argued that given that they are pro-opposition organizations government created 'irrelevant' problems in order to prevent their official registration. The reasons for refusal centred on the name of the organization and/or the content of their programmes (Author's interviews, November-December 2000, Baku).

6 For the full text, see http://88.88.88.15/az/az_htm/A1658.HTM.

7 For instance, the Head of the Azerbaijan Modernization Centre is the co-founder of the Symbolic Constitution Court and the Azerbaijan Committee of Democracy and Human Rights as well as a member of the High Council of the Musavat Party. He is also on the administrative body of the NGO Congress. The Head of the Committee of the Rights of Oil Workers is a member of the Women in Black Organization and the secretary of Movement for Electoral Reform and Democratic Elections.

8 For example, the Azerbaijan Branch of the Helsinki Citizen's Assembly was located in the Azerbaijan Social Democrat Party. The chair, Arzu Abdullayeva, was the founding member of that Party. The Musavat Party hosts the Committee for Human Rights and Democracy, headed by Cingiz Ganizade, who is also a party member and the chair of the Democratic Reforms and Human Rights Unit recently established in the Democratic Congress -a political bloc of opposition parties. The Head of the Azerbaijan Foundation Democratic Development and of the Protection of Women's Rights in the name of Dilara Aliyeva was a high ranked member of the People's Front Party of Azerbaijan.

9 The human rights organizations, gender organizations, journalist organizations, humanitarian aid and refugee organizations have regular meetings and discussions. In July 2000, the human rights organizations had several meetings on the issue of the number of political prisoners. In meetings of the journalist unions, 15 newspaper editors meet twice a month to discuss journalists' problems, the oppression of the journalists and other related issues. They make declarations and address to the president.

10 The prominent examples are the women's organizations and human rights organizations. For instance in February 2002, the human rights organizations in Azerbaijan initiated two federations to unite local NGOs working in the same field.

11 Interviews with Aflatun Amashov, Head of the RUH [Spirit] Journalist Union, Arif Aliyev, Head of the Yeni Nesil [New Generation] Journalist

Union, Aydin Xan, Head of the Union for New Writers and Artists, November 1999, Baku.

12 Interviews with Anar Rzayev, Head of the Writers Union, Haci Haciyev, Head of the Journalist Union, July 2000, Baku. Although the Journalist Union does not receive any financial assistance from the state, the Writers Union receives state funding for its executive body's salaries and publications. Both have not had any relations with international NGOs in Azerbaijan.

13 There was a TV programme where reporters interviewed 20 people on the street and asked them to define an NGO. One out of 20 correctly defined NGOs, five said they did not know and 14 stated 'organizations working against the state'. Space TV (July 12, 2000).

14 Three out of forty NGOs interviewed have regional branches in a few regions. Shortage of staff, difficulty in convincing people in the regions and the problems stemming from the local authorities are the main reasons cited for this.

15 Interview with V.P., December, 1999, Baku.

16 Interview with Ali Hasanov, Head of the Social and Political Issues Unit of the President, cited in Nelson, 1999, pp. 7-8.

17 Interviews with members of the NGO Congress, July 2000, Baku.

18 The Head of the RUH Journalist Union and New Generation Union have been invited to parliamentary sessions to discuss media law. The Head of INAM Pluralism Center was invited to the presidents' office after an international conference organized by his organization and asked to propose suggestions and collaborate with the President. The chair of the NGO Forum was invited to discussions on the Law for Social Organizations.

19 The Azerbaijani Foundation for Development of Democracy, the Human Rights Protection Committee, the Organization of Women in the name of Dilara Aliyeva, the Azerbaijan National Democracy Foundation were located in the headquarters of the PFPA. The Azerbaijani Committee for Human Rights and Democracy is located in the Musavat Party and the Azerbaijan National Committee of Helsinki Citizens Assembly was located in the headquarters of the Azerbaijani Social Democrat Party.

20 Fazil Memmedov, head of the registration unit in the Ministry of Justice, Space TV, interview (July 12, 2000).

21 Most of the human rights organizations that are not registered are the more active ones and well-known in the media and have regular contact with international organizations, such as: the Institute for Peace and Democracy, the Committee for the Protection of Human Rights and Democracy, the Human Rights Center, the Azerbaijani Branch of the Helsinki Citizens Assembly.

22 Interviews with the representatives of the NGOs, December, 1999, Baku.

23 Interview with Leila Yunus, December 1999, Baku.

24 This assessment has been made by the 1997 CSD survey, which filtered out organizations that do not work in the socio-economic sphere at the first stage (i.e., reducing the total number to about 2,000 via the exclusion of organizations focused on sport, religion, trade union organizations, etc.) and then evaluating the actual performance of organizations. In 1998, MBMD adopted a similar approach in its survey of the NGO sector and obtained approximately the same results.

25 In April 1997, a CSD survey surveyed 402 organizations after a preliminary selection of organizations that meet the four predefined DNP criteria. In a 1998 MBMD survey the number of organizations included is 530. After filtering out the organizations that are not engaged in activities focusing on civil society issues, 364 organizations remained.

* The term 'Civiliarchy' has been introduced into practice for the first time by this author. Civiliarchy (civil (lat.) + archy (Greek)) refers to the functioning of a political system, structuring and aiding the civil interrelations among its constituents. Civiliarchy is conceived of as directing institutions, a form of legitimacy and a system (Alexanyan, 1999, pp. 2-9; Alexanyan, 2001, pp. 227-240; Alexanyan, 2002, pp. 115-125).

** The concept of 'Civiliology' illustrates the interrelation between concepts such as 'culturology', 'traditionology', 'anthropology', 'theory of civilization', etc. It is possible to conceive of civiliology from two points of view: as a science about citizen or as a science about civilization (Alexanyan, 2002, pp. 115-125).

26 See Talmon, 1961, pp. 1-12, 34-45; Talmon, 1963, pp. 2-7, Aron, 1981, p. 35.

27 This paper was written in 2000. Some of the figures are different now (for instance the number of NGOs in Bulgaria), but the conclusions remain the same.

28 It is not accidental that the organizations are called 'non-profit' rather than 'non governmental' given that they are primarily concerned with (non) profit activity.

29 Admittedly, this applies to the top 15 of 80 NPOs in the region. It is possible that this 'division' into spheres of influence could block the access of other, or newly founded, organizations to funding. The 15 NPOs in question have come to regard themselves as a local 'Establishment'.

PART IV

1 The author would like to thank to LSE-Bilgi University fellowship program for having hosted this research at the LSE, the European Institute. The author also thanks to Ayça Ergun, Başak Çalı, Zeynel Besler, Dimitri Sotiropoulos, Tony Woodiwiss and Ayşe Güneş-Ayata for their comments and suggestions on earlier drafts of this article.

CONTRIBUTORS

Fethi Açıkel is an Assistant Professor of Sociology in the Faculty of Political Science at the University of Ankara. His research interests/publications cover the fields of Turkish identity/nationalism, political and historical sociology.

Ashot S. Alexanyan is a Deputy Dean in the Faculty of International Relations of the Yerevan State University, in Armenia. He is lecturer in the Department of Political Science of YSU. His recent fields of study include: civil society, and human political rights.

Ayşe Ayata is a Professor of Political Science and the Chair of the Centre For Black Sea and Central Asia at the Middle East Technical University, Ankara, Turkey. She is also a member of the Advisory Board of the Regional Bureau for Europe, the CIS, and the UNDP. Her recent publications include: From Euro-Scepticism to Turkey Scepticism: Changing Political Attitudes on the European Union in Turkey, *Journal of Southern Europe and the Balkans*, 5 (2), 205-222 (August 2003); Ethnic and Religious Bases of Voting in S. Sayarı & Y.Esmer, (Eds.), *Politics, Parties and Elections in Turkey*, Lynne Rienner Publishers: Boulder (2002) and Discipline, Success and Stability: The Reproduction of Gender and Class in Turkish Secondary Education in D. Kandiyoti & A. Saktanber, (Eds.), *Fragments of Culture: The Everyday of Modern Turkey*, I.B. Tauris & Co. Publishers: London (2002).

Tunç Aybak is the Director of Political and International Studies at Middlesex University. He lectures on European politics and Eurasian studies. His recent books include, *Politics of the Black Sea*, I.B. Tauris & Co. Publishers: London (2001). At present, he is working on a project on the new regional security challenges and globalization in the Black Sea region.

Sarah Birch is a reader in Politics at the University of Essex. Her recent publications include: *Electoral Systems and Political Transformation in Post-communist Europe*, Palgrave-Macmillan (2003) and (co-authored) *Embodying Democracy: Electoral System Design in Post-communist Europe*, Palgrave-Macmillan (2002).

Stephen Blackwell is a European Analyst in Jane Sentinel's Security Assessments. His recent publications include: Military-Media Relations and Defence Policy-making in Britain in M. Caparini (Ed.) *Media and Security Governance: the Role of the News Media in Security Oversight and Accountability*, Baden-Baden: Nomos Verlagsgesellschaft (2004); From Stability to Institutional Co-operation: Romanian Civil-Military Relations and the Accession Process to NATO and the European Union, *Romanian Journal of Society and Politics*, 2 (2) (September 2002) and Review Article: Romania and the Enlargement of the European Union and NATO, *Romanian Journal of Society and Politics*, 1 (2) (September 2001).

Işıl Çelimli is a PhD. candidate in the Sociology Department at Columbia University, in the City of New York. Her research interests are on urban sociology and the sociology of change.

Ayça Ergun is an Assistant Professor of Sociology at the Middle East Technical University, Ankara, Turkey. Her recent publications include: International Challenges and Domestic Preferences in the Post-Soviet Political Transition of Azerbaijan in M. P. Amineh & H. Houweling (Eds.), *Central Asia in Global Politics: Conflict, Security and Development*, Leiden: Brill Academic Publishers (2004) and, co-authored with B. Çalı, Global Governance and Domestic Politics: Fragmented Visions, in P. Muller & M. Lederer (Eds.), *The Challenging Global Governance Reader*, Palgrave-Macmillan (forthcoming in 2005).

Petya Kabakchieva is an Associate Professor in the Department of Sociology at Sofia University. Recently she is working in the field of the Sociology of European Integration. Her recent publications include: *The Social Impact of Seasonal Migration* [in English] (Co-publication with R. Guentcheva & P. Kolarski), IOM: Vienna (2003) and *Civil Society vs. State: the Bulgarian Case* [in Bulgarian], LIC Publication House: Sofia (2001).

Olga Kesarchuk is MA student at the Centre for Russian and Eastern European Studies at University of Toronto in Canada. She has graduated with her masters from the Political Science Department at the Central European University in Budapest, Hungary.

Eyüp Özveren is a Professor of Economics at the Middle East Technical University, Ankara, Turkey. His recent publications include: Black Sea and the Grain Provisioning of İstanbul in the Longue Durée in B. Marin & C. Virlouvet (Eds.), *Nourrir les cités de Mediterranée* (pp. 223-249), Maisonneuve & Larose: Paris (2003).

Luciana Salagean is currently a correspondent in the "Radio France Internationale" (RFI). Her recent publications include: *Tattoo – New and Old Cultural Values*, Pamplona: Thomson-Aranzadi (2002) and Homosexuals - Why is it so Hard to Accept Diversity? Romanian Attitudes to Shaping New Patterns in Sexual Minorities Issues in *Conference Proceedings, International Student Conference*, Civic Education Project: Budapest, Hungary, (May, 2000) available at http://195.38.96.112/projects/studcon/2000/ISC. pdf.

Neil Robinson is a Senior Lecturer in the Department of Politics and Public Administration, University of Limerick, Ireland. His recent publications include: *Russia, A State of Uncertainty*, Routledge: London, New York (2002), and (Ed.) *Reforging the Weakest Link: Global Political Economy and Post-Soviet Change in Russia, Ukraine and Belarus*, Aldershot: Ashgate (2004).

Oktay F. Tanrısever is an Assistant Professor in the Department of International Relations at the Middle East Technical University, Ankara, Turkey. His most recent publication is Turkey and Russia in Eurasia in L. G. Martin & D. Keridis (Eds.), *The Future of Turkish Foreign Policy,* (pp. 127-155), MA, MIT Press: Cambridge (2004).

Elena Triffonova is a Program Director at the Institute for Regional and International Studies, Sofia, Bulgaria. She is a Ph.D. candidate at Sofia University, "St. Kliment Ohridski," in the European Studies Department. Her most recent publication is Creation of Youth Community Council. Is the Mission Possible? in the brochure *Youth Community Council - Mission is Possible: Civic Capacity Development in Local Polity Making in Zavet*, IRIS: Sofia (2004).

INDEX